North U. Racing Tactics

Bill Gladstone

North U.
Racing Tactics
Seventh edition.
　　Bill Gladstone
© 1983 by Bill Gladstone

All rights reserved.
Reproduction (except for the Race Planner) by any means for any purpose without the written consent of the author is prohibited.

Published in 2010 by
North U.
Madison CT 06443 USA

ISBN 978-0-9770952-2-3

Printed in Hong Kong

Printing History
As *Performance Racing Technique*
First Edition	1983
Second Ed. 1st printing	1984
Second Ed. 2nd printing	1985
Second Ed. 3rd printing	1986
Second Ed. 4th printing	1987
Third Ed. 1st printing	1987
Third Ed. 2nd printing	1989
Third Ed. 3rd printing	1990
Third Ed. 4th printing	1991
Third Ed. 5th printing	1993
Third Ed. 6th printing	1994

As *Performance Racing Tactics*
Fourth Ed. 1st printing	1995
Fourth Ed. 2nd printing	1996
Fourth Ed. 3rd printing	1997
Fourth Ed. 4th printing	1998
Fifth Ed. 1st printing	1999
Fifth Ed. 2nd printing	2000
Fifth Ed. 3rd printing	2001
Sixth Ed. 1st printing	2002
Sixth Ed. 2nd printing	2003
Sixth Ed. 3rd printing	2005
Sixth Ed. 4th printing	2007

NORTH U.
RACING TACTICS
Contents

CHAPTER 1: STRATEGY, TACTICS, AND THE RACING PYRAMID ..1
    1.1 Tactics 2
    1.2 Why Do We Race Sailboats? 2
    1.3 The Racing Pyramid...2
    1.4 Performance Analysis 4

CHAPTER 2: RACE PREPARATION 5
    2.1 Introduction 6
    2.2 Get Ready to Race 6
    2.3 The Race Planner 8

CHAPTER 3: STARTING STRATEGY 13
    3.1 Introduction: Elements of Strategy 14
    3.2 Where to Start 15
    3.3 Approaches 21
    3.4 Conclusion 26

CHAPTER 4: STARTING TACTICS...27
    4.1 Introduction..28
    4.2 Tactical Information...28
    4.3 The Start 30
    4.4 Pitfalls 35
    4.5 Conclusion 38
    4.6 Building Starting Skills....................................39
    4.7 Starting Quiz Questions 40

CHAPTER 5: RULES AT STARTS 41
    5.1 Luffing at Starts...42
    5.2 Barging...44
    5.3 Other Starting Rules...46

CHAPTER 6: OFFBEAT STARTS...47
    6.1 Running Starts..48
    6.2 Reaching Starts 48
    6.3 Starts on One-Legged Beats.............................50
    6.4 Conclusion 51
    Starting Quiz Answers 52

CHAPTER 7: UPWIND STRATEGY 53
    7.1 Introduction to Strategy 54
    7.2 Predicting Conditions......................................54
    7.3 Wind 56
    7.4 Wind Shifts...58
    7.5 The Impact of Wind Shifts...............................70
    7.6 Current 72
    7.7 Strategy vs. Rivals 75
    7.8 The Land of Opportunity 75
    7.9 Local Knowledge 77
    Strategy Quiz 82
    Strategy Quiz Answer 84
    (Continued)

North U. Racing Tactics
Contents (cont.)

Chapter 8: Upwind Tactics *85*
    8.1 Introduction 86
    8.2 The Impact of Wind Shifts 86
    8.3 Tactical Principles 92
    8.4 Up the Beat in 3 Stages 96
    8.5 Tactical Weapons 100
    8.6 Rules Upwind 106
    8.7 A Tactician's Nightmare 110
    8.8 No More Tactics! 112
    8.9 Upwind Strategy and Tactics: Quiz Questions ...113
    Skill Building: Upwind Strategy and Tactics 114
    Upwind Strategy and Tactics: Quiz Answers 115

Chapter 9: Reaching Strategy and Tactics *117*
    9.1 Introduction 118
    9.2 Reaching Strategy 118
    9.3 Reaching Tactics 124

Chapter 10: Running Strategy and Tactics *133*
    10.1 Introduction 134
    10.2 Downwind Performance 135
    10.3 Running Strategy 136
    10.4 Running Tactics 146
    10.5 Jib and Main Racing 150
    10.6 Conclusion 150
    10.7 Quiz Questions and Skill Building 151
    Quiz Answers 152

Chapter 11: Downwind Rules,
Mark Roundings, and Finishing *153*
    11.1 Introduction 154
    11.2 Downwind Rules 154
    11.3 Mark Rounding Rules and Tactics 155
    11.4 Finishing Rules & Tactics 162
    11.5 Quiz Questions and Skill Building 164
    Quiz Answers 165

Chapter 12: No More Tactics *167*
    12.1 The Trouble with Tactics… 167
    12.2 The End 168

Appendix 1: Learning The Rules *169*
    App.1.1 The Rules 170
    App.1.2 The Four Right of Way Rules 170
    App.1.3 General Limitations 172
    App.1.5 Mark-Room and Other Rules 174
    App.1.5 Appeals and Protests 175
    App.1.6 Next Steps 176

Appendix 2: Special Topics *177*
    App.2.1 Mixed Fleet Racing 178
    App.2.2 Big Fleet Racing 179
    App.2.3 Distance Racing Strategy 180

Forward

North U. Racing Tactics is the most complete book on racing tactics. As such, the book covers a broad spectrum of topics, some of which you may find of more immediate interest than others. While the material in later sections builds on earlier chapters, each chapter is written to stand alone and can be read independently.

The Racing Rules are covered as part of each chapter on tactics. Those who are new to racing and the racing rules might want to jump to the Appendix: Learning the Rules for a primer.

Speed Reading

If you are looking for an answer to a particular question, you can skim quickly by reading the illustration captions and studying the illustrations. When you hit upon an area of particular interest, dig into the text for more details. You can also use this skimming technique for a quick review (Fig. 1).

Understanding the Illustrations

Most of the illustrations show the evolution of a tactical situation over time. Generally the checkered boat is the object boat discussed in the captions and text, with the black hulled boat or dark sailed boat as the key adversary. Other boats of varying shades and designs are used to fill out the scene.

A key to the symbols used to depict sequential action, the path of a boat, and an alternative path, the wind, windshifts, and current is shown at right.

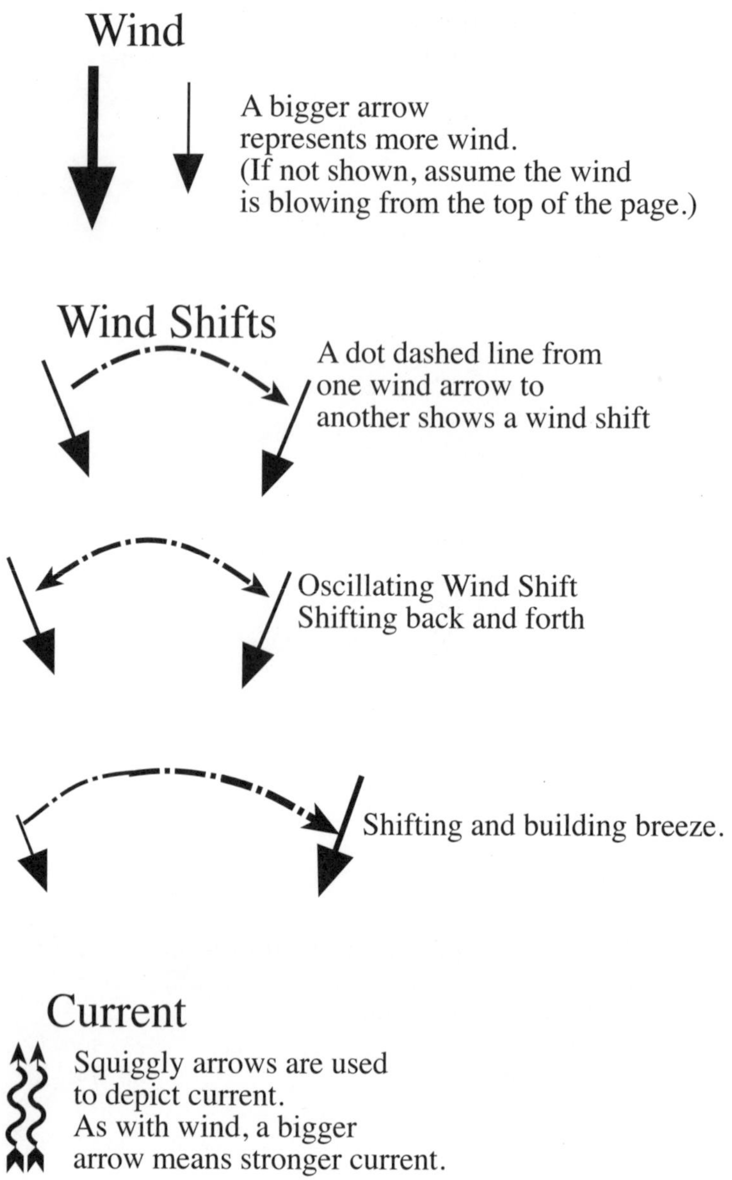

Wind

A bigger arrow represents more wind.
(If not shown, assume the wind is blowing from the top of the page.)

Wind Shifts

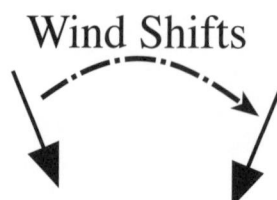
A dot dashed line from one wind arrow to another shows a wind shift

Oscillating Wind Shift
Shifting back and forth

Shifting and building breeze.

Current

Squiggly arrows are used to depict current.
As with wind, a bigger arrow means stronger current.

Wind moving down the course.
Here we see oscillations moving
down the course as patches of wind with
wind arrows to show direction

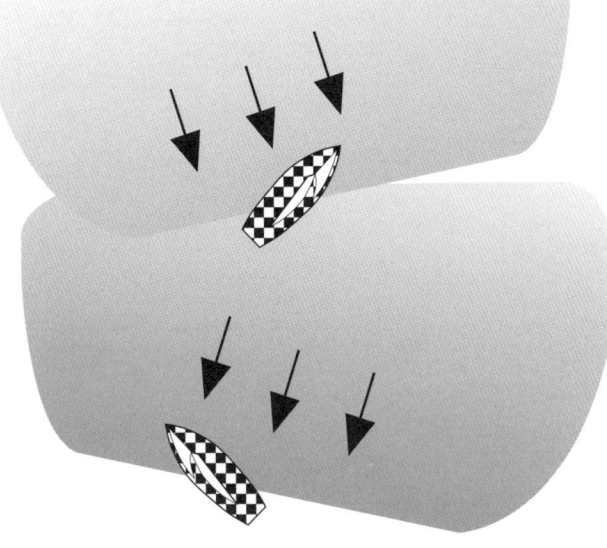

Boats and Motion

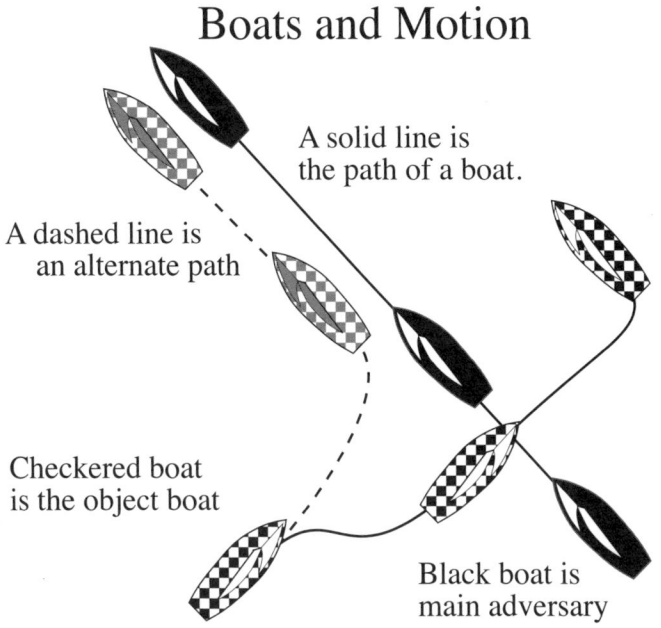

A solid line is
the path of a boat.

A dashed line is
an alternate path

Checkered boat
is the object boat

Black boat is
main adversary

Each boat on a path is presented in time sequence to other
boats on other paths. ie. The first boat on one path corresponds
in time to the first boat on any other path, and so on.

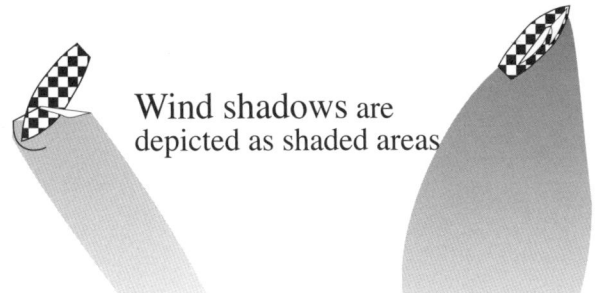

Wind shadows are
depicted as shaded areas

Other Symbols

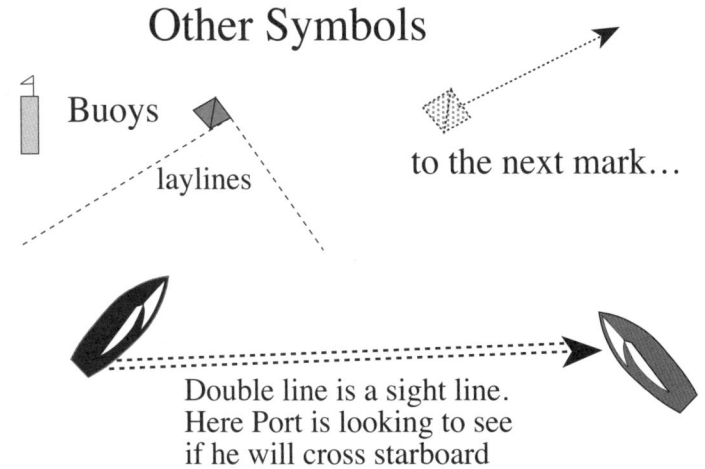

Buoys

laylines

to the next mark...

Double line is a sight line.
Here Port is looking to see
if he will cross starboard

Forward

Chapter 1: Strategy, Tactics, and the Racing Pyramid

1.1 Tactics
1.2 Why Do We Race Sailboats?
1.3 The Racing Pyramid
1.4 Performance Analysis

Tactics

Boat Speed

Boat Handling

Chapter 1: Strategy, Tactics and the Racing Pyramid

1.1 Tactics

This book covers sailboat racing tactics. *Tactics* in the broad sense means strategy, tactics, and rules. *Strategy* is the overall race plan. Strategy is based on wind, wind shifts, and current. Strategy does not include other boats. *Tactics* are the techniques used to implement strategy, to deal with other boats, and to comply with the rules. While strategy involves a plan, tactics are spontaneous. *Rules* are the International Sailing Federation *Racing Rules of Sailing* and the Sailing Instructions of a particular race. These are the rules of the game. You have to follow the rules to play the game.

1.2 Why Do We Race Sailboats?

Of course, successful racing involves much more than Tactics. Sailboat racing requires a broad mix of skills: There's tactics, and an understanding of wind and weather. We also need sailing and boat handling skills, specialized sail trimming skills, organizational skills to manage crew, and analytical skills to grapple with information. We need to be able to set goals and establish priorities, concentrate amidst chaos, ignore discomfort, and learn from our mistakes.

None of us can master all the skills, and every race challenges us in new ways, for no two races are alike. Part of the enduring appeal of racing is the breadth of the challenge it provides.

The appeal of sailboat racing goes beyond these challenges. We enjoy racing for the chance to be out on the water, for the thrill of working with the wind, for the challenge of competition, and for the camaraderie racing brings.

1.3 The Racing Pyramid

The ingredients to racing success can be viewed in a pyramid comprised of boat handling, boat speed, and tactics.

At the base of the pyramid is **boat handling**. You must be able to *sail* your boat well before you can *race* well. Next is **boat speed**. No matter what you race—cars, bicycles, horses, bobsleds, whatever—speed is essential. Because sailors are not always racing alongside their rivals, some underestimate the importance of speed in sailboat racing.

Tactics lies at the top of the racing pyramid. To race successfully you must work your way up the pyramid: Your boat handling must be second nature and your boat speed second to none. Tactics alone will rarely win races. Tactics just helps you beat boats with comparable boat handling and boat speed.

In *North U. Racing Tactics* we assume that your boat handling and boat speed are competitive. For more on boat handling and boat speed, refer to the companion volume, ***North U. Racing Trim***, which is available (surprise!) from NorthU.com, or your local chandler.

Before leaving this topic, one final point deserves mention: The foundation of the racing pyramid is **preparation**. It is difficult to sail well, and to sail fast, without a properly equipped boat (Fig. 1).

Fig. 1 - The Racing Pyramid.

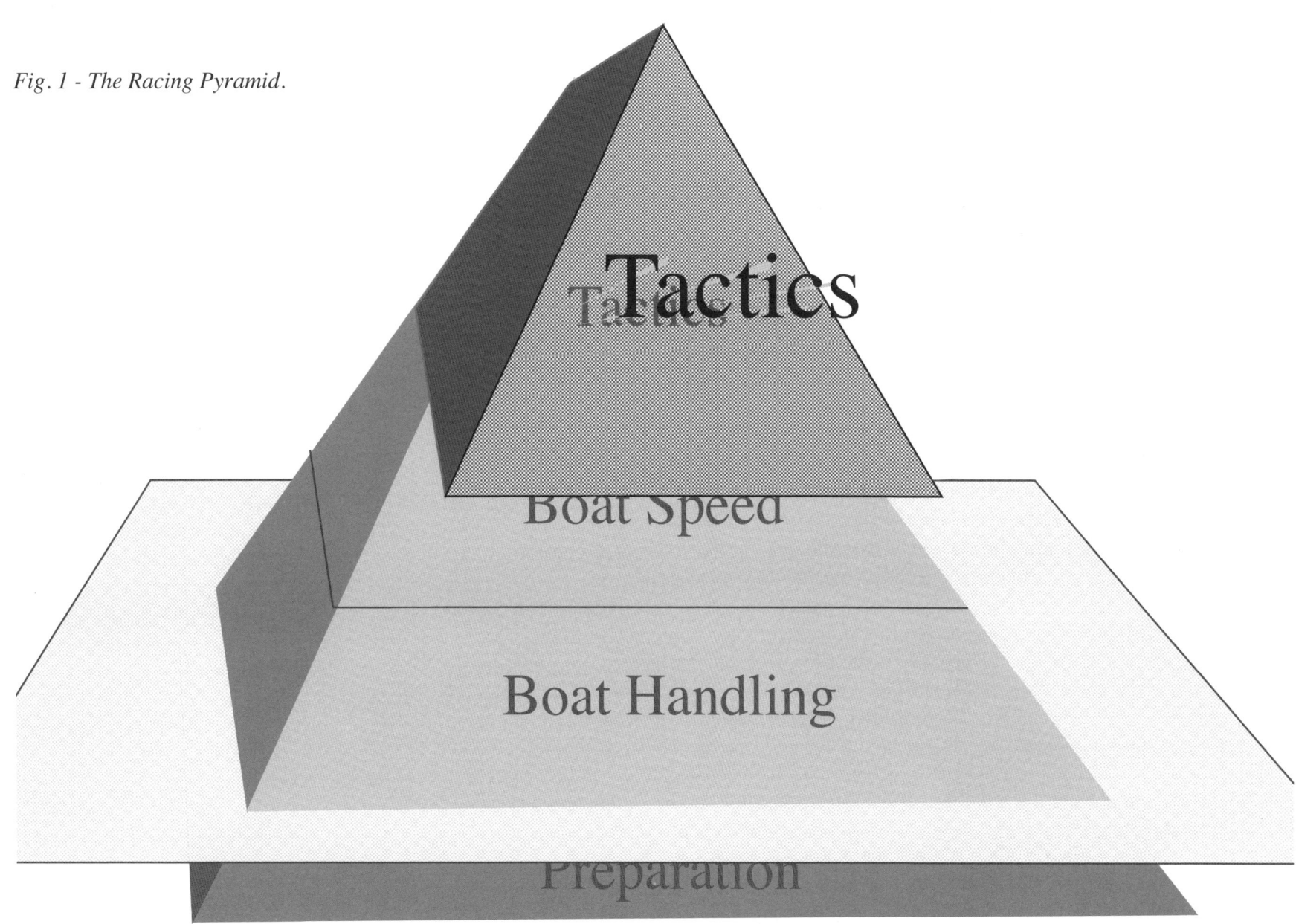

1.4 Performance Analysis

So, how are your skills?

The *Performance Analysis* presented here is intended to help you look at your racing skills and the overall skills of the crew on the boat you race. If you are a tactical king, you need to team up with a boat speed druid and a boat handling wizard. Of course, if you race single handed you'll need to be all these things!

Consider both strengths and weaknesses. Obviously, you want to eliminate weaknesses. As we shall see, there are also ways to shape races toward your strengths.

Performance Analysis:

Last year's fleet position: _____   Goal for next season: _____   **Strength   Weakness**

Tactics
- Upwind strategy, tactics, and rules .... _____   _____
- Downwind strategy, tactics, and rules .... _____   _____
- Starting strategy, tactics, and rules .... _____   _____
- Round the buoys and port-to-port / distance racing .... _____   _____

Boat Speed
- Upwind in light, moderate, and heavy winds .... _____   _____
- Helming, mainsail trim, headsail trim .... _____   _____
- Reaching in light, moderate, and heavy winds .... _____   _____
- Helming, mainsail trim, headsail trim .... _____   _____
- Running in light, moderate, and heavy winds .... _____   _____
- Helming, mainsail trim, headsail trim .... _____   _____

Boat Handling
- Do you have a full, regular crew? .... _____   _____
- Upwind: Tacks, reefs, and sail changes .... _____   _____
- Downwind: Spinnaker sets, jibe sets, jibes .... _____   _____
- Take downs, floater takedowns, and peels .... _____   _____
- Can you, personally, handle each position on the boat? .... _____   _____

Preparation
- Boat: Hull condition, keel & rudder shape .... _____   _____
- Weight distribution below decks .... _____   _____
- Rigging and hardware .... _____   _____
- Instrumentation (working, calibrated, integrated) .... _____   _____
- Sail inventory complete, and in excellent condition .... _____   _____

CHAPTER 2: RACE PREPARATION

2.1 INTRODUCTION

2.2 GET READY TO RACE

2.3 THE RACE PLANNER

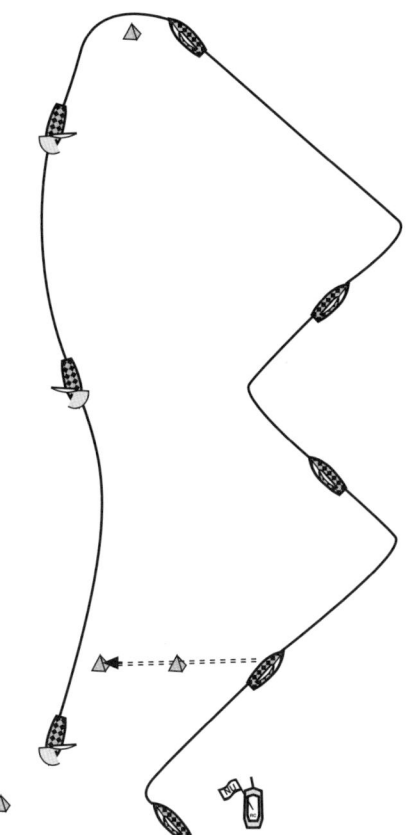

CHAPTER 2: RACE PREPARATION

2.1 Introduction

Many races are won or lost before they even start.

As boats head for the line some are ready to race and others are not. In this chapter we will look at things to do during the hour prior the start to get ready to race. Longer term preparation of the boat, crew, and equipment is covered in the companion text, *North U. Racing Trim*.

Every sailboat race is really several events in one. To succeed, you must understand the weather, harness the wind, and battle against opponents. To win, you will need to be ready for challenges of every type. You'll also need to figure out which are the critical variables for today's race.

2.2 Get Ready to Race

On the Way Out...

Race Day preparation begins with a routine to insure that everything needed is brought along and anything not needed is left ashore. Once on board, the time spent getting to the course area should be used to review any changes in technique or organization from previous races. New crew should be paired with regular crew and briefed on responsibilities. The boat should be rigged and, if conditions permit, sailed to the course area. Wind checks should be made periodically. Weather conditions and any special strategic situations (season/ series standings) should be discussed.

Pre-Race Checklist:

1. Collect weather and wind information.
2. Test sail selection and trim upwind.
3. Record close-hauled course and speed on each tack.
4. Sail the compass course for each leg of the race in sequence, noting wind speed and angle.
5. Tune up and test course sides with a tuning partner.
6. Set, jibe, jibe, jibe, and douse.
7. Plan sail selection and organize sails below decks.
8. Post start, course, and weather information.
9. Enter the marks of course into instrument system or as GPS waypoints.
10. Formulate an overall race strategy.
11. Discuss the strategy and basis with entire crew. Emphasize expected conditions to look for and things which might require a change in plans.
12. Check the starting line and plan starting strategy.
13. Set the prop and pump the bilge. Back down.
14. Review crew assignments; especially for new crew.
15. Locate any marks in sight.
16. Observe earlier fleets.
17. Get nervous & get used to it.
18. Get psyched—go team go!
19.
20.
21.

At the Starting Area...

Plan to arrive at the starting area one full hour before the race. During that hour you will have to plan strategy, make sail selections, and tune up. A routine checklist of pre-race responsibilities can make sure you touch all the bases. You can doubtless add to the list presented here.

One of the most valuable things you can do is to sail the entire course in miniature. This means sail the compass course of each leg in sequence. Here is what you will learn (Fig. 1):
- Are the windward legs balanced (with equal time on each tack) or are they skewed?
- As with upwind legs, are the downwind legs square to the wind, or are they unbalanced?
- If the course is a triangle or trapezoid, are the reaches close or broad? This will help determine tactics at the windward mark rounding and at the jibe mark. It will also help the crew position the spinnaker pole properly for initial trim.
- If the reach is a close reach, how much would the wind have to shift to make the leg a jib reach?

Sailing the course in miniature will give your crew the big picture, and allow them to plan ahead. The wind conditions are likely to change over the course of the race. Sailing the course in miniature will provide a base line to help you anticipate the impact of those changes.

If time allows then sail the full course to get a feel for geographic shifts and changes in conditions across the course. Also, if gate marks are set, get a bearing on the gate to aid in calculating the favored side of the gate.

Most of the information you need to gather prior to the start can be compiled in a Race Planner, such as the one shown in the next section. Of particular importance is the wind information you compile.

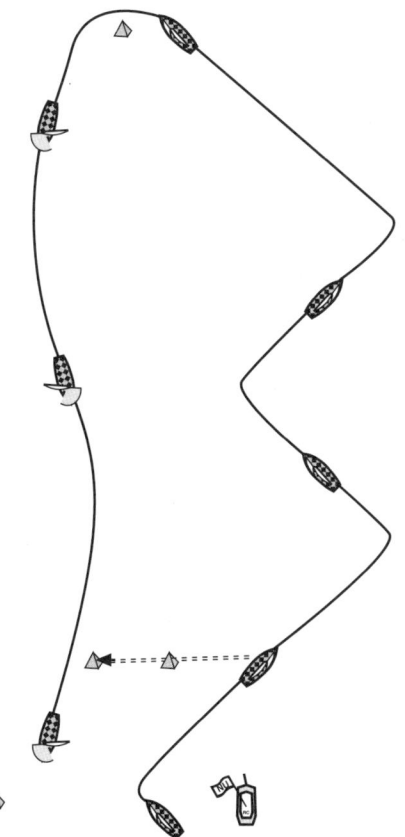

Fig. 1 - By sailing the course in miniature - or the entire course if time allows - you can anticipate the sailing conditions and plan strategy for upcoming legs. If gate marks are set then get the bearing of the gate line as you sail by.

2.3 The Race Planner

A standardized form, or Race Planner, can help you organize race information, and make sure you don't forget any details. A completed form is shown here. A sample blank is shown on the following page. Copy it, refine it, and send me ideas. You could be made famous in the next edition!

The form is divided into sections.

The Wind Graph

The purpose of the wind graph is to track the true wind direction over time. We do this not by luffing into the wind, but by recording our close-hauled compass course on each tack, and then averaging those numbers. For example, if our close-hauled course on starboard is 160°, while on port we sail 250°, then the wind direction is 205°. (In this example we are tacking through 90°, so on each tack we are sailing 45° off the true wind.)

Note: There are several reasons to work from close-hauled compass numbers rather then luffing into irons. For one, it allows us to tune up in race trim while at the same time gathering wind info. Second, luffing into irons beats up your sails; don't do it! Third, recent studies have shown that once the race starts, luffing into irons is "tactically disadvantageous." Since we'll be working from close-hauled compass numbers during the race, we might as well get used to using close-hauled numbers while we tune up.

How to Use It

During the hour prior to the start, and during the race, we'll record the time, wind speed, boat speed, and close-hauled compass course. Record starboard tack numbers under the Stbd heading, and port tack numbers under the Port heading. We'll then average those numbers to get the wind direction.

Here's the Trick

After recording the initial starboard number, if the next starboard number is to the right (higher) then record it on the next line, shifted to the right. If the next starboard number is to the left, then offset it to the left. Same for port, and ultimately, for the wind itself. In this way we create a graphic representation of the wind trend.

Wind Graph Example

The example on the following page shows a sample plot. Our initial port and starboard headings at 11:02 were 150° on starboard, and 240° on port. This corresponds to a wind direction of 195°. Subsequent readings on starboard of are 150°, 160°, 155°, 165°, and so on. On port-tack the sequence is 240°, 245°, 250°, then 260°, and so on.

After we record port and starboard numbers we average them and record a wind direction: 195°, 195°, 195°, 205°, 215°, 200° and so on in this example. After plotting wind direction and offsetting the numbers right or left, we can connect a string of readings into a graphic representation of the wind. This graphic will help us see trends and anticipate subsequent shifts.

This example shows the wind oscillating back and forth, and gradually shifting to the right - or so it seems.

Another Way

The process of plotting this information requires a lot of time and attention. An alternative is to purchase, install, calibrate, and maintain a set of integrated true wind instruments networked with a computer to record and display the information. When working well, these systems are awesome.

Race Planner

Wind Graph

Time	Wind Spd	Boat Spd	Stbd	Wind	Port
11:02	12	6.2	150	195	240
11:03	12	6.1		195	240
11:05	12	6.1			245
11:08		6.2	150	195	
11:12		6.1		160 205	250
11:18	13	6.2		215	250 260
11:22		6.3	155	200	250
11:27				165 210	250
11:30		6.2	155	200	
11:35	12			160 205	250
11:40		6.1		210	255
11:43				165 210	
11:44				215	260
11:48	12			170 215	
11:52				165 210	
11:55	13	6.3		170 215	
12:10	12			205	250
12:15	13			170 215	
12:20				165 210	
12:25				210	255
12:27				205	250

Race Info:

Race: **Spring Series**

Start Time: **Noon**

Start Area: **SA 3**

Class Flag: **#4**

Prior Class: **Farr 40**

Time Between Starts: (5) 10 15

Check in Required? (Yes) No

Course Info:

Leg	Dist.	Heading	Sails	Mark
1	1.75 m	195°	Lt 1	P
2	1.5 m	5°	.6	GATE
3	1.5 m	195°	Lt 1	P
4	1.5 m	5°	.6	GATE
5	1.75	195°		FINISH
6				

Starting Line:

Timed length of line: **1:35**

Compass course of line: **105°/ 285°**

Line +/- 90°: **195°**

Wind Direction: **205°**

(diagram: 195° 205° / 105°/285°)

Weather Forecast:

Wind Direction, Wind speed:
  South, going SW, 10 to 15 knots

Tide (Ebb/Flood); Sky, Seas:
  Strong Flood at start. Ebb starts at 2:28

Finish: 2:43:17   Boat **Moondance** Time **0:38** Ahead   Boat Behind **Lumpy Gravy** Time Behind **1:43**

Time : :   Ahead

Use the back of form for post race notes on trim, boat handling, wind, current, and equipment.

Race Info

In this section, list critical race details. It will save you the embarrassment of digging for the Race Book or Sailing Instructions as you watch everyone in your class start five minutes early…

Course Info

List the distance and compass heading for each leg of the course along with which sails you anticipate using.

Starting Line

Use this to plot the set up of the starting line, and by comparing that to the wind direction, you can determine which is the upwind (favored) end of the line. In the example shown, the right end of the line is 10° favored.

Weather Forecast

Essential meteorological data should be recorded here, along with the marine forecast. This often provides an amusing juxtaposition to the actual, observed weather.

The Back of the Planner

The back of the race planner should be used for post-race comments. Immediately after the finish, review the race leg by leg. Go over trim, tactics, and crew work; record new ideas. List any equipment problems (and think through any excuses you may need to explain away the race back at the bar). Confirm the schedule for the next practice (you do practice, don't you?) and race. Also print a diagram of your local race area on the back of your race planner. The chart can then be used after each race to record any local knowledge tricks you pick up concerning wind or current.

Keep a Notebook

Compile your race planners in a notebook, so that you can refer back to them over time. You may be surprised how often conditions repeat themselves. Your race planners will serve as the basis for developing and refining your local knowledge.

The ultimate value of this pre-race information will become clear as we refer back to it during the race strategy discussions which follow.

Race Planner

Wind Graph

Time	Wind Spd	Boat Spd	Stbd	Wind	Port

Race Info:

Race

Start Time

Start Area

Class Flag

Prior Class

Time Between Starts
 5   10   15

Course Info:

Leg	Dist.	Heading	Sails	Mark
1				
2				
3				
4				
5				
6				

Starting Line:

Timed length of line: _____

Compass course of line: _____

Line +/- 90°: _____

Wind Direction: _____

Weather Forecast:

Wind Direction, Wind speed:

Tide (Ebb/Flood); Sky, Seas:

Finish: Boat   Time   Boat   Time
Time   :   :   Ahead   Ahead   Behind   Behind

Use the back of form for post race notes on trim, boat handling, wind, current, and equipment.

On the back of your race planner, photocopy a chart of your race area. After each race diagram what you've learned about wind and current. Also note what you've learned about trim, boat speed, boat handling, and tactics. In addition, note any work the boat needs prior to the next race, and go over your upcoming race and practice schedule.

Chapter 3: Starting Strategy

3.1 Introduction: Elements of Strategy

3.2 Where to Start

3.3 Approaches

3.4 Conclusion

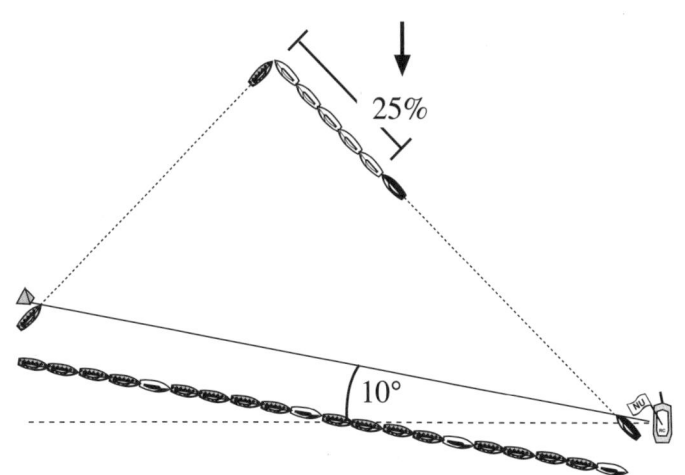

Chapter 3: Starting Strategy

3.1 Introduction: Elements of Strategy

The start of a sailboat race is one of the most exciting and demanding moments in sports. Starts require judgement, timing, and teamwork. They require an understanding of wind and weather, and knowledge of strategy, tactics, and rules. Starts demand dexterity at close-quartered maneuvering. Finally, starts require the ability to stay cool and concentrate in an environment packed with distractions. These requirements create a uniquely thrilling, and at times baffling, challenge.

Given so many areas of concern, our success will depend on our ability to prioritize—to determine which factors are critical to a particular start. The goal is to hit the starting line at the gun at the favored end, with speed and clear air, and freedom to maneuver at will.

The starting signal is but the midpoint of the start. A good start is one which finds us in the front row, free and clear, not just at the gun, but a or two minute later, after the sprint off the line.

To succeed we must create order from the chaos of the starting line. First we need a Starting Strategy—a game plan based on the information gathered during our race preparation. Once we have a plan, then starting tactics will be used to implement the plan. This chapter will look at starting strategy—how to make a plan. The next chapter, on Starting Tactics, will show us how to execute the plan.

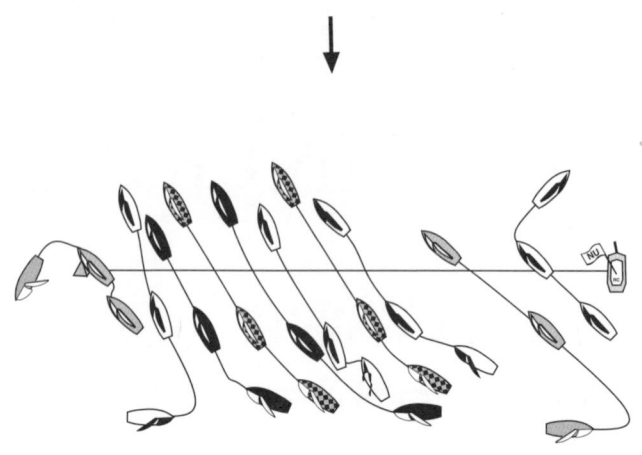

Fig. 1 - Starts are chaos. To succeed, we will first need a starting plan (strategy). Then we will need to execute the plan (tactics) despite all the distractions. A good start is one which finds us free to pursue our race strategy a minute or two after the gun.

The importance of a good start cannot be overstated. While it is not necessary to win the start in order to win the race, a good start is usually required. A good start gives the freedom to pursue strategic objectives without interference (Fig. 1). A poor start means compromising strategy and setting off in the wrong direction, or sailing in bad air to pursue strategic goals.

In this chapter we will concentrate on upwind starts. Chapter 6 covers Offbeat Starts.

Fig. 2 - Simply put, start right to go right, start left to go left, and start in the middle to keep your options open.

3.2 Where to Start

Starting strategy means deciding where on the line to start. When deciding where to start, consider three factors:
1. Race Strategy for the First Leg.
2. The Set of the Line.
3. Making it Work.

Race Strategy will effect starting strategy, as we shall see. The Set of the Line refers to the angle of the line to the wind. In Making It Work we will look at balancing race strategy, line set, and other concerns.

First Leg Strategy

Race Strategy for the first leg is the first factor to consider in deciding where on the line to start.

If strategic considerations suggest sailing up the right hand side of the beat, then a start at the right end of the line is preferred. By starting at the right end we are free to tack and go right immediately after starting. Clear air is relatively unimportant, as we will be tacking away. Freedom to tack and go right is the first priority.

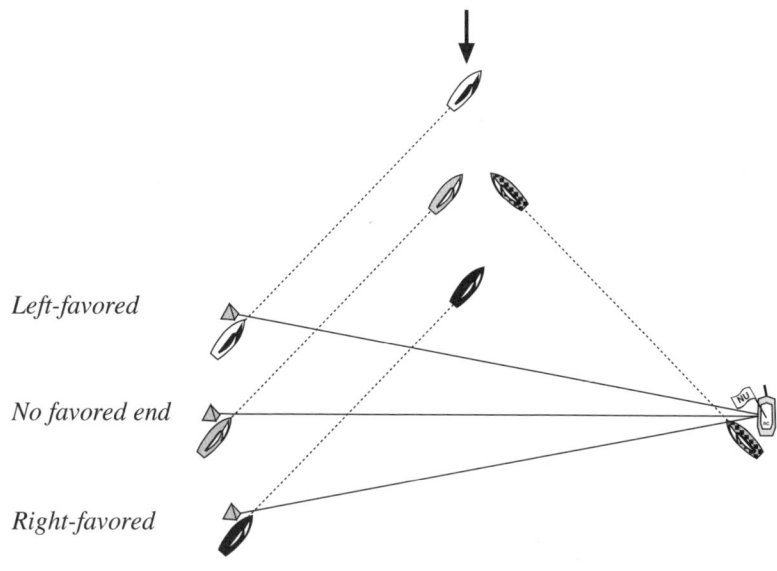

Fig. 3 - The upwind end of the line is favored, as it is closer in sailing distance to the windward mark.

If our race strategy says go left, then a start near the left end is called for. The advantage here is not as strong as starting right to go right. More critical than the exact position is clear air, and the freedom to continue to the left unimpeded.

If there is no clear advantage to either side, then a midline start is indicated. There are several advantages to a midline start. From a starting perspective, it is often the easiest and least crowded place to start. From a race strategy perspective, a midline start gives the greatest flexibility, as it offers the freedom to go either way. For further discussion of Upwind Strategy, see Chapter 7.

Simply put: Start right to go right, start left to go left, start in the middle to keep your options open (Fig. 2).

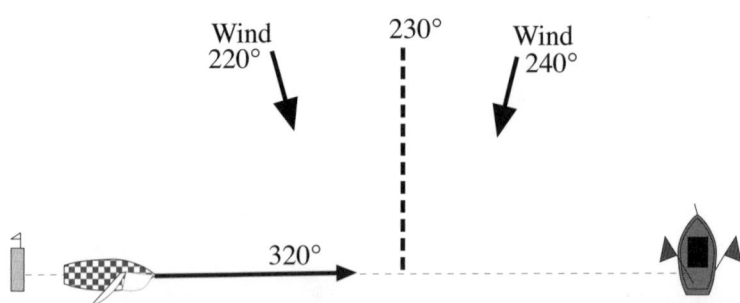

Fig. 4 - To find the favored end, compare the compass course of the line to the wind direction. If the line is 90° from the wind then the line is square. If the wind is less than 90° from the line you are headed toward the favored end; greater than 90° and you are sailing away from the favored end.

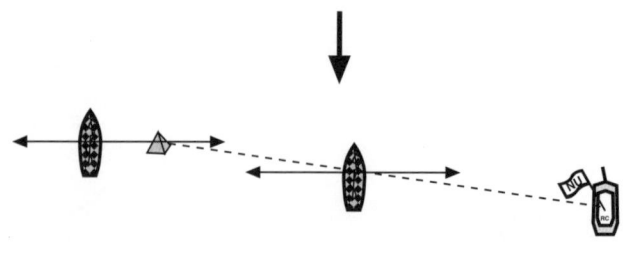

Fig. 5 - You can determine the favored end–and ruin your sails–by luffing into irons, either on the line or off one end.

The Set of the Line

The set of the line means the angle of the line to the wind. Since we are racing upwind, there is an advantage to starting at the end which is furthest upwind—we call this the favored end. A starting line set perpendicular to the wind does not have a favored end. When the line is not square to the wind then one end—the upwind end—is favored (Fig. 3).

Two questions come to mind:
Q1. How can you figure out which end is favored?
Q2. How much difference does it make?

Q1. Which End is Favored?

There are several ways to find the favored end of the starting line. Some are better than others:

1. Compare the compass bearing of the line to the wind direction. You can then plot which is the favored end. Once you know the bearing of the line, you can update your calculations as the wind changes. For example, in the illustration, the line is set at 320°. If the wind direction were 230° the line would be square to the wind. With the wind at 240° the right end is 10° favored. With the wind at 220° the left end is 10° favored (Fig. 4).

2. Luff into irons on the line (or off one end). Sight across your boat (using the traveler bar, e.g..); your sight will be square to the wind. While this is a popular technique, I recommend against it for two reasons: First, you must redo it every time the wind shifts; second, it is hell on your sails—the worst thing you can do to them (Fig. 5).

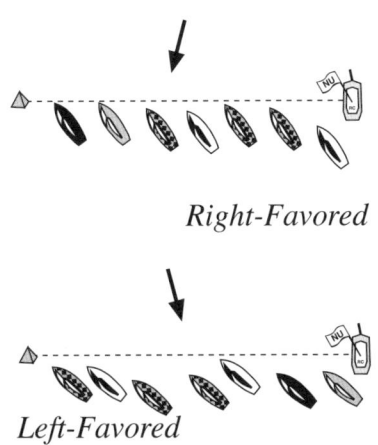

Fig. 6 - You can determine the favored end by observing other starts. If the fleet comes off the line bow to bow, the right is favored; bow to stern, then the left is favored.

3. Observe other starts. If the fleet lines up bow to bow off the line, then the windward end is favored. If the fleet lines up bow to stern, then the pin end is favored (Fig. 6).
4. Sail past one end of the line close-hauled, and observe the relative distance as you pass abeam of the other end. This offers only a rough measurement.

No matter which technique (or combination) you use, you must recheck the line if the wind shifts. The first technique is preferred because it allows you to quickly recalculate after a wind shift. It also allows you to determine how many degrees off square the line is set, and the magnitude of the advantage, as we shall see.

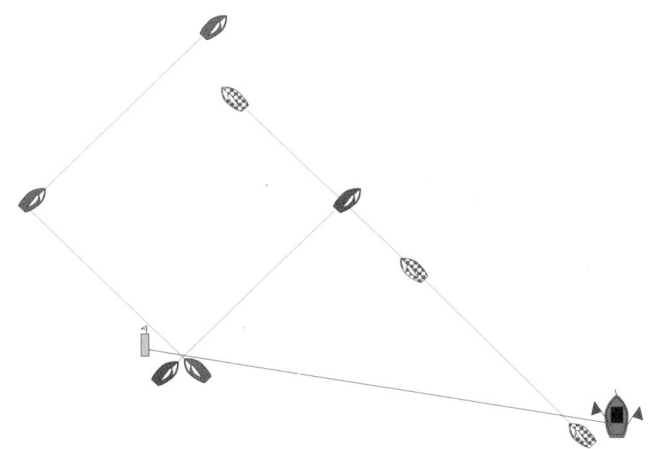

Fig. 7 - You need not start on port tack to take advantage of a left end favored line. You will realize the advantage when you tack.

Q2. How Much Difference Does It Make?

Two boats starting from opposite ends of a square line will be equally far from an upwind mark. If they were on converging tacks, they would hit bow to bow. If the line is not square to the wind, then one will start ahead, as shown in Figure 3.

You don't need to start on port tack to take advantage of a pin-favored line. You will realize the advantage when you tack to port (Fig. 7).

How Far Ahead?

For a line 5 degrees off square (most are), the advantage is 12.5% of the distance between the boats. If the line is 10 degrees off square (not uncommon), the advantage is 25% of the distance between the boats.

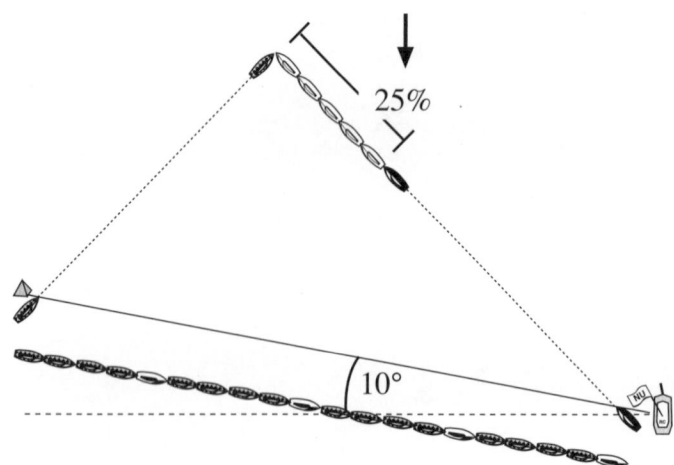

Fig. 8 - For a line that is 10° off square, the advantage at the favored end is 25% of the length of the line— That's 5 boat lengths on a line 20 lengths long!

On a typical starting line, 20 boat lengths long, and 10° off square, the advantage from end to end is 5 boat lengths! A 5 length lead off the line is no small matter—clearly the set of the line is an important factor in our decision where to start (Fig. 8).

Mark Position and Favored End Not Related

Not so clear is the fact that the position of the windward mark does not determine the favored end of the line. Boats starting at the upwind end will be in the lead, and will be able to cross boats starting from the downwind end and lead them to the mark. Even though the downwind end may be closer as the crow flies, it will be further in upwind sailing distance (Fig. 9).

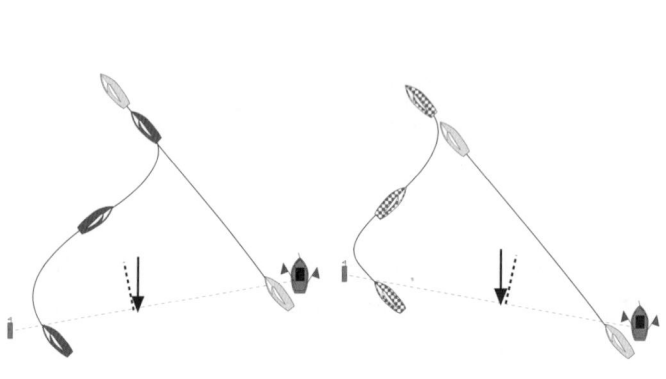

Fig. 9 - The position of the windward mark does not determine the favored end of the line. The set of the line relative to the wind, not the mark, determines the favored end.

The position of the mark may be a factor in our first leg strategy, and thus may impact our decision on where to start, but it does not determine the favored end of the line. The favored end is a function of wind direction—not mark position.

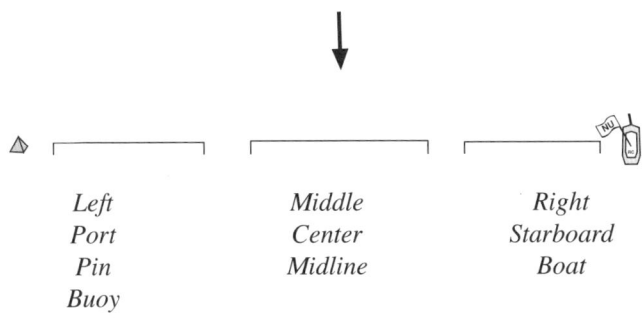

Fig. 10 - Pick a section of the line for your start. Your exact starting spot will depend on how the start plays out tactically. Each section has many names.

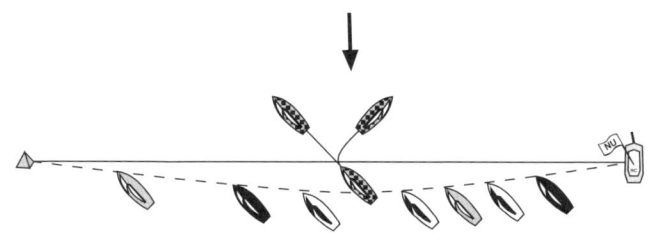

Fig. 11 - Midline starts are preferred if you do not have compelling reasons to push toward an end.

Making It Work

Where to start? In addition to our first leg strategy and the set of the line, there are a collection of other factors which we will lump under the heading of Making It Work. Wind shifts, crowding, and clear air are among the issues we must consider.

A start near the favored end, but clear of congestion, is best. It provides the advantages of the favored end without risking clear air and the freedom to maneuver and accelerate. Remember—you don't need to win the start the win the race; you just need a good one. We'll look at a couple of situations to get a feel for how to decide where to start.

Pick a Section

You don't so much pick a spot on the line as you pick a section: left, middle, or right (Fig. 10).

Midline Starts

Unless there are strong reasons to push toward an end, a midline start is the best choice (Fig. 11). The advantages include minimal crowding on the approach and strategic flexibility once you clear the line. You can set up for your start with a variety of approaches (details in the next section), and you can often get a jump by avoiding midline sag.

Start Near the Favored End

When your choice is one of the ends, it is best to target near—but not right at—the favored end. A favored end draws a crowd, and you will get much more consistent starts by staying out of crowds. Slide down the line just far enough to clear the crowd, and you will have a much easier time getting a good start. In fact, you may end up with the best start, as the boats in the crowd deprive each other of the air and room necessary to accelerate off the line.

Even when one or more boats do get good starts right at the favored end, many more are buried. By hedging toward the middle of the line, you dramatically increase the odds of getting a good start.

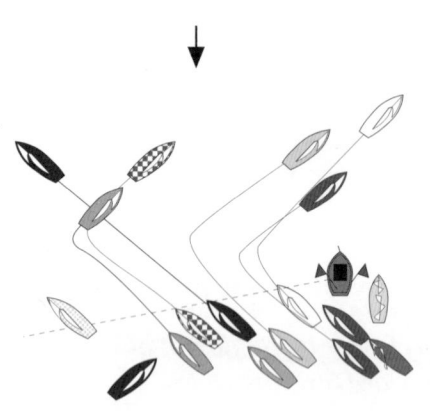

Fig. 12 - To go right, try a start just below the crowd at the boat end. You can get off the line with clear air and be a leader going to the favored side.

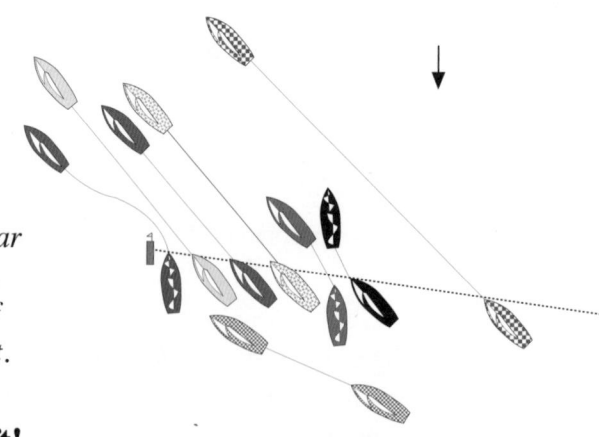

Fig. 13 - To go left, a start with clear air is essential—you can't tack out. Once again, setting up just clear of the crowd helps assure a good start.

Go Right!

If your goal is to start right and tack out immediately, it may be worth it to go for a start right at the boat. If you get the perfect start congratulations—and more power to you!

Even if you end up in the second row it's OK, since you'll be tacking out. Sounds good—but in reality the front row boats will be tacking immediately, and you will have to delay your tack to avoid tacking in bad air. A position in the front row a little bit down the line will allow you to sail full speed until you do tack, and may actually allow you to tack sooner! Plus, you avoid the hazards of barging (see Chapter 5: Starting Rules for more on barging), and of other crowd-related problems (Fig. 12).

How badly do you need to be the first boat to tack out? What are the odds of pulling it off? Can you afford the risk of being buried? How does that compare with the much higher percentage play of being the third boat to tack by starting down the line?

Go Left!

If everything favors the left side, then get ready to battle! There is little margin for error in these starts, and few spaces in the front row when the pin end is favored. The boat furthest left may be the only one with clear air, but any hesitation may allow the next boat up the line to roll over the top. Again, a start part way up the line may be the easiest way to get the second best start (Fig. 13). You'll be able to create space for clear air and room to accelerate. In fact, a jam up at the pin may leave you with the best start! Plus you control the center and the first tack. We'll look at the tactics of this position in detail in the next chapter.

Hit the Shifts

The best start in shifty conditions is one which allows you to sail to the shift with speed and affords you the room to tack when the shift arrives. Blast off from the middle of the line, tack if the next shift is coming from the right, and sail fast. When racing to a shift, speed is more important than pointing, and room to tack is critical if you are going to take advantage of the shift when you get to it. Stay clear of crowds and sail fast.

3.3 Approaches

The next step, after deciding where on the line to start, is to decide how to get there. We must select our approach. The approach we choose will form the basis of our starting plan. There are a variety of approaches available, each with advantages and disadvantages. It is best to be well-versed and comfortable with each, so we can select the one which best fits the prevailing strategic and tactical circumstances.

The approaches covered in the following pages include:

- *Reach Out and Back*
- *Half Speed Approach*
- *Vanderbilt Start*
- *Triangle Approach*
- *Port Tack Approach / Pin End Start*
- *Port Tack Approach / Midline Start*
- *Port Tack Start*
- *Luffing Start*
- *Elvstrom Start*
- *Dip Start*

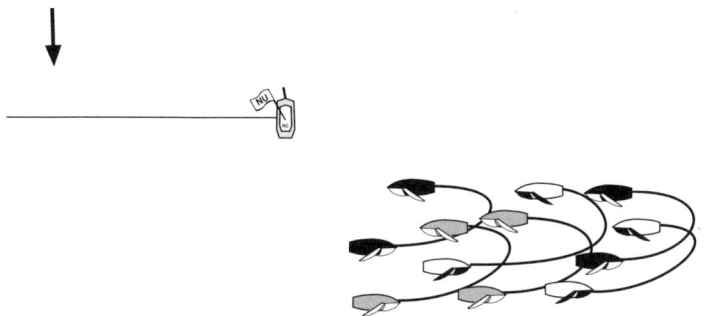

Reach Out and Back

The most commonly used approach is the *Reach Out and Back*. Often the fleet moves én mass, reaching out on port tack one and a half to two minutes before the start. At around a minute everyone tacks back and reaches to the line, trimming up to close-hauled for the last fifteen to thirty seconds.

Advantages

The Reach Out and Back is simple.

Danger!

This approach creates clumps of boats. You want to avoid crowds. This is also a barging set up. There are better approaches.

The Secret to Success

The key is to hold a position with clear air in the front row. Try to leave room for acceleration ahead and to leeward by sweeping down and luffing up, effectively stalling while those ahead sail further down the line. Then use the space to accelerate. The biggest problem is keeping the space for yourself. Some boats will try to go over and under you to steal it; others will come in on port tack.

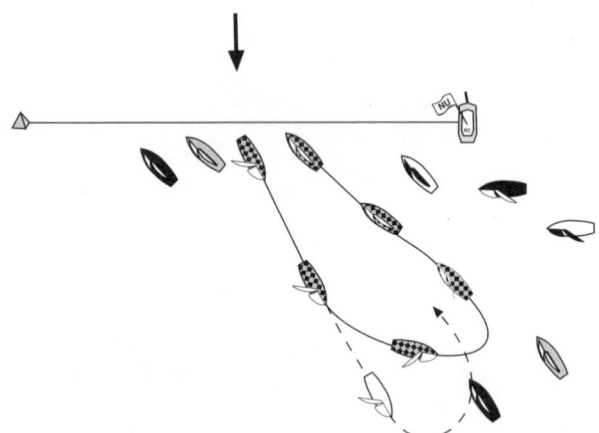

The Half Speed Approach.

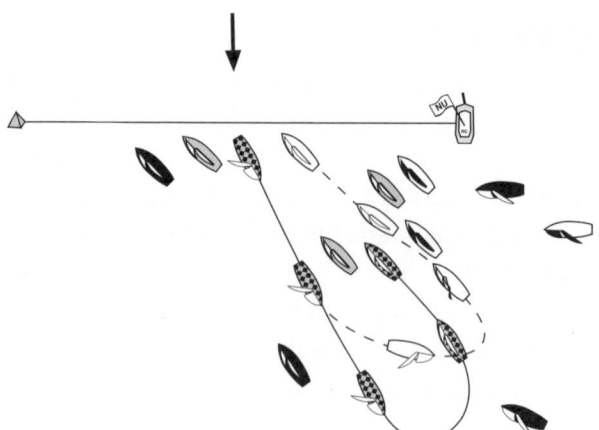

Vanderbilt Start with Half Speed alternative.

Half Speed Approach

The *Half Speed Approach* is popular and effective. Sail away from a spot on the line and turn back early to allow for the congestion and bad air of the fleet. Once headed for the line, speed is adjusted to properly time the approach. The object is to approach at half speed with final trim coming early enough to reach full speed and hit the line at the gun.

Advantages

The half speed approach is relatively simple and reliable–a good choice in moderate to heavy air. It gets you set up early and puts you in the front row. This approach is effective in any part of the line. For a right-hand end start, you can bottle up the crowd reaching in above you.

Danger!

Tacking kills speed. Jibing carries you away from the line. Allow plenty of time for your turn. At the same time, beware setting up too close to the line, without room to accelerate. Also, avoid this approach in light air, or in a heavy boat which is slow to build speed.

Another problem with the half speed approach is that you must sail on port tack into oncoming starboard boats and find room to make a full 180° turn.

The Secret to Success

In order to be able to accelerate readily to full speed it is important to maintain at least half speed throughout the approach. Another trick to knowing when to "pull the trigger" and accelerate to full speed. Truth is, time, speed, and distance judgement is the secret to success in most starts, not just this approach.

In big fleets there is rarely sufficient room to be fully accelerated at the gun. The key is to hold a position with clear air in the front row. Boats tend to push to the line early to keep clear air. While you might prefer to hang back to leave room to accelerate, you have to stay in the front row to keep clear air.

The Half Speed Approach shares the basic out-and-back geometry of the Vanderbilt Start (coming up next), but has some distinct advantages.

Vanderbilt Start

The *Vanderbilt Start* is a popular but flawed approach. The basic plan is to sail away from the line on a port tack broad reach on the reciprocal of your starboard tack close-hauled course. You then tack or jibe, and return to the place from which you departed.

Advantages

The attraction of this approach is its simplicity.

Danger!

The problem? It doesn't work. At least not in a competitive fleet it doesn't, as it lacks flexibility. If anything throws off your timing, you will be late.

One flaw is that you cannot make your turn at the appointed place and time because other boats will be there. If you somehow find room for your turn, you will lack the clear air necessary to accelerate; and the crowds will block your path.

The Secret to Success

In a small, uncompetitive fleet you might succeed with this start, but you would do better to practice a technique (like the Half Speed Approach) which will be of more use when you move up.

If you insist on using this approach, remember that the speeds out and back are not necessarily equal, and you must allow sufficient time for your tack or jibe. The Vanderbilt start was developed for big boat match racing. Congestion and disturbed air make it a poor choice for fleet racing.

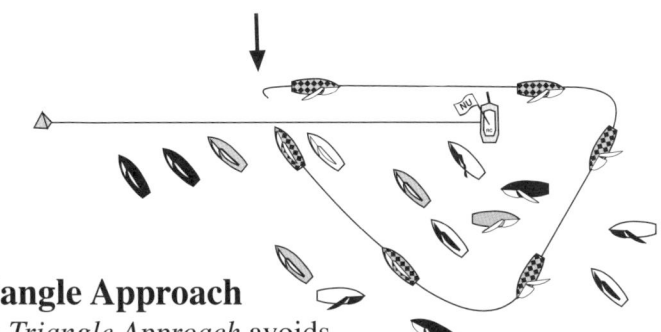

Triangle Approach

The *Triangle Approach* avoids the problem of searching for room to tack or jibe in a crowd. Initiate the triangle at the spot from which you want to start. Sail from your starting spot on a port beam reach, along the line and its extension. Next, jibe to a starboard broad reach and sail down to the final approach layline. Finally, head up to close-hauled for the run at the line. Each leg of the triangle is of about the same duration–usually 30 to 45 seconds each for a 30-foot boat, scaled up or down for larger or smaller boats.

Advantages

The turn onto your final approach doesn't slow you down and doesn't take much room. You are also very maneuverable as you reach in. The triangle approach allows more room to accelerate than other approaches and provides flexible timing in variable conditions. Recommended for light to moderate air. Works anywhere on the line.

Danger!

Don't be late. If you are late, you may not have time to get through the crowd and around the bargers.

The Secret to Success

If you fear you are running late on leg two, cut the corner. Often legs two and three turn into one long continuous sweeping turn.

Chapter 3: Starting Strategy

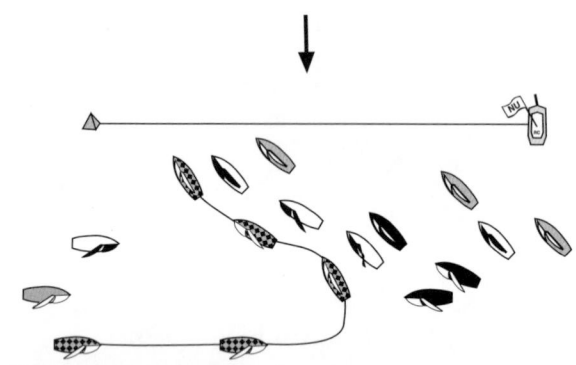
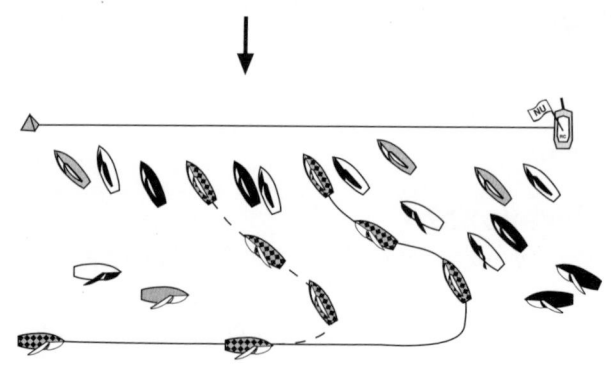

Port Tack Approach for a Pin End Start

From the starting pin, sail up the line on port tack, toward the fleet. As you near the pack of starboard tack boats working down the line, tack to leeward of the crowd and lead them back toward the pin.

Advantages

A port tack approach allows you to set up late and is the easiest way to judge the timing for a pin end start.

Danger!

Where do we begin? There are the obvious port-starboard and tacking-too-close risks, the risk of not finding a space to tack into, and the need to tack and accelerate late in the sequence. This can be particularly difficult in light air.

The Secret to Success

This is an excellent set up for a pin end start. Note the time as you sail past the pin, and keep track of the split time as you sail up the line. It may be necessary to duck some early starboard tackers and then jump into the next gap. Obviously, good crew work is essential to a smooth tack and quick acceleration. Your approach should set up three to four boat lengths from the line. Also, to carry speed into the tack, head up and trim on port before tacking to starboard.

Port Tack Approach for a Midline Start

As with the pin end start, come in from the left end of the line about three boat lengths below the line. As you near the pack of starboard tack boats, duck the early bunches and tack into a gap.

Advantages

A port tack approach allows you to set up late and avoid clumps of boats which have set up early. It protects you from attack, and allows you to attack others if you choose.

Danger!

As with the Port Approach for a Pin End Start, there are right-of-way hazards and the challenge of tacking and accelerating late in the sequence.

The Secret to Success

This is a great set up for a midline start. Your tactician should be looking ahead to find a gap. Once you find a gap, the key is to tack into the windward edge, leaving room to drive off to leeward and accelerate. Allow plenty of time to search out a gap, tack, and get up to speed. Again, good crew work is essential to a smooth tack and quick acceleration.

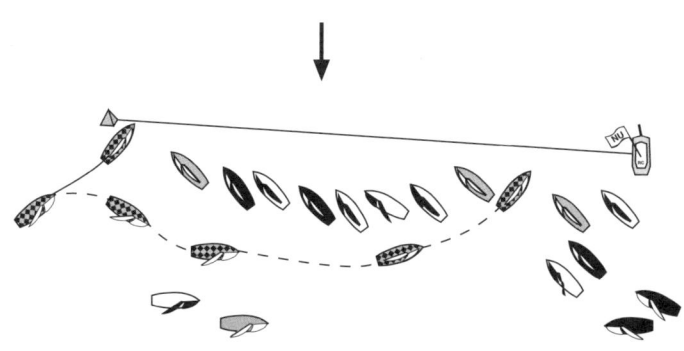
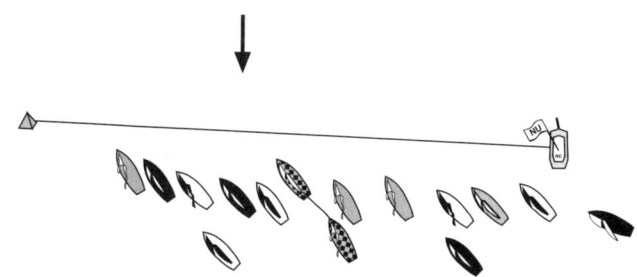

Port Tack Start

Approach the line on port tack, shoot through a gap, and cross the fleet. This approach requires great timing and nerves of steel.

Advantages

If the line is port end favored and the right-hand side of the course is advantaged, a port tack start lets you blast off toward the favored side.

Danger!

Are you Crazy? Poor timing or unsteady nerves can lead to disaster. Other boats doing the same thing can make it messy.

The Secret to Success

Timing, anticipation, and a bail out plan. It is always better to duck boats – even if you duck the entire fleet – than to slam in a last second tack. Look ahead as the fleet sets up and pick your gap. Close reach with lots of speed and trim into your gap. Be ready to search for a new gap on a moments notice. An adverse current can hold up the fleet and make it easier to succeed with this approach. (It has also been suggested that this approach be reserved for times when you are sailing someone else's boat.)

Luffing Start

Select a spot and luff near the line. Trim for speed in the final seconds before the gun. The object is to secure a spot on the line.

Advantages

In a crowded fleet on a short line, this is one way to secure a spot in the front row.

Danger!

The dangers are not leaving enough room to accelerate, and having other boats sail over and under you before you can respond; or being too far back and falling into bad air.

The Secret to Success

Preserve as much space as possible ahead and to leeward, while preserving clear air and holding your space in the front row. You'll need this room to accelerate.

This approach is popular in dinghies, centerboard boats and some one-design keelboats, particularly in large fleets where it is difficult to find room on the line. It is not practical for any but the lightest keelboats. If your boat is relatively light in a mixed fleet, set up to leeward of the crowd, luff everyone, and then blast off while others wallow.

Lufing boats tend to drift to leeward. *Fore-reaching* – holding close-hauled trim while sailing above close-hauled – is an effective way to minimize leeway and create accleration room to leeward.

Chapter 3: Starting Strategy

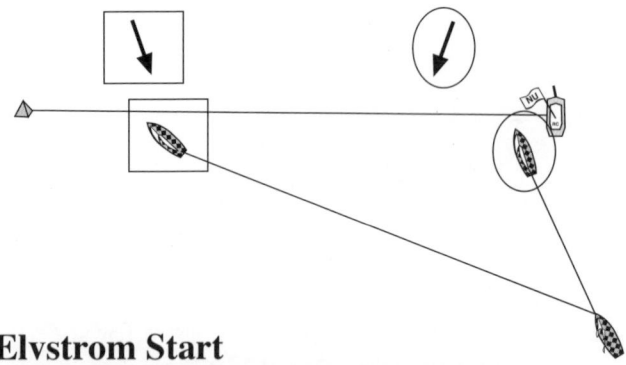
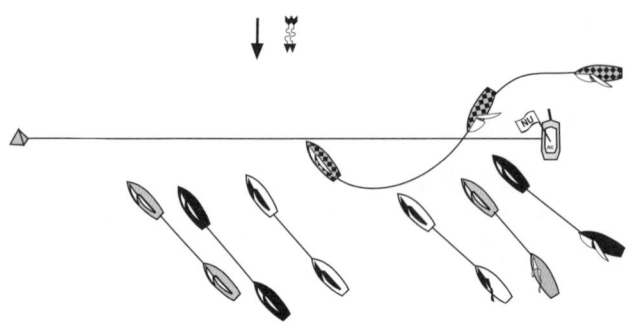

Elvstrom Start

This is an approach I observed Paul Elvstrom using in shifty conditions. He positioned himself to leeward of the R.C. Boat and luffed on the starboard tack layline. If the last shift before the start was a lift, he sailed it to start at the favored boat end of the line; if the last shift was header, he sailed it to the favored pin end.

Advantages

In shifty conditions, this approach allows a last minute decision based on the final shift before the gun.

Danger!

Timing is tricky. Be sure to allow enough time to get to the line in a header—and be sure you will be able to fetch.

The Secret to Success

The beauty is that while the rest of us luffed on the line and battled to hit the first shift after the start, Elvstrom was a step ahead, hitting the last shift before the start.

Dip Start

Approaching from the wrong side of the line, find a gap and dip into it from above.

Advantages

When the line is difficult to approach from below due to light wind and strong current, you drop into a front row seat.

This approach is useful only when the line is difficult to approach in the conventional way.

Danger!

The danger of being over early or of being luffed by leeward boats limits the usefulness of this approach. Also illegal if the One Minute Rule is invoked.

The Secret to Success

The Dip Start can succeed in light air and adverse current. A large R.C. boat with the line site near the bow increases the chances of success, as does a pin favored line.

3.4 Conclusion

Starting strategy is a game of choices, requiring a balance between overall strategic goals, line set, and crowding. Once the strategic decision has been made on where to start, we must select an approach appropriate to the conditions. This strategic plan lays the groundwork for our start.

We now turn to *Chapter 4: Starting Tactics*, to turn our plans into reality.

Chapter 4: Starting Tactics

4.1 Introduction
4.2 Tactical Information
4.3 The Start
4.4 Pitfalls
4.5 Conclusion
4.6 Building Skills
4.7 Starting Quiz Questions

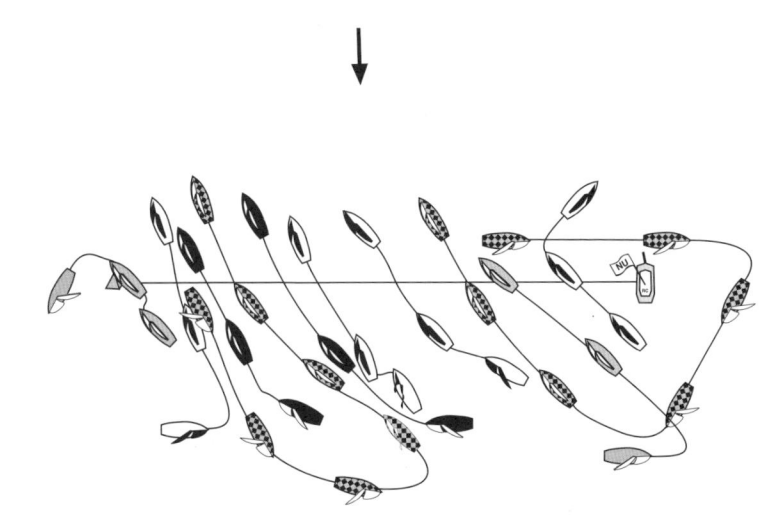

Chapter 4: Starting Tactics

4.1 Introduction

With our strategic plan set, Starting Tactics will be used to execute a start which meets our strategic goals. Our goal is to arrive at the selected section of the line at the gun at full speed with clear air and no interference from other competitors. No mean feat (Fig. 1).

This chapter will look first at the tactical information we need and how to gather it. Next, we will look at the start itself—those final fractions of a minute which can unravel the best laid plan. This section includes the final approach, the critical sprint off the line, and some common pitfalls.

4.2 Tactical Information

We gather tactical information (Fig. 2) about the line to help us execute our approach. This is different from the strategic information we gathered to decide where on the line to start.

The information we need includes:

The timed sailing length of the starting line (Fig. 2a).
This information will help us judge our timing as we set up for our start and as we make our final run at the line. It can also help us figure out if other boats are close enough to pose a threat to our plans.

Laylines to each end of the line (Fig. 2b,c).
Knowing the layline to each end, particularly if you plan to start near the end, will help you set up. Obviously, you want to be inside the right end layline to avoid barging, and inside the left layline to fetch. But you also

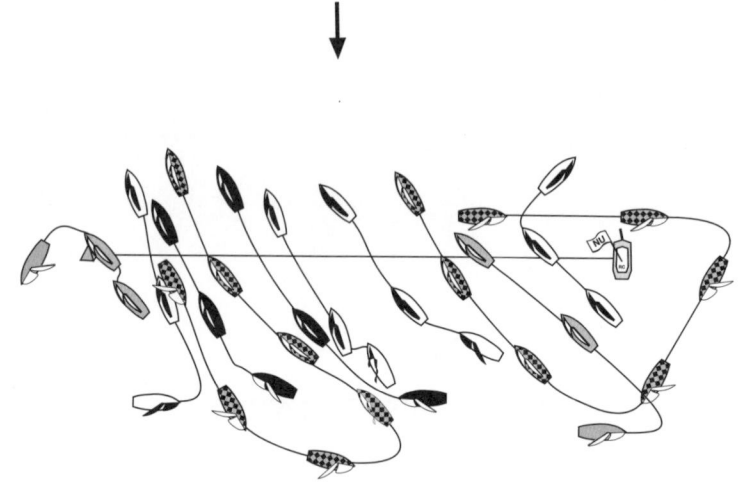

Fig. 1 - Tactics will give us the tools to hit the line at the gun in clear air at full speed at the favored end.

can use the layline to position yourself up or down the line. For example, if you want to start five boat lengths down the line, you need to make your turn five lengths after crossing the layline, not five lengths after passing under the end of the line.

Line Sights off each end of the line (Fig. 2c).
Line sights to each end of the line can help us judge how close to the line we are. This is particularly useful for midline starts or when other boats obstruct our view of one end. Compass bearings are not an effective way to judge the line, as it is not practical to sight the line with a hand bearing compass as you approach. Line sights using a range to an object on shore or to a nearby

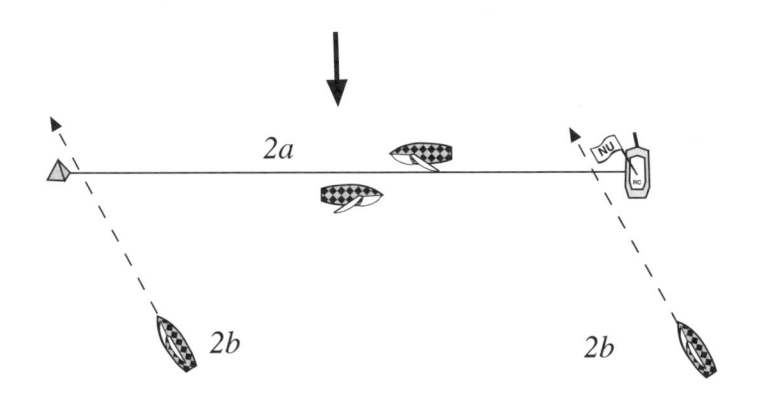

Fig. 2a,b - Tactical Information.
2a - Time the line. (Check both directions to test for current.)
2b - Check the laylines.

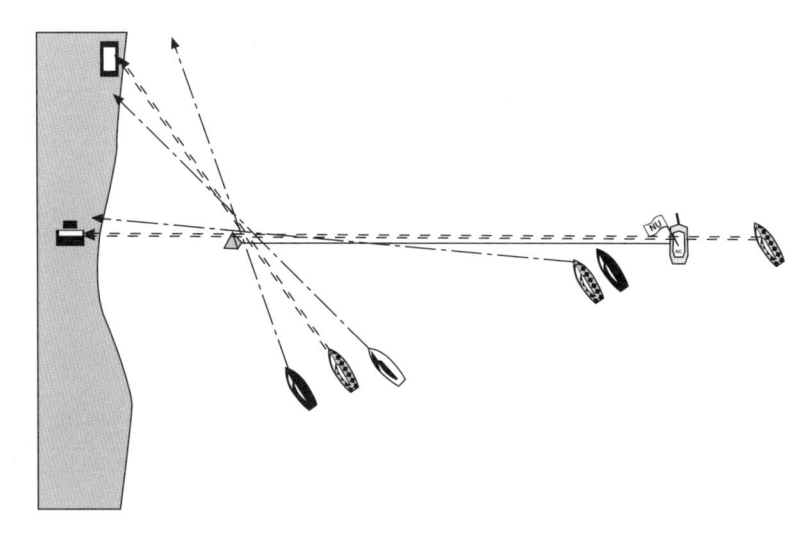

Fig. 2c - Get line sights off the ends and laylines. The line sights can help you call the line even when your view of one end is cut off. Layline sights can help you set up inside the laylines

anchored boat (such as a judges boat or spectator boat off the pin end) are what we want. If you are near the committee boat on your final approach, the eyes of the line caller offer a definitive reference.*

This tactical information will help us execute our start. For our starting plan, we will need to choose from one of the approaches described in the previous chapter.

---

* Secret note to Race Committee personnel: If you are a line sighter, sight to leeward of the line to hold the fleet back until the gun.

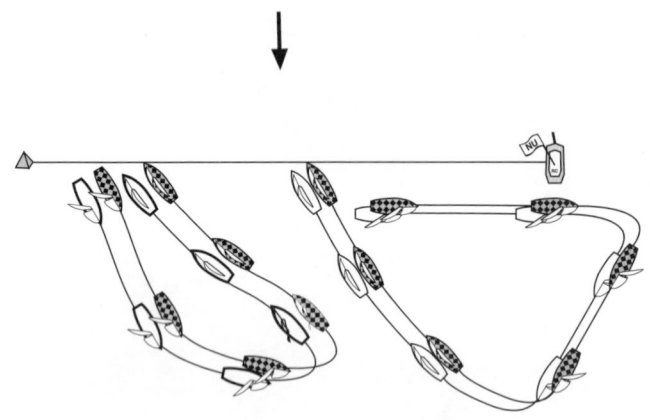

Fig. 3 - The Practice Start: Whichever approach you choose, do a practice run to prepare for the real start.

4.3 The Start

Regardless of the approach we choose, the details of timing, speed, and clear air can be a struggle. Our approach gets us set up. We have taxied into place. Next is our sprint down the runway and the climb out.

The Practice Start

A practice start helps assure success. A dress rehearsal of our planned approach (Fig. 3) lets us:
1. Confirm lines of sight and bearings on the line.
2. Check laylines.
3. Confirm wind direction and close hauled headings.
4. Approximate timing for the final approach.
5. Check sail trim for acceleration off the line.
6. Confirm crew organization and communications.

A practice start is an important part of preparing for our final approach. Obviously, it lacks some of the frenzy of the real thing, but it offers a valuable base line.

I often us the three minute signal for our practice start.

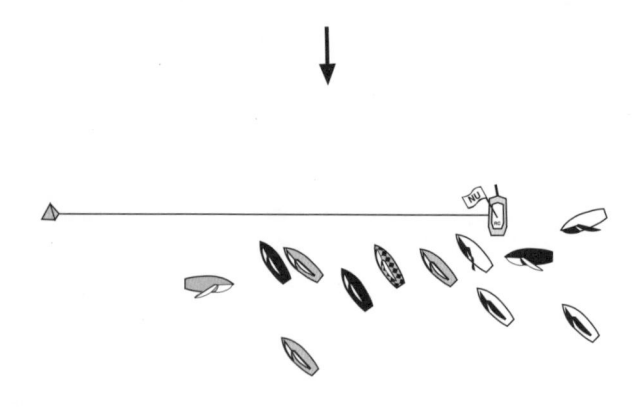

Fig. 4 - The Final Approach: Sail your boat. Ignore the chaos around you. Appoint a spokesman to handle inter-boat "dialogue."

The Final Approach

Our goal is to hit the line at the gun, with full speed, clear air, and no interference from other boats. Here are some things you can do to accomplish this: Sail your boat, create room, control speed, kill time, keep clear air, accelerate, sail faster than full speed, defend your space, start near a marshmallow, call the line, call time, speed and distance, and get off the line.

1. Sail Your Boat

On the final approach you must charge the line. This is no place for the timid. Push hard to hit the line with full speed at the gun. Don't hold back. With the practice run under your belt, you should be able to communicate easily with the crew and concentrate on speed and timing. Do not let the histrionics on boats nearby distract you. Appoint a "spokesman" to handle boat-to-boat "conversation." If the tactician, helmsman, and sail trimmers sail the boat, you will leave the chaos in your wake (Fig. 4).

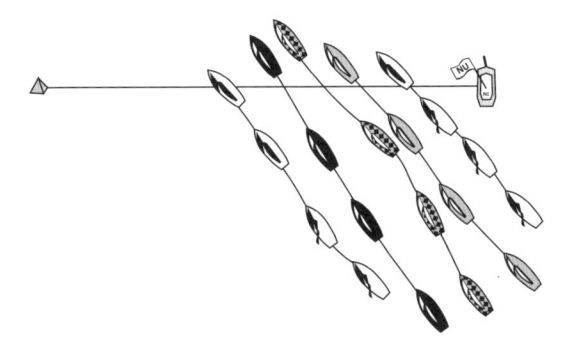

Fig. 5 - To create room, first squeeze up. Then drive off to accelerate.

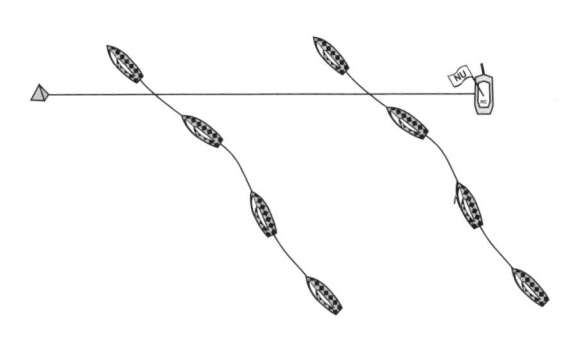

Fig. 6 - To control speed luff the jib first. This keeps the bow up and helps create room. Or fore-reach, sailing above close-hauled with close-hauled trim.

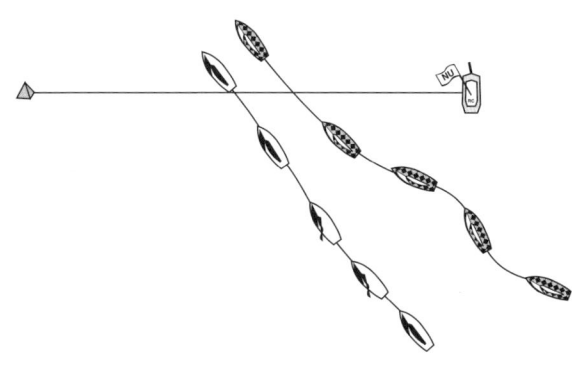

Fig. 7 - Oversteering is an effective way to kill time.

There are several techniques you can use during the final approach which will help you start with speed.

2. To Create Room

Perhaps the single most important thing you can do on the final approach is create a double space to leeward. You then use part of this space to drive off and accelerate to full speed. Your goal is to save part of the space for after the start, so you won't have any interference from leeward. By carving a double space, you can accelerate more quickly and avoid the danger of sailing down into bad air. You create room by pinching up under boats to windward (Fig. 5).

3. To Control Speed

If you need to slow down during your approach, luff the jib first and keep the main trimmed. This creates weather helm, holding the bow up and preserving space to leeward (Fig. 6).

Remember that it takes a long time to trim a genoa—call for trim early so you have full trim when you need it. Time your approach so you hit the line at full speed. Trimming at the gun is too late.

4. To Kill Time

Rather than slow down, a better way to burn off extra time is by over-steering and sailing extra distance (Fig. 7). Keep your speed. Steering erratically will keep others away, preserving space and clear air. (My crew tell me I'm great at over-steering!)

5. To Keep Clear Air

Near the line it is important to keep clear air. You want to keep your bow even with those around you. If you fall into bad air, it is difficult to accelerate. At the same time, you want to hold back with room to accelerate to the line. Boats which are too close to the line will not have room to accelerate without

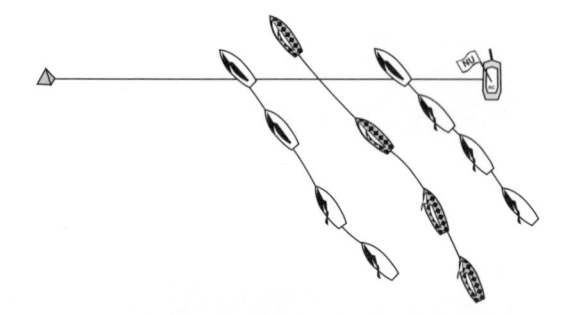

Fig. 8 - To keep clear air hold your bow up. But hang back to keep room to accelerate.

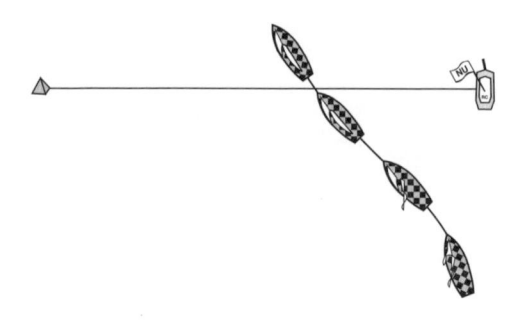

Fig. 9 - To accelerate from a luffing position drive off by trimming the jib first, then trim the main.

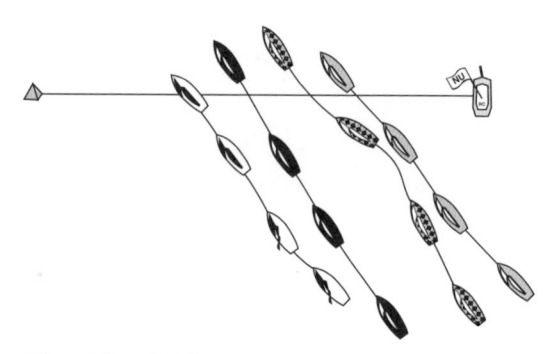

Fig. 10 - With enough room you can accelerate to faster than close-hauled speed and then trim up.

being over early; boats which are too far back will be in bad air. This is a difficult balance to strike (Fig. 8).

The more room you can preserve in front of you for acceleration the easier it will be to preserve space to leeward, which you can use later if needed. If you use up your forward space, you will be forced to drive down and give up some of your cushion to leeward. You may even be driven down into the exhaust of the boat to leeward.

6. To Accelerate

To accelerate from half speed, bear off a few degrees from close-hauled. Trim the jib first to drive the bow down, then trim the main. If the main comes in too early it creates weather helm, making it difficult to bear off and accelerate. It also may push the bow up and over early. Trim the jib to accelerate, trim the main to squeeze up to course as speed builds (Fig. 9).

Setting up with a space to leeward helps insure a good start. Without the space to drive off it will be difficult to accelerate. You may end up backwinded by boats close to leeward, or blanketed by boats driving over on top of you. If you have a good double space you can start with full speed and keep clear air off the line. In fact it may be possible to start going faster than full speed.

7. Faster than Full Speed?

Full speed is passé. Our goal is to hit the starting line at faster than full speed. But how?

If you have room to leeward to drive down the line you can accelerate on a close reach to speeds faster than close-hauled. When you trim up to course you will carry the extra speed for a few boat lengths—enough to squirt you out in front of the pack as you come off the line (Fig. 10). We won't settle for full speed anymore—we want to come off the line faster than full speed!!

Fig. 11a *Fig. 11b*

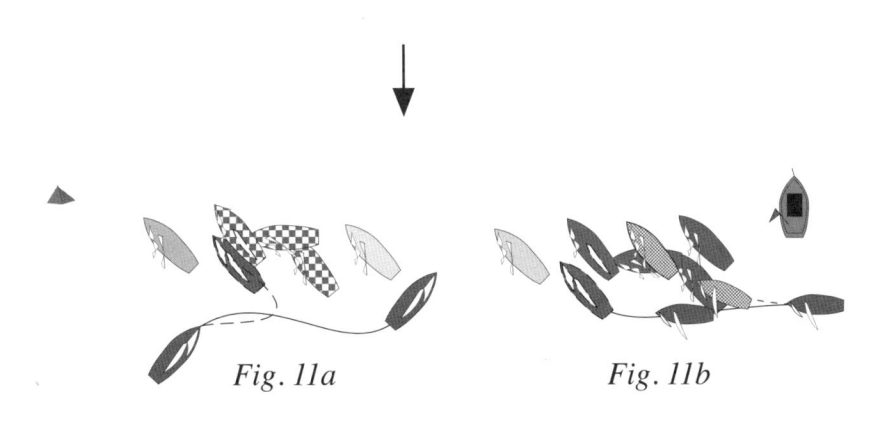

Fig. 11a - To defend your space from a port-tack poacher, rotate your boat across your space with your sails luffing.
Fig. 11b - When a starboard tack shark attacks, lure him in above you, or let him pass, and then head up sharply.

Fig. 12 - Start near a marshmallow.

8. To Defend your Space

Once you are set up with a space to leeward, you may have to defend it from those who would steal it away. This may happen while you are killing time, luffing, before you make your final mad dash to the line. Suppose you see a port tack boat sailing down the line, eyeing your space; or you see a starboard tacker ducking sterns, looking for a space to cut in. How can you defend you position? With sails luffing, turn your bow down and stretch your boat across your space. Unless the space is huge (big enough for two), this should scare off the treasure hunters. The port-tack boat should continue down the line; while the starboard tacker may take the space to windward, rather than leeward. Once the threat has passed, trim the main hard and put the helm over to bring your bow up. You may let your neighbor to windward off the hook with this move, but you should be able to save your space (Fig. 11a,b).

If you have already started to build speed on your final dash, then don't worry about others sailing into your space. The port tacker won't be able to tack and accelerate into your spot before you drive over him, and the starboard boat won't be able to drive through you far enough to be a threat. As you trim up, you will gas him.

Another way you can protect your territory is with sweeping turns up and down. This is an effective way to kill time and preserve your space.

9. Start Near a Marshmallow

Another useful technique is to find a "marshmallow" to set up nearby (Fig.12). If you can surround yourself with slow boats, you will be assured of less interference coming off the line. (Kinda' makes you wonder about all those times you found yourself near the fleet champion at starts last season, don't it?)

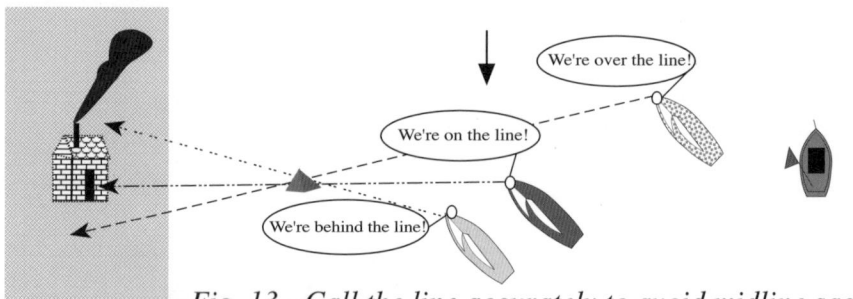

Fig. 13 - Call the line accurately to avoid midline sag.

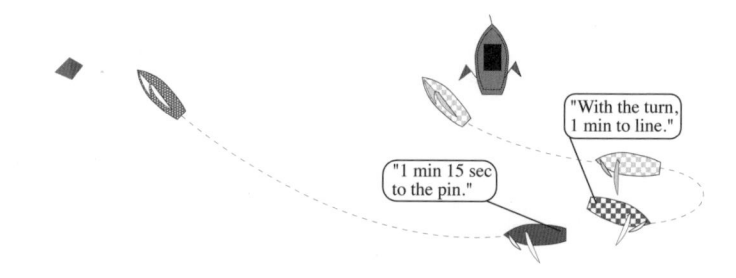

Fig. 14 - You should always know your time to the line. With practice you will be able to make accurate calls.

10. Call the Line

A crew member in the bow pulpit should signal information about other boats and distance to the line. Point at other boats with fingers, and hold fingers up to give boat lengths to the line. Signal where to go with a thumb: up to accelerate, down to slow, windward to head up, and leeward to bear off. The bow crew needs a watch to call the start effectively. As soon as she (or he) knows you will be clear, she/he should get off the bow (Fig. 13).

11. Calling Time, Speed, and Distance

Calling starts is tricky—you need to know when to put the hammer down. Too early, and you'll be over, or you'll have to stall at the last moment; too late and you'll be buried by those around you. At every moment during the sequence you should know how far from the line you are (Fig. 14). As you sail away this includes time for a turn.

It isn't easy, but with practice you will find you are able to guess time to the line quite accurately. It is an important skill.

12. Getting Off the Line

The starting signal marks the midpoint of the start. We've dashed down the runway—now for the climb out. The final seconds before the start, and the two minutes after, are often a pure sprint for clear air. Speed is the key ingredient. A little ex-

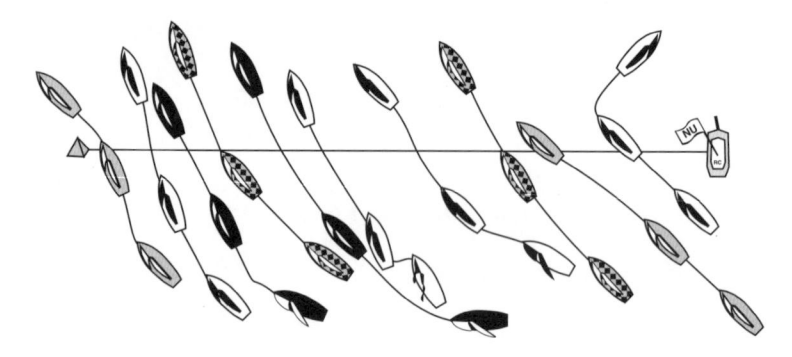

Fig. 15 - At the gun blast off the line and Sail Fast. Only those with speed will be free to pursue strategy unimpeded. Others will have to compromise strategy to keep clear air.

tra speed or pointing here translates into a big advantage. Make sure you are tuned up before the start; concentrate on sailing your boat; ignore others. Try to start faster than full speed if possible, and blast off. Settle the crew and concentrate on steering and trim.

The tactician should watch the compass and the fleet for shifts and room to tack. Being a shade slow or a little low eventually leads to bad air, and problems multiply. Keep clear air and keep moving. Nothing else matters (Fig. 15).

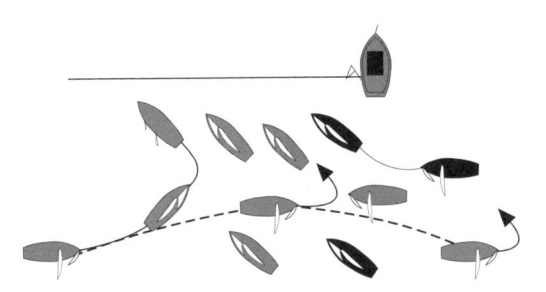

Fig. 16 - Don't get caught in a crowd going the wrong way.

Fig. 17 - Don't duck boats if you aren't sure you have plenty of time to come out the other side.

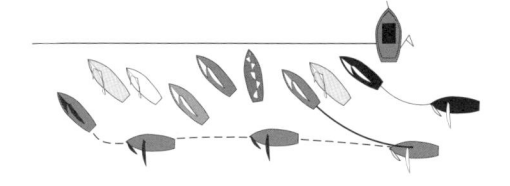

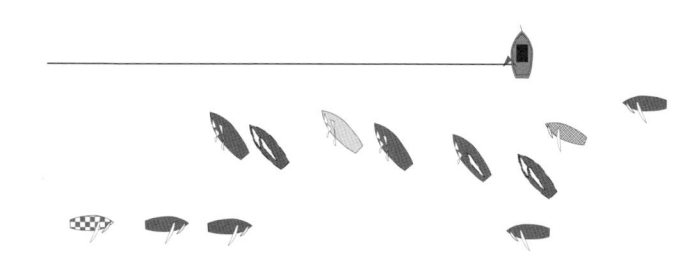

Fig. 18 - On a port tack approach match up the boats to the available spaces - and turn back early if there are no vacancies.

4.4 Pitfalls*

Sailboat races are won by the crew making the fewest mistakes. Nowhere is this more true than around the starting line. The most common mistake is being late for the start. Much less common is being over early. Listed below are the most common reasons for being late, and other assorted mistakes and pitfalls: Caught going the wrong way, son of caught going the wrong way, too far from the line, too late, too early, barging, can't fetch the pin, buried at the start, bad air, tunnel vision, above a pincher, below a footer, and rules.

1. Caught Going the Wrong Way

You're reaching down the line on port tack, looking for a place to turn around. As the pack gathers for a run at the line it can be impossible to find room to turn in the crowd. To keep clear air, look ahead and turn before you get into the crowd. Otherwise, by the time you emerge from the other end and get turned back you will be late, and behind everyone. Turn back early. Point your bow toward the line (Fig. 16).

2. Son of Caught Going the Wrong Way

This happens on starboard tack. Ducking sterns of other starboard tack boats stalling ahead. Once you start to duck you may never emerge. It is safer to keep your bow headed for the line. Don't duck unless you are sure you have plenty of time to come out on the other end (Fig. 17).

3. No Vacancy

You are on a port tack approach, the third of three boats reaching up the line, searching for gaps in the crowd. Count the gaps ahead – if there are only two spaces (or fewer) remaining, then turn back early. Don't continue up the line if there aren't as many spaces as boats in the hunt. (Fig. 18).

---

*Author's Note: We of course have *never* personally experienced *any* of the troubles described here. This section is based *entirely* on observation and hearsay, and may lack the veracity of the balance of our writing.

Fig. 19 - As the leading boat on a port tack approach you need to overturn your tack to keep from being squeezed by the trailing boat.

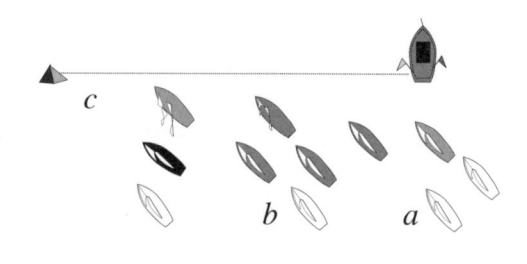

Fig. 20a - Don't get too far from the line.
b - Don't be late.
c - Don't be too early either!

4. Squeeze
If you are the lead boat on a port tack approach then beware the trailing boat tacking when you do, and putting you in the squeeze. Over turn on your tack to force the trailing boat to spin its tack, and then trim up hard to open a gap. (Fig. 19).

5. Too Far from the Line
When the fleet gets between you and the line there is no way to get through, and you get only bad air. In most conditions it pays to stay within a few lengths of the line. In light air or adverse current stay right on the line. It is easy to get pushed away and hard to get back (Fig. 20a).

6. Too Late
You approach too late, get bad air, and can never accelerate. Has this ever happened to you? Me neither.

Once, when I was stuck in a streak of late starts I adjusted my timing to try to be five seconds early. It is easier to kill time than to recreate it. Set yourself up to be a few seconds early (Fig. 20b). Don't be late!

7. Arrive Too Early
You either end up over early, or you stall and start with no speed and get run over. Timing is tricky–close enough to control part of the line, but far enough back to have room to accelerate (Fig. 20c).

8. Barging
Stay below the layline to the windward end. Any time your final approach is from above the layline, you are asking for trouble (Fig. 21b). Barging is reviewed in Chapter 5: Starting Rules.

9. Can't Fetch the Pin
When you find yourself outside the layline to the pin, bail out. At the first sign of trouble jibe around. Tacking to port is suicide. You may be able to come away with a decent start, instead of being wrapped around the pin as the gun fires. For a pin-end approach, you must know the layline and stay above it (Fig. 21a).

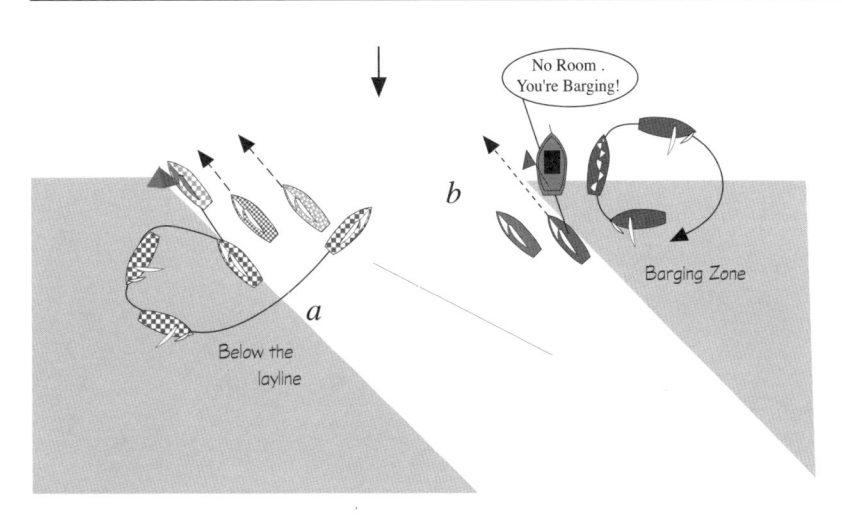

Fig. 21a - If you find yourself below the pin layline, an early bail out can save you. b - Stay between the laylines and don't barge.

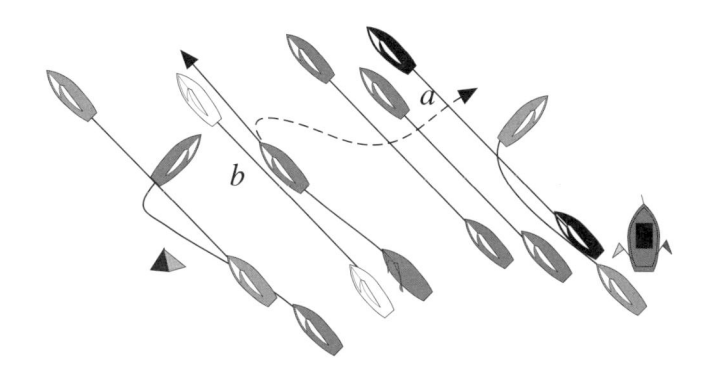

Fig. 22a - If you are slow to "pull the trigger," you can get buried at the start.
Fig. 22b - Once buried, you can hang on or tack out.

10. Buried at the Start

"Everything seemed fine, then we trimmed to go and nothing happened. We shot out the back of that fleet so fast you'd think we came out of a cannon." If you're off the pace by one instant, those around you get the jump.

Sails don't come in instantaneously. From the thought "I need speed" to the reality takes 5 steps: Thought, Call, Trim, Accelerate, Speed. Call for trim before you need it (Fig. 22a).

11. Starting in Bad Air

Coming off the line in bad air requires a quick evaluation of options. Can we tack? Can we squeeze up or drive off into clear air? It can take minutes before things open up and you have a chance to clear out. If you are unsure what to do, consider your overall strategy. If you want to go right then it may be worth ducking a few sterns to get out that way. If you are on the favored tack or if you are headed for the favored side, it may be worth eating bad air for a short while—though it will seem an eternity (Fig. 22b).

If you'd like to tack out, watch out for boats inside you preparing to do the same. Try to spare yourself the utter frustration of being tacked on just as you try to clear your air.

The tactician should have a contingency plan in mind in the event of a bad start. Think about it before it happens, then see to it that it doesn't.

12. Tunnel Vision

You hit the line right on time and get so excited you over steer and over trim and pinch and . . .

Over-trimming at starts is very common. All that energy and excitement—plus you are trying to squeeze every last bit of performance out of the boat. Until you are at full speed in clear air and open water, over-trimming squeezes the life out of your performance instead.

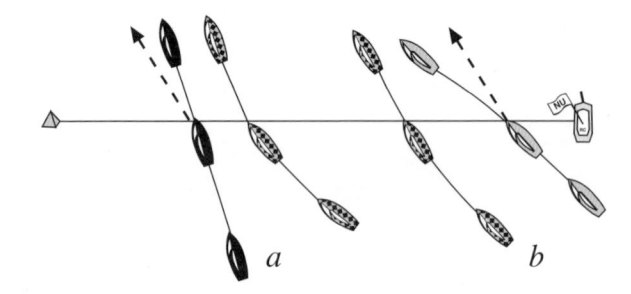

Fig. 23 - A pincher (a) below you can ruin your start—and his own. Try to gas off a footer (b) before the speedster rolls over you. Sometimes you have to beat pinchers and footers at their own game before you can sail your boat properly.

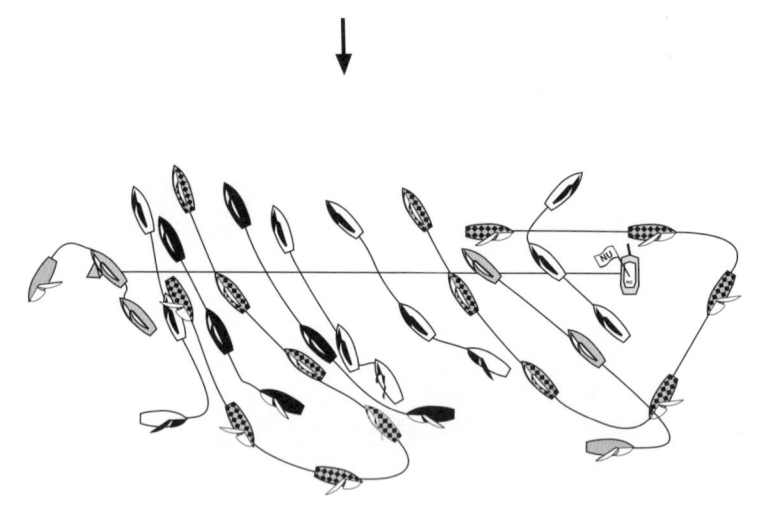

Fig. 24 - Starts require a good plan, great teamwork, and impeccable timing.

13. Start above a Pincher

You come off the line fine, but the guy below you sticks his boat up and pinches. He is slow, but just fast enough to sneak under you and give you bad air. As he ruins your start it is little consolation that he is hurting himself too (Fig. 23a).

14. Start below a Footer

This can be a problem, or a blessing. If we are inspired to new heights of performance in order to hold off the speedster, this can work to our advantage. If the speedster rolls over the top of us then, we have a problem (Fig. 23b).

15. Rules

In addition to the regular racing rules, there are some special rules which apply only at starts. Know the rules, and be aware that others may not.

Starting rules are such an important topic that they deserve a chapter all their own, which is next.

4.5 Conclusion

Starting Tactics guides us through the most important and exciting part of sailboat racing. It is no wonder more and more regattas are being run on short courses, with multiple races each day: Everyone wants more chances to start.

Starts take teamwork built around a sound, flexible plan directed toward clear strategic goals. Get the information you need, practice your approach, and don't be late (Fig. 24).

Following are some ideas on how you can build your starting skills:

4.6 - Building Starting Skills

Stop and Go Drill
Park your boat (near a buoy) on a close-hauled course with sails luffing, then trim and accelerate to full speed. (How long – in time and distance – did it take to reach full speed?) Experiment to find the best angle and trim sequence (jib before main, but by how much) for different wind and sea conditions. Work on the stopping part too. Have crew push out on the boom to create an air brake. You may need this someday when you're headed for a gap which closes up in front on you - and you'll need an alert word to call for it: "Air Brake!"

Fore Reaching
Fore Reaching is a way to park and hold position and slow down without luffing. With sails trimmed close-hauled, head up above close-hauled, but not into irons. The jib will go soft, but not backwind – sort of a super pinch mode. Great for holding height and slowing down at the same time.
The jib trimmer should be ready – with the sheet in hand – to luff the jib if it starts to back. Otherwise you may be thrown into an inadvertent tack!
To accelerate out of fore reaching bear off to close hauled or just below and ease the sheets a few inches.

Add Timing
Using a short (five minute) starting cycle, repeat your stop and go or fore reaching drill with the goal of passing a buoy at full speed at the gun. Luff or park far enough from the buoy to have room to get up to full speed. How long does it take (in time and distance)?
Circle back and do it again every five minutes.

Time / Speed / Distance
How long will it take us to get to the line from here? You will be practicing this in the timing drill above. Do it everywhere you go—in and out of the harbor, as you approach a buoy or crab pot or another boat. With a little practice you can refine this all-important starting skill.

Don't be late
If you are habitually late for starts, build in an extra five or ten seconds into the sequence. That is, plan to start five seconds early. It is much easier to waste time than it is to retrieve time that is lost when you are late. (You've noticed that too, I bet.)

Rotate Positions
During practice, rotate crew positions to get an idea of what each crew member is doing. How hard is it to grind in the jib? How tricky is it to call the line (much less stay on board) when working the point on a wavy day?

Watch Other Starts
Try a position off the pin end to see how other fleets sag and accelerate. Try watching from behind the line to see how others approach and create room to accelerate. Rather than try to watch the entire fleet, focus your attention on one or two boats for the last minute or two of the sequence.

Practice Partner
Adding just one more boat can make all the difference. Set a short (2 length) line and practice starts.

4.7 - Starting Quiz Questions

(Answers appear on page 52)

1. While setting up for a port tack approach, you notice another boat appears to be doing the same thing. What should you do?

2. You are setting up for a boat end start using a triangle approach and notice a surprise wind shift which makes the pin end favored. What should you do?

3. How can you tell which end is favored and how much difference does it make?

4. The right end is 10° favored, but the left side is favored upwind. Where should you start?

5. What is the purpose of sailing the course in miniature before the start? Why do a practice start? What else should you do during the hour before the race?

6. How can you tell if you are over early when you can only see one end of the line?

*7. You are approaching the line close hauled. A rival skipper to leeward is yelling at you: "UP UP **UP***!"*
How should you respond?

8. You are close hauled approaching the stern of the committee boat and you hail an inside boat which is barging. Moments later the gun fires and the return hail is, "Now we want room." What should you do?

9. You are the third smallest boat in a PHRF start with twenty boats. How will your size affect your strategy? What if you are the largest boat?

10. What are the best ways to waste time if you are early on your approach?

Chapter 5: Rules at Starts

5.1 Luffing at Starts

5.2 Barging

5.3 Other Starting Rules

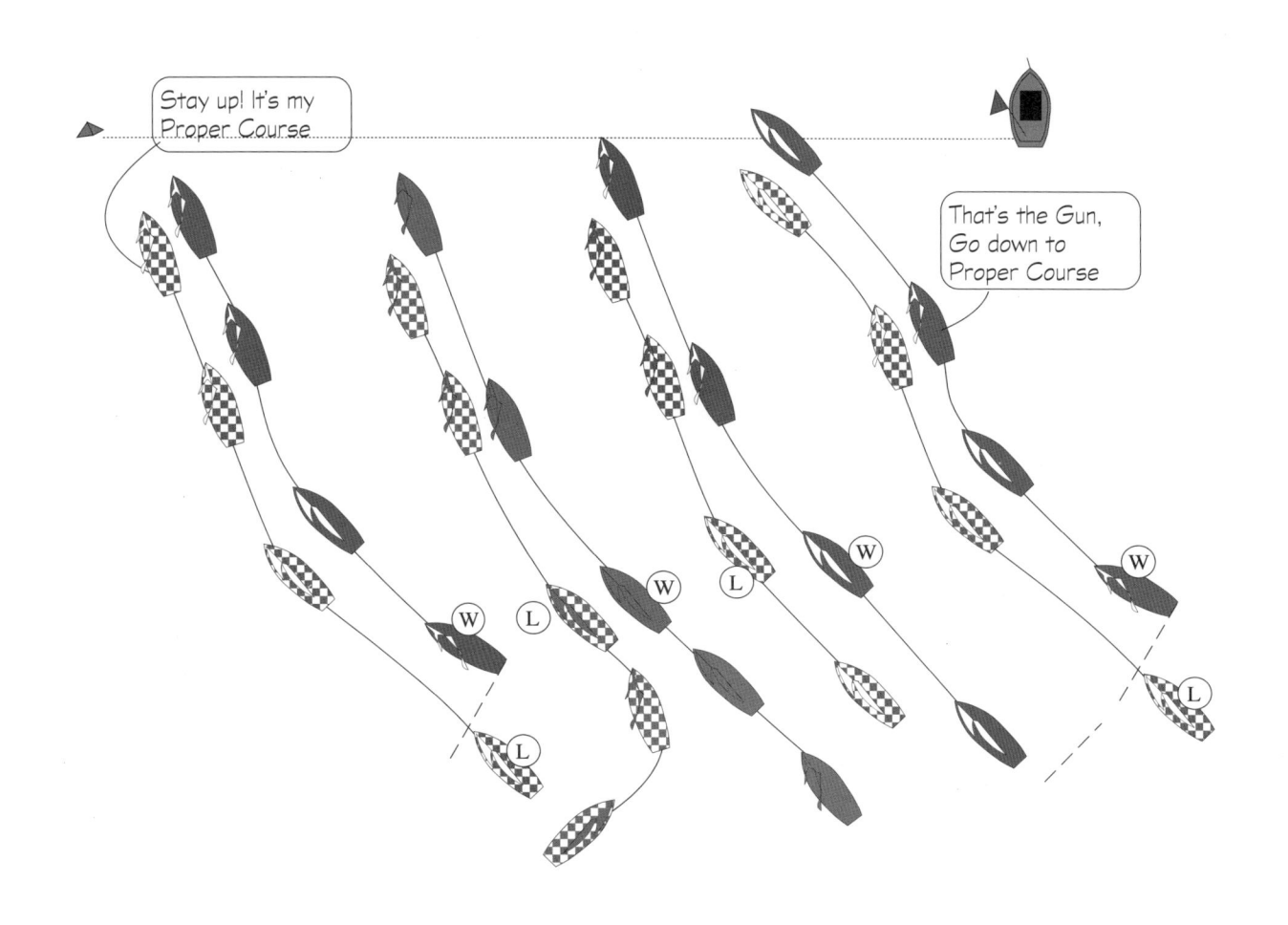

Chapter 5: Starting Rules

Starting Rules are a mix of the regular racing rules—such as starboard / port, overtaking, and While Tacking—which always apply; and special rules which apply only during starts (Fig. 1). These special rules include exemption from the Mark Room and Obstruction Rules (Section C preamble), restarting (Rules 21.1 & 29.1), and the one minute rule (Rule 30.1). The luffing rules are now the same before starts as they are during the race though in practice some differences remain as we shall see.

If you'd like an overview of the rules and their underlying principles, jump to Chapter 12 - Learning the Rules.

5.1 Luffing at Starts

As written, the luffing rules are the same before starts as they are during the race. In practice there are differences, as there is no proper course before the start.

Here is how the luffing rules work (Fig. 2):

The leeward boat has right of way (Rule 11) and may luff as she pleases, limited only by the need to give the windward boat room to keep clear (Rule 16).

If the leeward boat established her overlap from astern, then after the starting signal, she shall not sail above her proper course (Rule 17).

If the windward boat established an overlap from astern, or if the leeward boat tacked into the overlap, then she may luff and she may sail above her proper course even after the starting signal. (Why she would want to is another question.)

When you find yourself as a windward boat in a luffing situation, the definition of keep clear requires that you respond promptly to a luff. Head up as far and as fast as possible or necessary. Failure to respond to a luff will likely result in disqualification.

A leeward boat may luff to clear the pin as long as she allows the windward boat room to keep clear. Even after the starting signal, a leeward boat may luff above close hauled, as starting is her proper course.

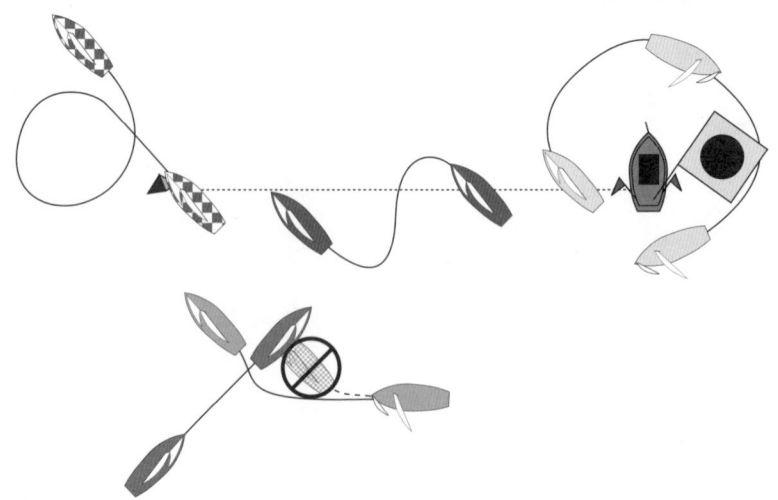

Fig. 1 - Starting Rules are a mix of regular racing rules and special rules which apply only at starts.

Definitions:

The definitions in the *Racing Rules of Sailing* can clarify some common confusion and misunderstanding of the rules.

Proper Course is the course a boat would sail to finish as quickly as possible in the absence of the other boats referred to. Note that *A boat has no proper course before her starting signal*.

One boat **keeps clear** of another if the other can sail her course with no need to take avoiding action and, when overlapped on the same tack, if the leeward boat could change course without immediately making contact with the windward boat.

Room is the space a boat needs in the existing conditions while maneuvering promptly in a seamanlike way.

Fig. 2 - Luffing at Starts

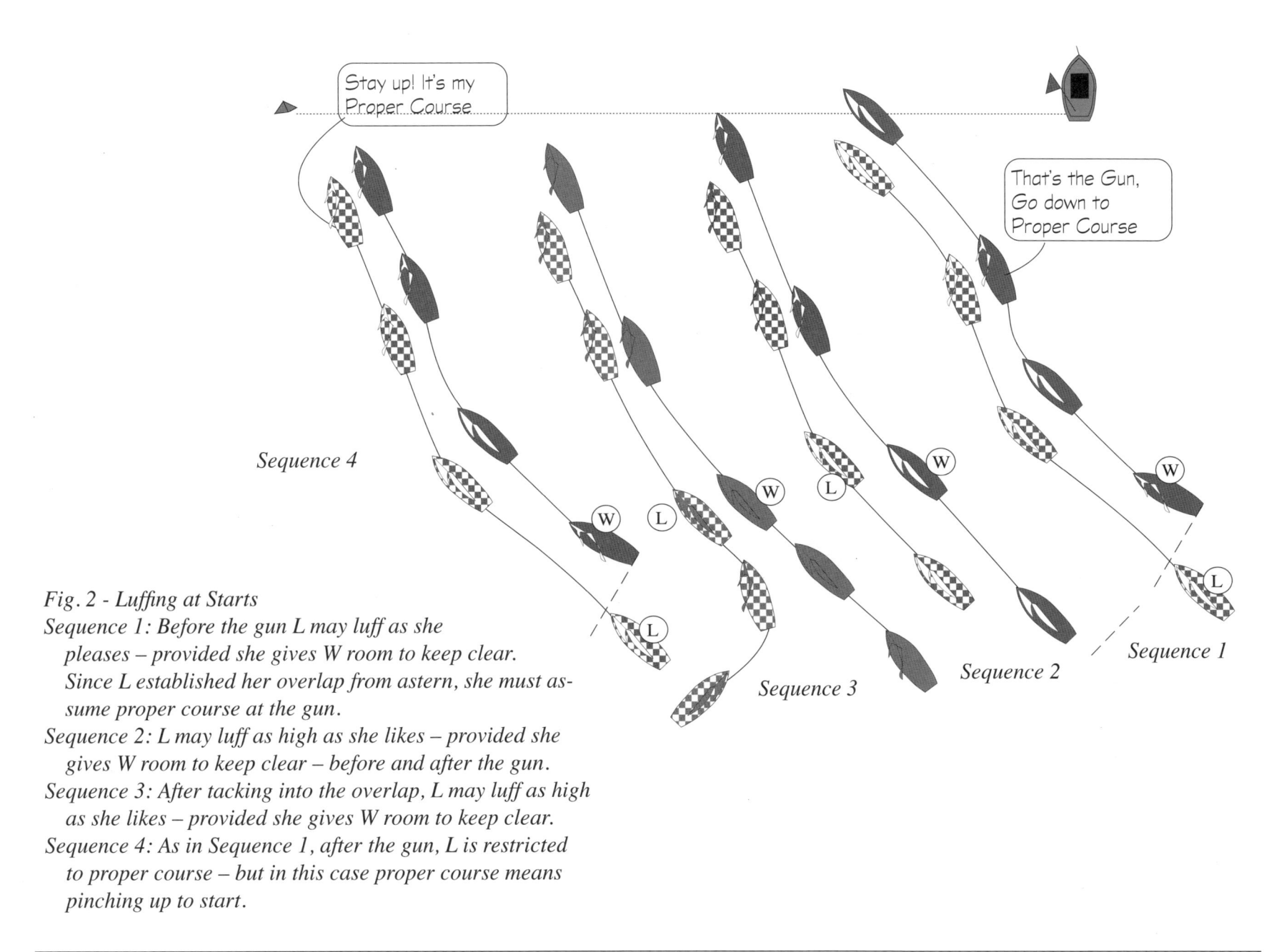

Sequence 1: Before the gun L may luff as she pleases – provided she gives W room to keep clear. Since L established her overlap from astern, she must assume proper course at the gun.

Sequence 2: L may luff as high as she likes – provided she gives W room to keep clear – before and after the gun.

Sequence 3: After tacking into the overlap, L may luff as high as she likes – provided she gives W room to keep clear.

Sequence 4: As in Sequence 1, after the gun, L is restricted to proper course – but in this case proper course means pinching up to start.

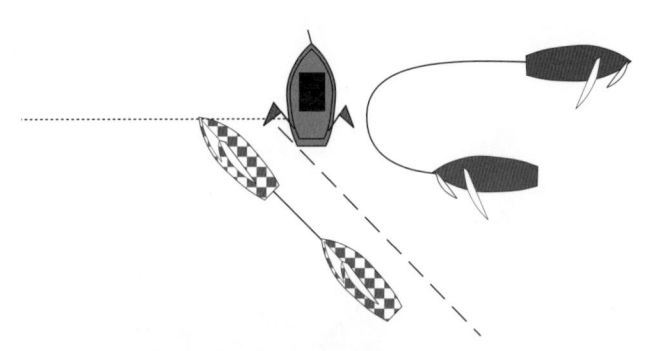

Scenario 1 – A leeward boat sailing close-hauled may close out a windward / inside boat at the start..

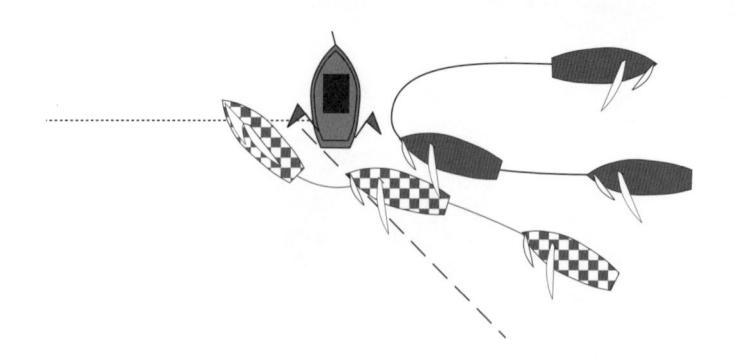

Scenario 2 – Likewise, a leeward boat sailing a reach may peel off a windward / inside boat at the start..

5.2 Barging

A leeward boat need not give an inside boat room when approaching the line to start, as the Mark Room rules do not apply (Section C Preamble).. (An inside boat is entitled to room when the fleet is noodling around before the start.)

The windward / leeward rule (Rule 11) applies. It is constrained only by the need to leave room for the windward boat to keep clear (Rule 16).

If the overlap was *established from clear astern*, then the leeward boat is further restricted to not sail above proper course after the starting signal (Rule 17). (By definition there is no proper course prior to the starting signal.)

If L's turn to proper course creates room for W to start (as in Scenario. 4, at right) that is W's good fortune; but if L's turn to proper course leaves no room for W then W is NOT entitled to room (see Scenario 5)

The anti-barging rule is detailed in the situations presented on this and the facing page.

Confused? Here's a tip: Don't barge.

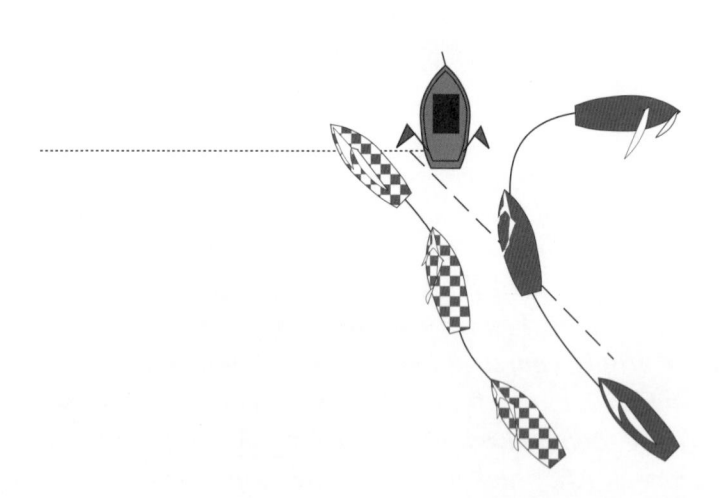

Scenario 3 - A leeward boat may sail above close hauled to close out a windward boat at a start. Even after the starting signal the leeward boat can sail above close-hauled except…

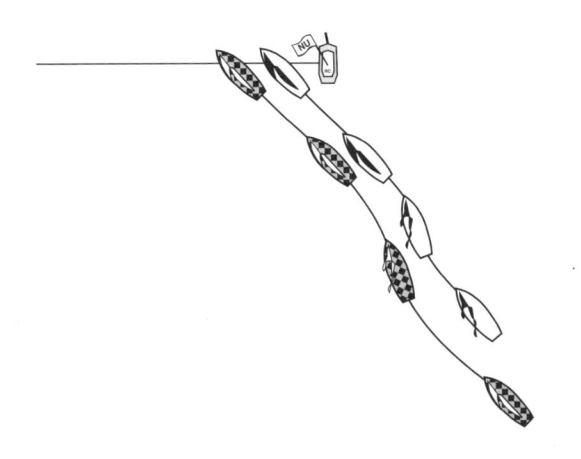

Scenario 4 - ...if and only <u>if the overlap was established from astern</u> then <u>after the starting signal</u> a leeward boat may <u>NOT</u> sail <u>above close hauled</u> to close out a windward boat...

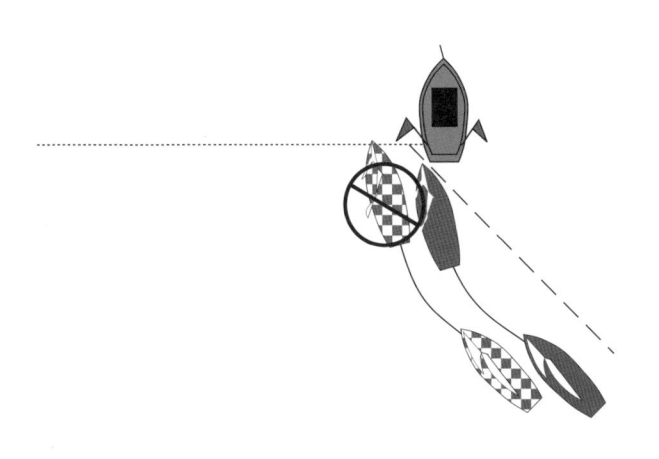

Scenario 6 - When a leeward boat changes course she must leave the windward boat room to keep clear. Rule 16.1.

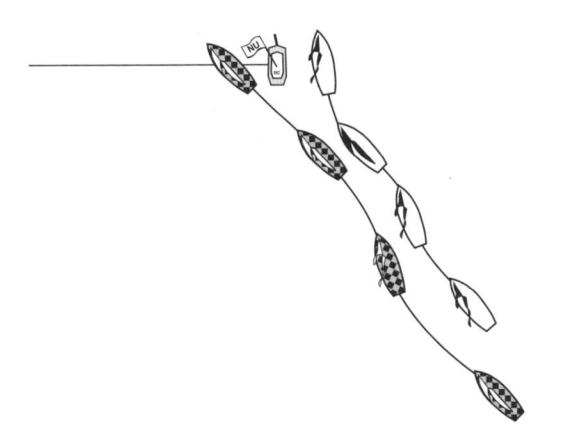

Scenario 5 - ...but if (with <u>the overlap was established from astern</u>) the leeward boat's turn to <u>close hauled</u> leaves no room for the windward boat the windward boat is NOT entitled to room.

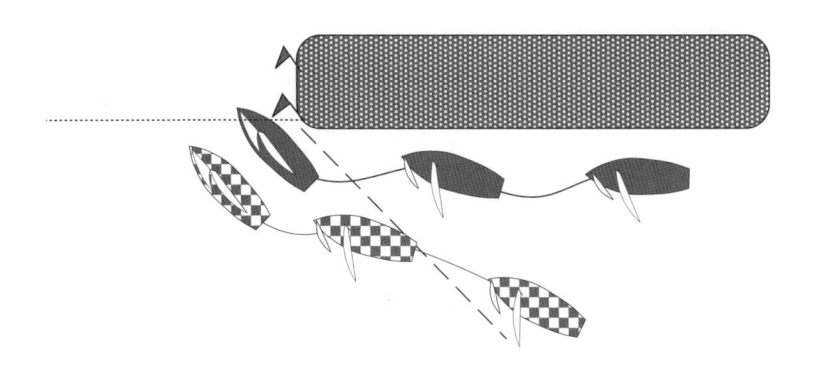

Scenario 7 - When the starting mark is not surrounded by navigable water, then Rule 19 - Room to Pass An Obstruction applies and the inside boat gets room.

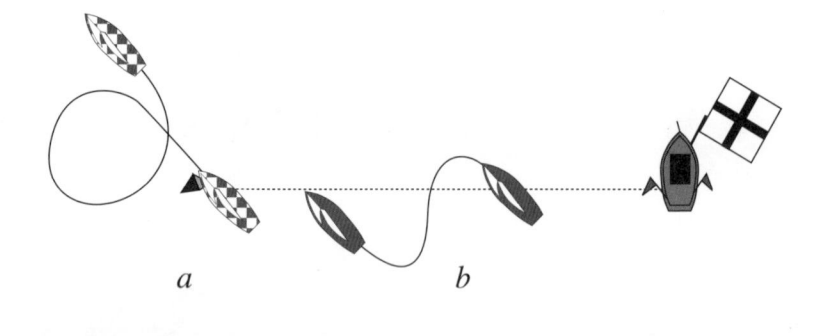

Fig. 3a - If you hit a starting mark, you must do a 360°.
Fig. 3b - If you are over early, you must restart.

5.3 Other Starting Rules

If you hit a starting mark you may exonerate yourself by doing an immediate One-Turn Penalty (Rule 31, Fig. 3a).

A boat which is over early must restart by returning to the proper side of the line (Definition of *Start*). The Race Committee must fly code flag X (white field with blue "+") if a boat or boats is over early (Rule 29.1) but is not required to hail individual boats — you must judge for yourself whether or not you have started properly. . While returning to restart, you must stay clear of those who have started properly (Rule 21.1, Fig. 3b).

The one minute rule is in effect when code flag "I" (a yellow field with a black "eye") is displayed as the preparatory signal four minutes before the start. You may not cross the line from the wrong direction after the one minute signal. A dip start or dip restart is not allowed. You must clear yourself by sailing around the end of the line (Rule 30.1, Fig. 4a).

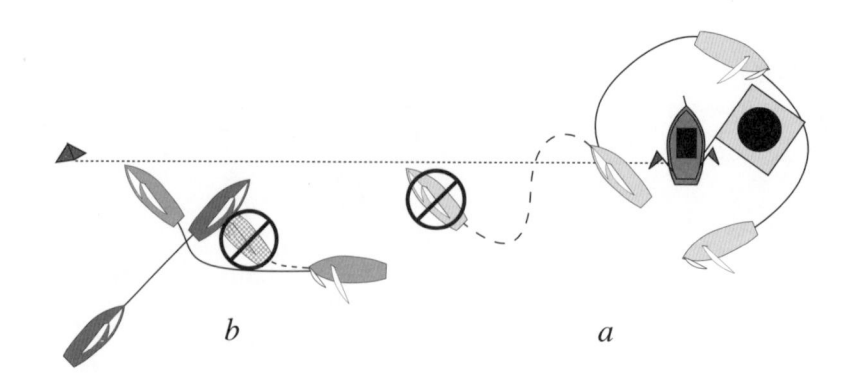

Fig. 4a - If the "I" flag is flying, then you may not cross the line from the course side during the last minute prior to the start or after the starting signal. You must clear yourself by sailing around the end of the line.
Fig. 4b - When changing course, a starboard-tack boat must give a port-tack boat room to keep clear.

As mentioned above, the starboard/port, overtaking, and tacking-too-close rules apply during starts just as they do on the course. In starboard/port (Rule 10) situations the starboard boat may do as she pleases, constrained only by the need to leave port a way to keep clear (Rule 16, Fig. 4b).

The starting rules are intended to bring order to a crowded starting line. They are fairly effective, at least for upwind starts. Offwind starts create a whole new set of tactical concerns and rules dilemmas, as we will see in the next chapter.

Chapter 6: Offbeat Starts

6.1 Running Starts

6.2 Reaching Starts

6.3 Starts on One-Legged Beats

6.4 Conclusion

6.5 Starting Quiz Answers

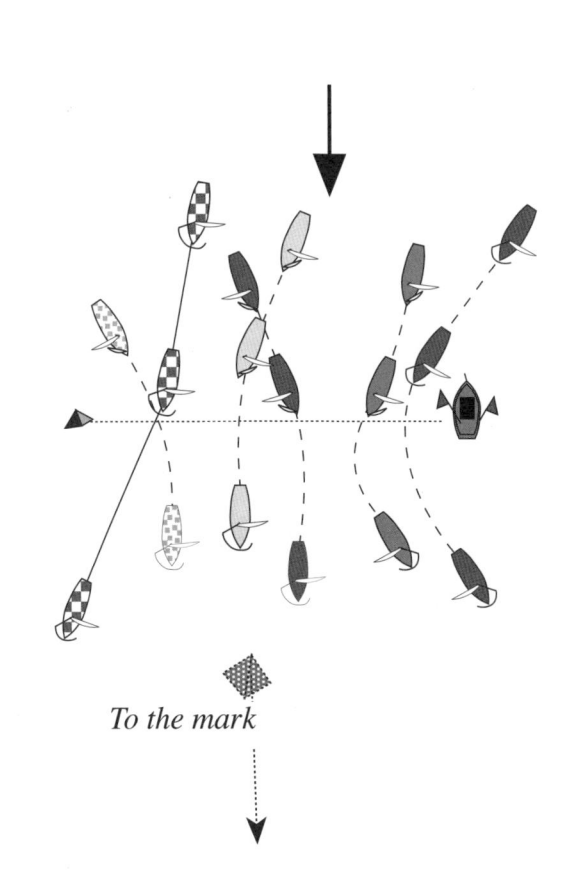

To the mark

Chapter 6: Offbeat Starts

While reaching and running starts are far less common than upwind starts, the keys to success are familiar: Planning, timing, and judgement are critical as always. Offwind starts lack some of the order of upwind starts; they can be unpredictable, and some of the techniques differ from those we use upwind. Below are a few thoughts on starts in a variety of wind angles, from straight downwind to reaches and one-legged beats.

6.1 Running Starts

As chaotic as upwind starts are, they pale by comparison to running starts. Starting near the ends enables you to reach out to the side for clear air, but you are then committed to that side for the first part of the race. Starting in the middle of the line leaves you in bad air. Pick a side which will give you clear air, and try to anticipate crowds and wind shadows (Fig. 1).

One of the most common mistakes in downwind starts is delaying the spinnaker set. To hit the line at full speed you must have your spinnaker up and drawing on your approach. Hoist your spinnaker in stops (rubber bands or thin yarn). Break it out and trim for full speed as early as you can—thirty seconds to one minute before the start—to get a jump on those who wait for the gun before hoisting. As a small boat in a mixed fleet, this is a great time to draft on the stern wave of a larger boat.

Sailing up the line on a starboard beam reach gives you right of way. Expect bad air and crowds to slow your progress, so set up early. If you approach on a broader reach timing is trickier. Be prepared to duck boats to leeward. At the other end, approach on starboard and then jibe after you clear the line.

Fig. 1 - For starts on a run, timing is tricky. Set the spinnaker early and sail fast. Control your approach by oversteering, but keep speed. Pick a side to get clear air.

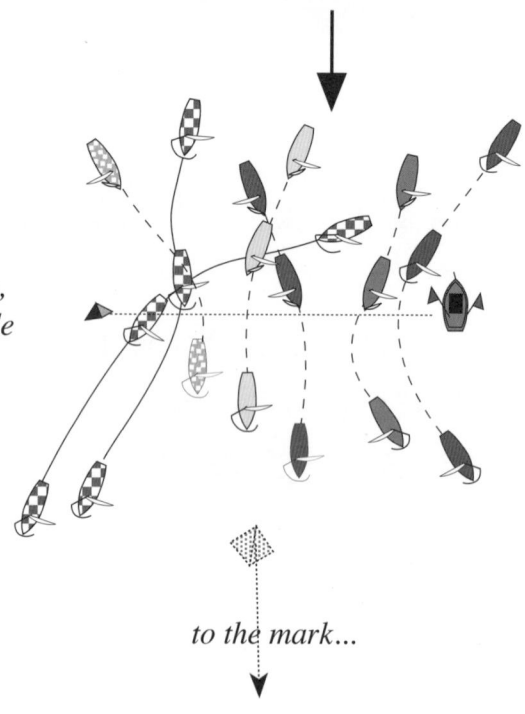

to the mark...

If the mark is not positioned downwind then clear air is available only at one end. Approach with the right of way and expect a crowd. It can get ugly.

6.2 Reaching Starts

Tactics on reaching starts depend on the exact wind angle of the line and to the mark.

Wind Forward of the Beam

The fleet will tend to bunch up at the upwind end, often without reason. As long as the wind is forward of the beam, a start near the leeward end is often better. You can reach up in front of the crowd, and off in puffs. That is, if the puffs get to you. The danger is that boats above you will get the breeze first and roll over you before you get it. From the leeward position you have right of way. A good start is essential. If you fall into bad air, you risk being rolled by one boat after another.

As a small boat in a mixed fleet, the leeward position may not work out, as you'll get rolled by faster boats. In hull speed conditions there is an opportunity to hitch a ride on the quarter wave or stern wave of a larger boat by dropping in from close to windward (Fig. 2).

Wind Aft of the Beam

With the wind abaft the beam and the rhumb line perpendicular starting line, clear air is available only at the weather end, and everyone knows it. Reaching up the line will give you luffing rights on those reaching into the line from above, but no wind.

Don't be surprised if the entire fleet does not respond to your hail to clear out as you charge up the line. In a crowd boats are insulated by their neighbors, and often there is no way to respond. Boats with right-of-way and no air are often bowled over by the mass of boats reaching in.

A start which gets your nose out in front of the crowd and into clear air can mean winning the race. Here again there is an opportunity for small boats to draft in the stern wave of larger boats (Fig. 3).

Fig. 2 - On a reach when the wind is forward of the beam, a start at the leeward end of the line gives the best sailing angle. An on time, full speed start is essential. There is a danger of getting rolled by one boat after another if you fall into bad air. In a mixed fleet, there are particular problems for small boats.

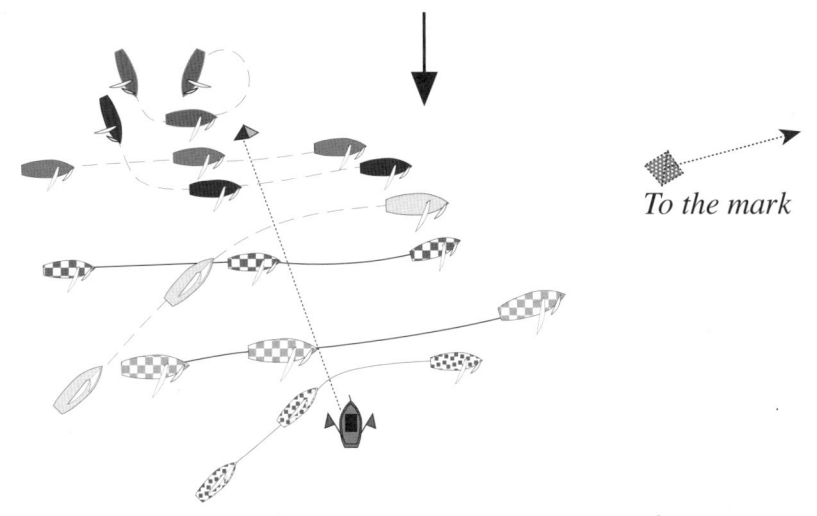

Fig. 3 - When the wind is abaft the beam, then clear air is available only at the windward end. The battle there can be unruly, with right-of-way boats bowled over by the sheer mass of intruders.

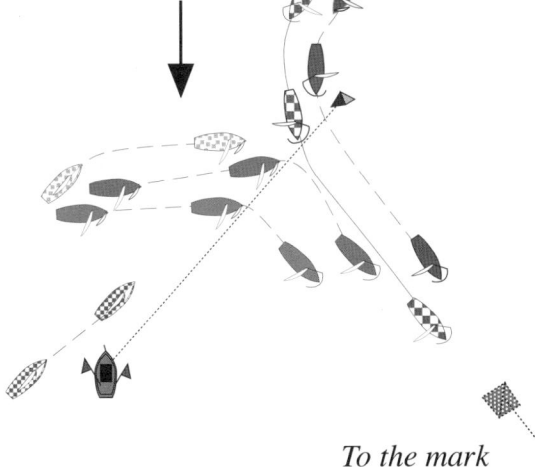

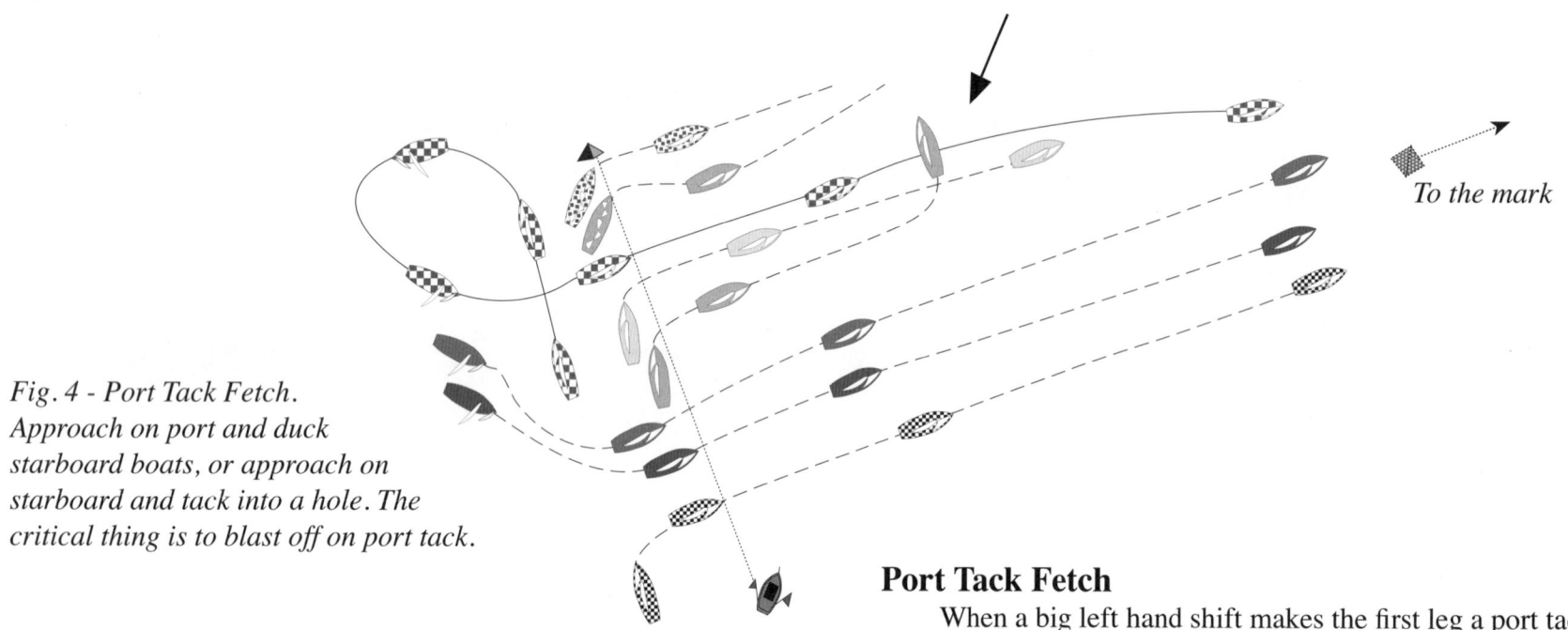

Fig. 4 - Port Tack Fetch. Approach on port and duck starboard boats, or approach on starboard and tack into a hole. The critical thing is to blast off on port tack.

6.3 Starts on One-Legged Beats

When a big wind shift turns the first leg of a race into a fetch or near fetch, starting tactics change. Typically the line is square to the mark (and original wind) and heavily skewed to the new wind.

Ideally, when there is a big shift before the start of a race, the Race Committee will delay the start and reset the course, but that is not always the case. When a shift turns the first leg into a one-legged beat, the goal of starting strategy is to get off the line, with speed, sailing on the tack to the mark. The exact position on the line is not important. Lets take a look at the two cases: Port tack fetch and starboard tack fetch.

Port Tack Fetch

When a big left hand shift makes the first leg a port tack fetch (or near fetch), blast off the line on port tack. The fleet tends to bunch up at the port end to the line, barely fetching or not fetching the line on starboard tack. Avoid the jam up, and start in the middle of the line.

Two approaches are recommended. One is a port tack approach, ducking starboard tackers, and finding a gap in the crowd. The other is a starboard approach. Sail up the line on starboard, find an open space, and tack. Allow time to build speed on port. Regardless of approach, the goal is to reach in and blast off!

From a midline position you will be ahead and to leeward of the pack. If the breeze backs further, you may fetch. If the breeze clocks, you will lead the fleet into the header. Meanwhile, the pack at the port end will be jammed up, sailing the wrong way, and unable to tack out (Fig. 4).

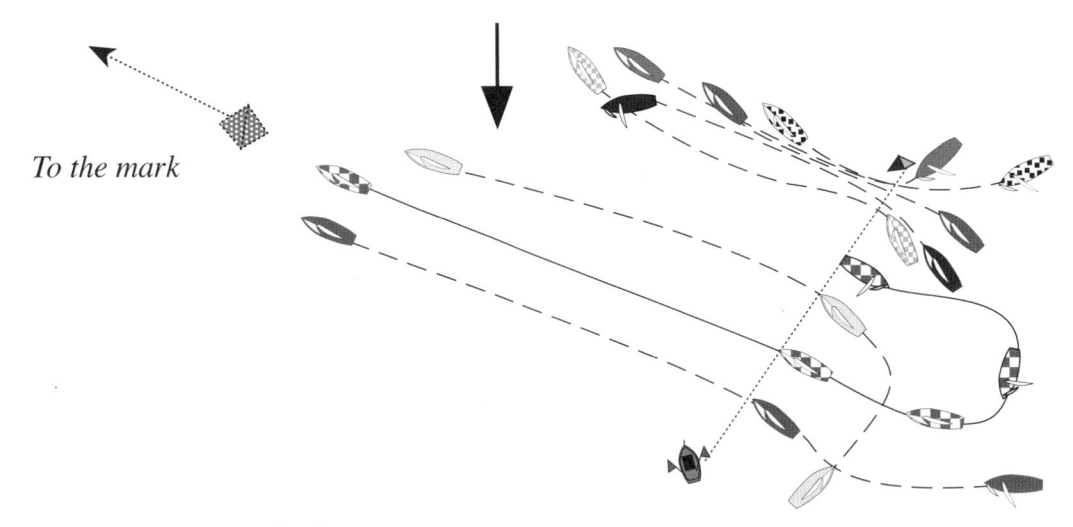

Fig. 5 - Starboard Tack Fetch. Once again, position on the line is not important. A fast, clear air start is the goal. Avoid the crowd at the windward end, and take the preferred position to leeward.

Starboard Tack Fetch

When the breeze clocks to create a starboard tack fetch, the same principles apply. Blast off the line on starboard tack. Your position on the line is not important—getting away clean is. Avoid the crowd at the starboard end; boats in the crowd push each other up as they fight for clear air, and they end up sailing extra distance. Take off from the middle of the line. You will be ahead and to leeward of the crowd; you will be inside (for a port rounding) if the leg becomes a fetch; and you will lead the fleet into the header if the breeze backs. A timed out and back approach is best (Fig. 5).

One-Legged Beats

The tactics for starts on one-legged beats boil down to starting with speed on the tack toward the mark. Position on the line is not important, but clear air is. This strategy applies to any reaching start with the wind forward of the beam and the line perpendicular to the leg.

6.4 Conclusion

Starts are critical, and offbeat starts are no exception. Offbeat starts provide a great opportunity for those who can take advantage of their unique characteristics. It is remarkable how the start can shape the entire race, even a distance race. Try to anticipate the actions of other boats, and get in position to start with clear air and good speed.

Starting Quiz Answers

1. While setting up for a port tack approach, you notice another boat appears to be doing the same thing. What should you do?

Start up the line early to put some space between you. If the rival follows immediately, the loop back behind him, and get into the push position.

2. You are setting up for a boat end start using a triangle approach and notice a surprise wind shift which makes the pin end favored. What should you do?

Change your plan. You should know the timed length of the line. Modify your approach to pretend you've already completed leg one of the triangle. Time your approach to be in the lower third of the line.

3. How can you tell which end is favored and how much difference does it make?

Compare the compass course of the line to the wind direction. You can plot it on the race planner. A line 10° out of square offers an advantage equal to 25% of the length of the line.

4. The right end is 10° favored, but the left side is favored upwind. Where should you start?

Try the middle, or even upper third of the line. The key is a clear air lane which will allow you to get to the favored left side.

5. What is the purpose of sailing the course in miniature before the start? Why do a practice start? What else should you do during the hour before the race?

Whoa there - one at a time. We sail the course in miniature to be able to anticipate the mix of starboard and port upwind, and the wind angle downwind. This in turn helps us plan strategy.

A practice starts helps with timing, crew organization, and psyche. See Chapter 2 for a list of things to do prior to the start.

6. How can you tell if you are over early when you can only see one end of the line?

Use a line sight to an object off the extension of pin end. If you can only see the boat end, look into the eyes of the line caller. If your bow is sticking out, you're likely over early.

*7. You are approaching the line close-hauled. A rival skipper to leeward is yelling at you: "UP UP **UP!**" How should you respond?*

If the other boat is close, then respond and head up, but you don't need to say anything. Sail your boat. You must stay clear and the other boat must give you room to do so.

8. You are close-hauled approaching the stern of the committee boat and you hail an inside boat which is barging. Moments later the gun fires and the return hail is, "Now we want room." What should you do?

Tell him, "No room, NO WAY!"

If the inside boat forces their way in, get the attention of the RC while you give them room. Get the RC to witness that you gave room to a barging boat. Avoid collisions.

9. You are the third smallest boat in a PHRF start with twenty boats. How will your size affect your strategy? What if you are the largest boat?

As a smaller boat you will have to fight to hold a clear lane to the favored side. It can be a struggle. At times it seems you must choose between going the right way in bad air, the wrong way in clear air, or tacking too much.

As a big boat, punch out, get clear air, and put your speed to work. If you get stuck in the mix it can be hard to break free.

10. What are the best ways to waste time if you are early on your approach?

We are all uniquely qualified in our ability to waste time.

CHAPTER 7: UPWIND STRATEGY

7.1 INTRODUCTION TO STRATEGY
7.2 PREDICTING CONDITIONS
7.3 WIND
7.4 WIND SHIFTS
7.5 THE IMPACT OF SHIFTS
7.6 CURRENT
7.7 STRATEGY VS RIVALS
7.8 SHORT STORY: THE LAND OF OPPORTUNITY
7.9 LOCAL KNOWLEDGE:
    EXAMPLES, HOMEWORK, AND QUIZ

Chapter 7: Upwind Strategy

7.1 Introduction to Strategy

Strategy vs Tactics

Strategy is our racing plan based on wind, wind shifts, and current. Tactics, on the other hand, are techniques we use for positioning and control of other boats or groups of boats. Strategy involves the big picture; tactics focuses in close. Strategy is long term and planned, tactics is more immediate and spontaneous.

Strategy is Wind, Wind Shifts, and Currents

There are three factors in planning strategy. We look for better wind. We try to take advantage of wind shifts. And we try to get favorable (or not unfavorable) current. The relative importance of each factor depends on how variable each is (Fig. 1).

7.2 Predicting Conditions

Our strategy is based on the expected conditions. The more accurately we can predict the wind and current, the more confidently we can form our strategic plan. As we discussed in Chapter Two, our predictions are derived primarily from our own observations during the hour before the start, and our experience sailing in a particular area. We revise our predictions as we continue to observe conditions during the race.

The figure shows a sample Wind Graph based on our pre-race observations. By carefully tracking the wind we can more accurately predict the wind for the race (Fig. 2).

Predictable vs Unpredictable

One issue in our strategic planning is our confidence in our forecast. When conditions are highly predictable, we can pursue our strategy with conviction. When we are unsure of what to expect, our strategy will change. First, we would not pursue the strategy as wholeheartedly. Second, we would devote more than the usual amount of attention to watching for changing conditions which might require us to change our strategy.

Our strategy will depend on the predicted conditions and our confidence in that prediction. When we are able to predict conditions accurately and confidently, our strategic planning is relatively easy. In practice our predictions often prove less

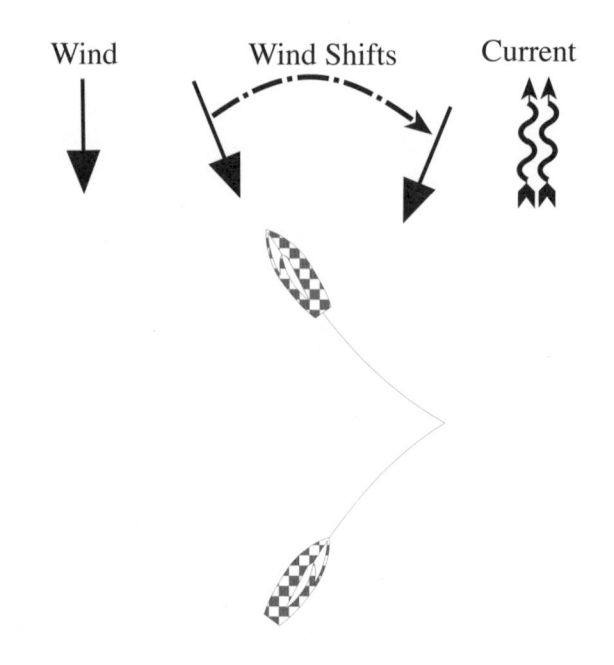

Fig. 1 – Strategy vs Tactics. Strategy is our racing plan based on wind, wind shifts, and current. Tactics, which we cover later, involves implementing our strategy and dealing with other boats.

Fig. 2 – Plan strategy based on observed and predicted conditions. The numbers listed here show a history of conditions prior to the start and during the first leg of a race. This information will help us plan and update our strategy. We plot the numbers to get a visual image of the wind pattern. This particular wind chart shows a very regular pattern of oscillations.

than accurate, and our planning boils down to playing the odds to reduce risks and increase possible gains.

Strategy and Conditions

As we said, our strategic planning revolves around the expected conditions. When we know what to expect, we will be able to make a firm plan. When our forecast is uncertain, then our plan will be less well defined.

Strategy and conditions are related in another way. The more variable the wind and current, the more important strategy will be to our success. In stable conditions boat speed will be the dominant concern. Our focus depends on what we see as the key to success in today's conditions.

Wind Graph

Time	Wind Spd	Boat Spd	Stbd	Wind	Port
11:15	8	5.2		220	265
11:18	8	5.1	180	225	
11:20	8	5.1	185	230	
11:21	9	5.6		230	275
11:25	9	5.5	175	220	265
11:30	9	5.5		220	265
11:35		5.6	170	215	260
11:43	8	5.0	180	225	270
11:45		5.2		225	270
11:50	9	5.5	185	230	275
11:55		5.6	175	220	265
12:01	9	5.5	170	215	260
12:07	8	5.2	175	220	265
12:12	9	5.5	180	225	270
12:15	9	5.5	185	230	(Start)
12:20	8	5.1	180	225	270
12:23	8	5.1		215	260
12:25	9	5.5		220	265
12:28	9	5.5	185	230	
12:30	8	5.1	180	225	
12:33	8	5.1		215	260
12:35	9	5.5		220	265

7.3 Wind

Wind Strength

Find more wind. Sail in stronger wind more of the time and you can't lose. There are several things to look for to find more wind.

Look for wind on the water. Stand up in your boat and look upwind. Puffs create dark patches on the water. It is tricky to distinguish shadows, changes in bottom color, and differences due to sunlight; but the wind is there if you can pick it out.

The wind changes near shore. Most of our racing is done close enough to shore that winds vary across the course. Often there is better wind near shore. When the wind is blowing onshore the thermals near shore create more wind. In an offshore wind the thermal mixing near shore sometimes pushes the stronger winds from aloft down to the surface. At other times the wind is lighter near shore. By paying attention and keeping records, you will be able to anticipate the change in wind as you get near shore.

Clouds often bring more wind. In partly cloudy conditions, there is often more wind at the edges of the clouds, and less wind directly under the clouds. In a clearing northwest wind with rows of cumulus clouds, there are usually down drafts of stronger wind around the clouds. If you see frontal clouds or building cumulus go to them—there is wind at the edges, but less wind beneath them.

The Favored Side

A windward leg will often have a *favored side*. Boats sailing to one side will have an advantage due to favorable wind, wind shifts, or current. Sometimes it is difficult to anticipate which side is favored. After observing the first leg we will have a better idea for the second time around. *If* conditions don't change, then we would expect the same side to be favored again. Also, after seeing particular conditions in a local area a number of times, we will be able to anticipate which side will be favored (Fig. 3).

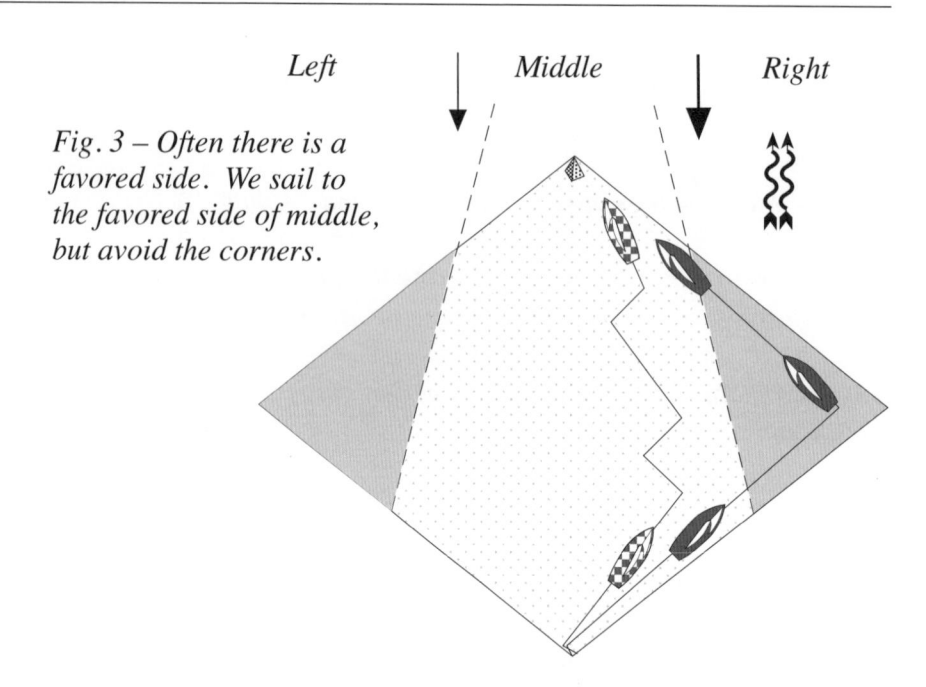

Fig. 3 – Often there is a favored side. We sail to the favored side of middle, but avoid the corners.

Time Out for Terminology

Before we go on about the *favored side* a few details of terminology must be cleared up: The *favored side* of the course carries some strategic advantage. The *favored tack* takes you to the *favored side*. This should not be confused with the *long tack*, which is the predominant tack on a skewed beat, (i.e. a beat where we spend more time on one tack than the other. Often it is strategically correct to sail the long tack first – that is, the long tack is often the favored tack. At other times the favored tack might be the short tack (Fig. 4).

Which Side is Favored?

How can you tell which side is favored before the race? Here are some ways:

- Your own experience. Local knowledge can help you guess the favored side based on past experience in similar weather.
- Testing. Sail to the sides of the course prior to the start. Is there better breeze, or a consistent shift to one side? Even if you can't sail up the beat you can test wind strength by reaching out off the extension of the line for a couple of minutes.
- More testing. Test with a tuning partner. Each boat sails to one side for a prescribed amount of time – say 3 minutes – and then tacks back. Who's ahead?
- Observe earlier starts. In a multiple fleet event watch those who go off before you do.
- Pay attention for the first few minutes of the race. If an advantage is apparent, it is not too late to go after it.

Why is This Side Favored?

Hopefully we will know not only which side is favored, but why. Knowing the reason will help us determine if conditions have changed and the advantage has changed as well. If current is the factor, for example, then a change in the tide can reverse the advantage. If the advantage is due to the geography of the surrounding shore, then the advantage will endure until the wind changes. Knowing not just which, but why one side is favored will help as we look ahead to plan our downwind strategy.

Right, Left, & Middle

In our discussion of strategy we will divide the windward leg into three vertical segments; representing the left, right, and middle of the course. When our strategy favors one side or the other it is generally best to sail to the right or left of the middle, but not beyond. There are several reasons to avoid the extreme sides. For one, our strategy may prove to be wrong and a total

*Fig. 4 – Don't confuse the **long tack** with the **favored tack**. On a skewed beat, the favored tack is not necessarily the long tack.*

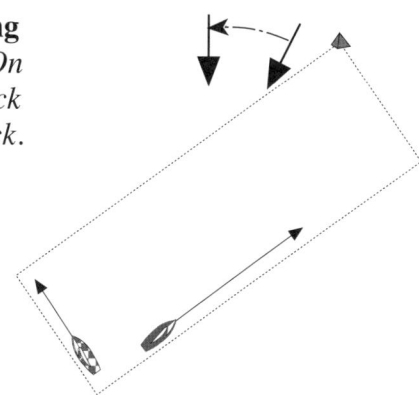

commitment would make it difficult to recover. Second, as we shall see, there are strategic and tactical reasons to avoid the corners, since they can leave us out of position and with few options. We would only sail to the extreme sides if:

- We are confident about our strategy and
- We must go to the extreme to get the advantage.

Caught on the Wrong Side: Now What?

What should you do if you sail to the favored side, get half way up the beat, and realize it is not the favored side after all? That is a tough question. Often it is surprising how close you end up to the leaders if you bail out half way up the leg and cut your losses. On the other hand, the ultimate frustration is bailing out early and then seeing those who stuck with it come out ahead in the end. Curses.

Of course, never having made such a mistake myself, it is hard to offer insights. I can offer a few ideas based purely on the experience of others:

- Don't overcommit to begin with—play the middle. (Now you tell me!)
- Hedge your bets. When in doubt stay with the pack.
- Be realistic about how things are going; don't kid yourself.
- While you ponder what to do sail toward the middle, not further into the corner.

7.4 Wind Shifts

The second strategic factor is wind shifts. Shifting winds allow us to reach the windward mark more quickly than we can in steady winds.

When the Wind Does Not Shift

When the wind is steady then the distance we must sail to an upwind destination is fixed. We will sail X distance on starboard tack, and Y distance on port tack to get to the mark. If the mark is straight upwind, then X and Y will be equal. If the leg is skewed, then they won't be equal.

You can sail all port tack, and then tack to starboard, or all the starboard tack first, or you can tack back and forth. In the end, you will sail X distance on starboard tack and Y distance on port tack to get to the mark. (Fig. 5.)

When the Wind Shifts

The wind shifts, and it is good. Wind shifts allow us to shorten the distance we sail to an upwind mark.

When the wind shifts, our close-hauled compass courses change. With each shift one tack is lifted up above its earlier course, and the other tack in headed below its previous course. When one tack is lifted the other is headed, and vice versa. (Fig. 6).

Our goal upwind is to sail each tack when it is lifted. By sailing the lifted tack, we sail a more direct route to our upwind destination (Fig. 7).

Sail to the Shift

The fundamental upwind strategy is to sail toward the new wind or wind shift. As we will see, this strategy keeps us on the lifted tack. The application of this principle changes with different types of shifts; but the fundamental rule—sail to the shift—never changes.

Fig. 5 – Regardless of its path, in the absence of wind shifts, each boat will sail the same distance on port tack and the same distance on starboard tack. The distance on each tack is fixed. The distance on port tack will match the distance on starboard tack only if the mark is directly upwind. If the mark is 1 mile directly upwind then the distance on each tack would be .71 miles for boats tacking through 90°.

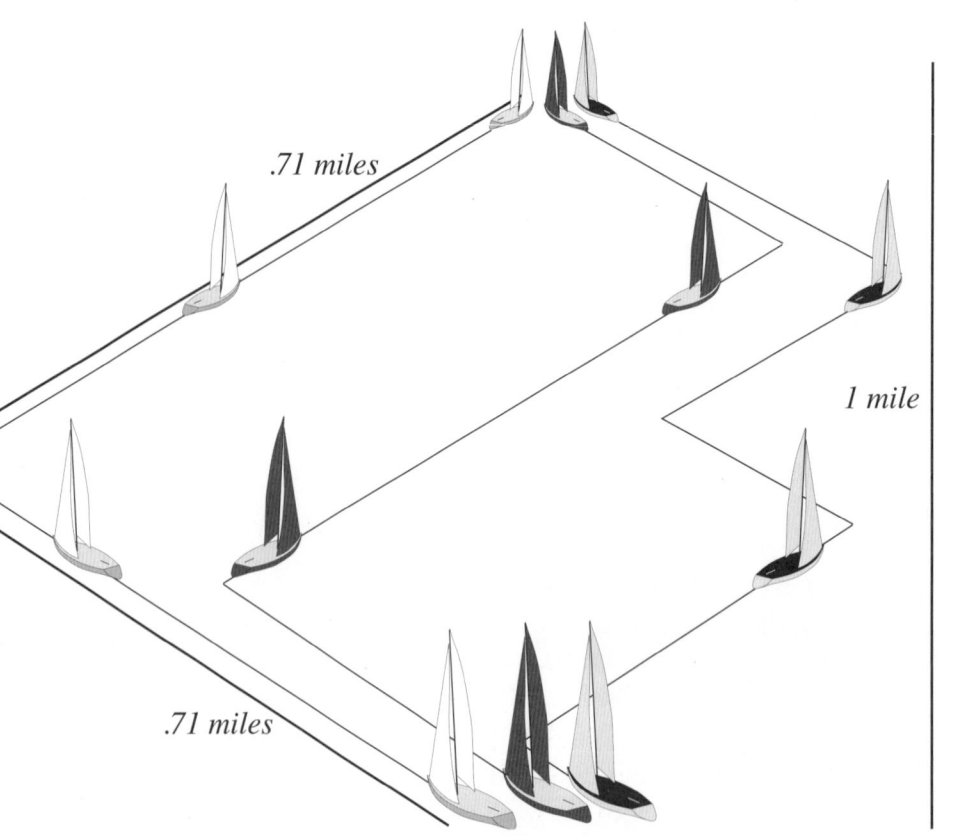

*Fig. 6 – As the wind shifts, one tack will be **lifted** up toward the mark while the other tack will be **headed** away from the mark. With the wind shifting to the right, (at right) starboard tack is lifted, and port tack is headed.*
A shift to the left (below) lifts port.

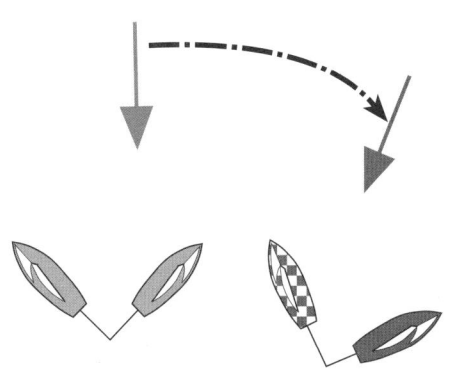

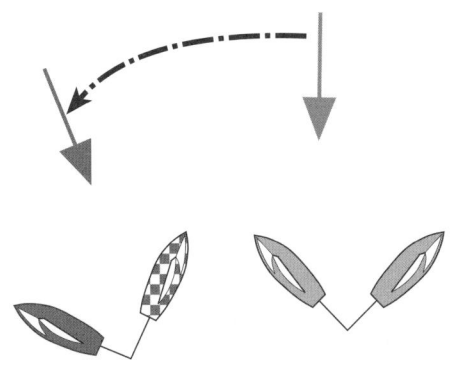

Fig. 7 – Sailing the lifted tack shortens the sailing distance to the windward mark.

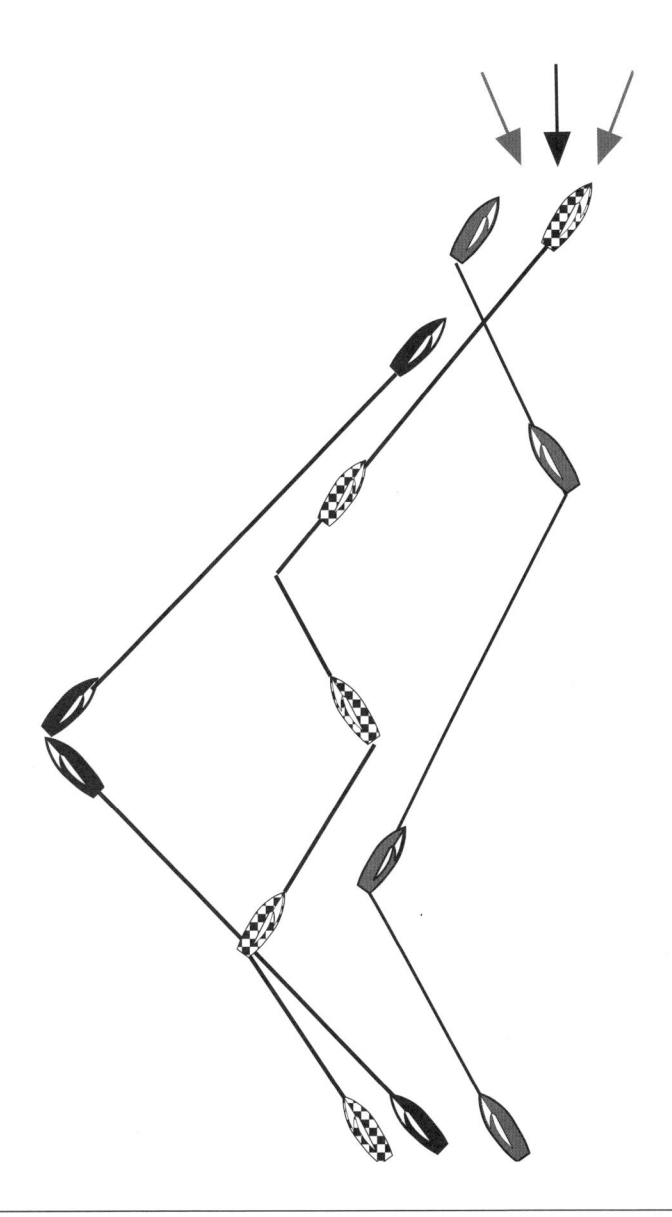

Tracking Conditions

In order to take advantage of wind shifts you must keep track of them. The best way to keep track of wind shifts is to track your close-hauled compass course. Keep a record of compass headings and establish a range of highs and lows for each tack. By recording the shifts, you can look for patterns (see Fig. 2, earlier) and anticipate upcoming shifts.

Of course, reading the compass only tells about a shift after it has arrived. In addition to the compass, observe the wind on the water and watch its effect on other boats. Work to recognize and predict shifts before they arrive.

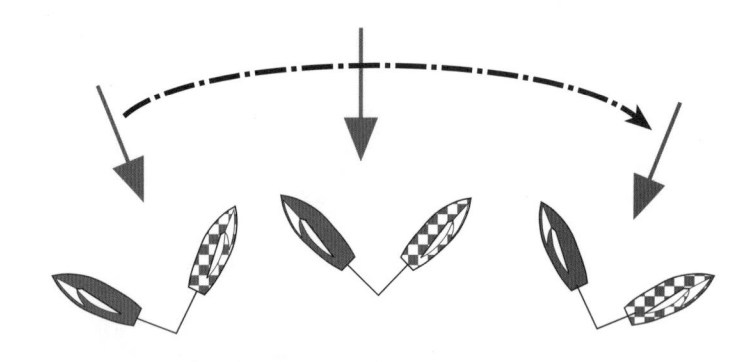

Fig. 8a – In a persistent shift the wind shifts continuously in one direction.

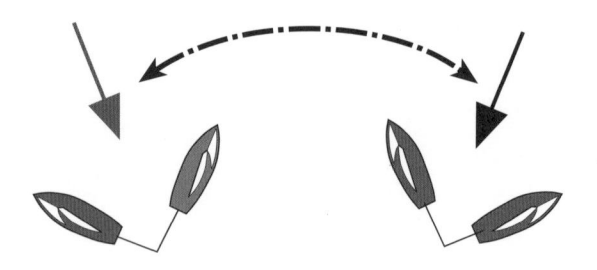

Fig. 8b – In oscillating shifts the wind swings back and forth

Types of Shifts

Wind shifts are generally categorized in two types: persistent and oscillating. Persistent shifts swing gradually in one direction, like the hands of a clock. A shift to the right is a clocking shift, or "veer;" a shift to the left is called a "back." Oscillating winds shift back and forth, like a pendulum. (Fig. 8 a, b)

From experience we know the real world is more complex than simple oscillating or persistent shifts. For starters we are going to look at strategy in these two textbook types of shifts. After that we will look at other variations.

Persistent Shifts

The basic strategy in a persistent shift is to sail to the new wind. As the wind gradually shifts, one tack will gradually deteriorate, while the other improves. If the wind is shifting to the right, then port tack will be at its best early and deteriorate over time, while starboard tack will get better and better. We would sail port tack first, before it is too badly headed, and sail starboard tack later, when it is most lifted. (Fig. 9)

Oscillating Shifts

The basic strategy in an oscillating breeze is to tack with the shifts. As the wind shifts, one tack is lifted so we can point closer to the mark (or average wind) while the other tack is headed further away. When the wind shifts again the advantage will be reversed; whenever one tack is lifted the other is headed. Each time we come about we are sailing toward the next expected shift – sail to the shift. When the wind is from the right, we sail lifted on starboard tack, toward the next shift, which is expected from the left. When the left shift arrives starboard tack will be headed, and port lifted. We tack again and sail lifted on port, toward the next shift, from the right, and so on. (Fig. 10)

By coming about when headed below the average course and sailing on the lifted tack, we can take advantage of the wind shifts to improve upwind performance. We use the term staying in phase to describe the process of tacking on the headers and sailing on the lifts.

Sometimes the wind shifts gradually back and forth. This is seen most often when the winds are coming over open water. We tack as we are headed below the average heading. At other times the shifts hit all at once. We see this when the shifts are coming off shore, or in the northwest winds after a cold front.

On starboard tack a higher compass reading is a lift, a lower number is a header. On port lower is a lift, higher is a header. It is most important to recognize headers since they suggest it is time to tack. Use the phrase Port, Higher, Header as an aid to remember the correlation between compass readings and shifts.

Get in Phase

By collecting wind information before the race and updating information as the race progresses, we should know at any moment whether we are sailing a lifted, headed, or average course. If conditions change, our lifted and headed numbers will have to be adjusted.

Out of Phase

Sailing in oscillations seems pretty straightforward. If the shifts come in a regular cycle and no one gets in your way, it should be easy to stay in phase. Somehow it doesn't always work that way. If you find yourself out of phase, sail the tack which takes you closest to the mark, or towards the next puff, while you sort things out.

Unbalanced Legs

Tacking as the wind crosses the average works great if the wind spends equal time on each side of average and the mark is straight upwind. This is not always the case. When the leg or shifts are not balanced, then the crossover angle for tacking must be adjusted to match. For example, if the leg is skewed to three times as much starboard as port, then we'll need to sail on starboard for three quarters of the wind range, and port for one quarter.

Similarly, if there are other strategic considerations, our tacking angles may be skewed. For example, if there is better wind or current to one side of the course, we would sail toward the favored side during average winds, and sail away from that side only at the extreme end of the shift spectrum.

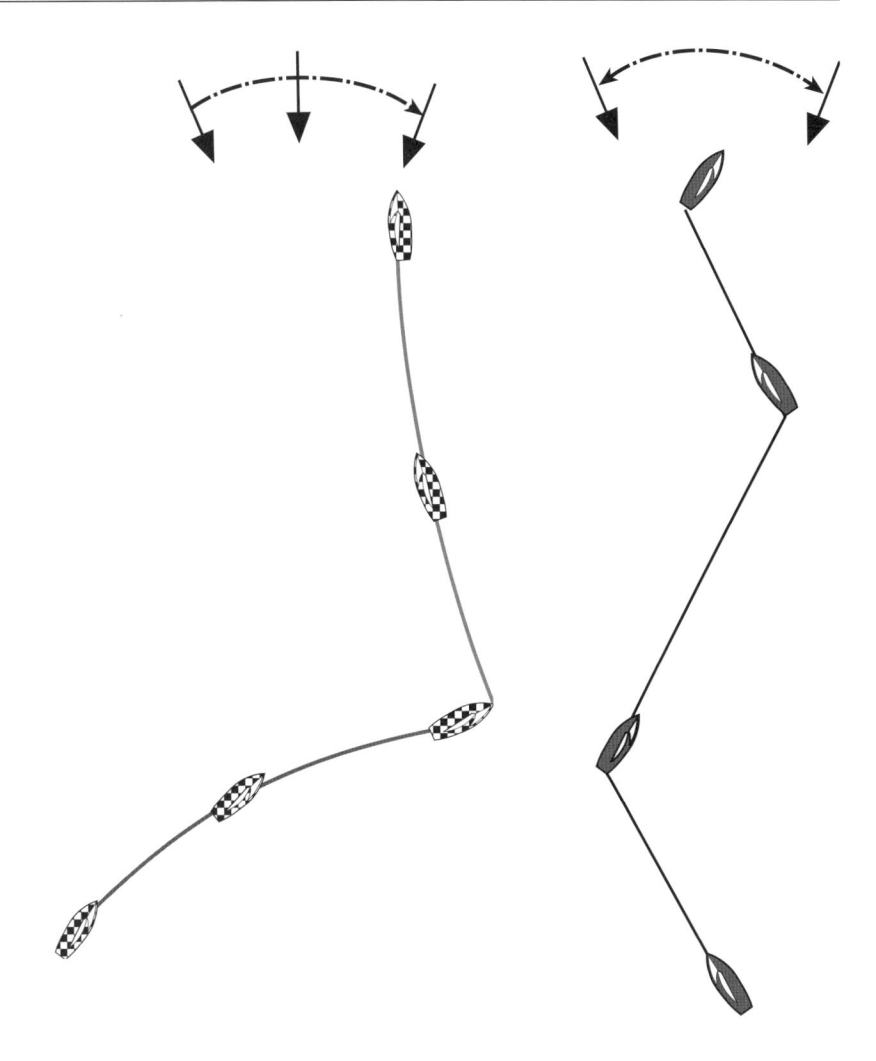

Fig. 9 – In a persistent shift we sail toward the shift.

Fig. 10 – In oscillating winds we do the same thing over and over, always sailing toward the next shift.

Persistent Shifts

The strategy in a persistent shift is to sail toward the new wind. If the wind is shifting to the right, then go right. If the wind is shifting left, go left.

Sail Headed

In a persistent shift, one tack is continuously getting headed while the other is getting lifted. Our strategy is to first sail the tack which is getting headed, then sail the tack which is getting lifted. Why? The tack which is getting headed is getting worse all the time. It is headed now, but will be headed more later. Sail it now before it gets worse. The tack which is getting lifted is improving all the time. If we sail it now we will be missing a better lift later.

Are you Sure it's a Persistent Shift?

How hard is it to split with the fleet and sail into a header? Without our pre-race info, weather forecast, and/or observation of other boats on which to build our strategy, it would be crazy. Even with good information and a well thought out plan, it is hard to stick to your guns as the fleet tacks away. If you know what is coming, then go to it. Position yourself to the favored side of the fleet.

The Rewards

How much do you gain by sailing into a persistent shift? It depends how far the wind shifts and how far you are separated from your competition; but in a word – plenty.

PERSISTENT EXAMPLE

We know from our Wind Graph that the wind is gradually backing. Our starboard tack readings for the hour before the start show a trend: 30° > 25° > 20° > 15°. The port tack compass readings are similar: 120° > 115° > 110° > 105°. Starboard is getting progressively headed, while port is getting lifted. The forecast tells of a low passing to the south. We expect the wind to continue to back (Fig. 11).

Sail to the Shift

Coming off the starting line on starboard tack our compass reads 10°. A few minute later it reads 5°, and soon after that, 0°. With each little header some of our competition tacks away. Some tacked to port on the first header off the line. Others have gradually bailed out as the header continues.

Eventually, with the compass reading 0°, we tack over. Our course on port tack is 90°. We are short of the layline to the mark. Gradually we are lifted, first to 85°, then 80°, 75°, and finally 70°. We are lifted to the mark, far ahead of those who tacked out early.

When Should We Tack?

The choice of where to tack is a little tricky. Theoretically we want to tack so we will be lifted exactly to the mark. This curved lifted layline would give us the full advantage of the shift without sailing any extra distance. This is a tough call, to say the least. A more realistic approach is to tack short of the layline. Then, as you approach the mark, tack out again, and take another guess. Don't overstand or you'll be sailing extra distance. As you get closer to the mark, you should be able to make a more accurate layline call.

Another (tactical) perspective on where to tack is to maintain position between the fleet and the shift. Don't sail to the corner – just get a controlling position.

So Much for the Competition

Coming off the starting line on starboard, we gradually got headed. Some of the fleet played the header as an oscillating shift, and tacked out. They expected to be headed again (on port tack) before tacking back to starboard. This was a big mistake. We knew from our Wind Graph that we were in a persistent shift. We used persistent shift strategy by sailing into the header, towards the new wind.

The boats which tacked out early kept getting lifted further and further on port tack, which made starboard tack look

Wind Graph

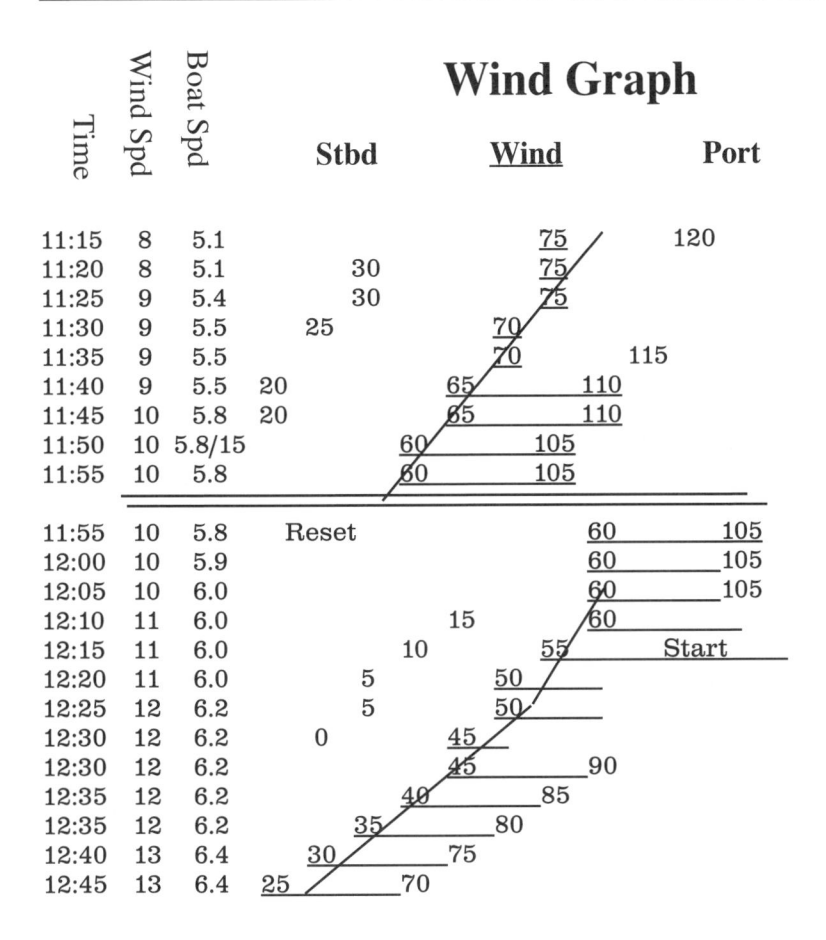

Time	Wind Spd	Boat Spd	Stbd	Wind	Port
11:15	8	5.1		75	120
11:20	8	5.1	30	75	
11:25	9	5.4	30	75	
11:30	9	5.5	25	70	
11:35	9	5.5		70	115
11:40	9	5.5	20	65	110
11:45	10	5.8	20	65	110
11:50	10	5.8/15		60	105
11:55	10	5.8		60	105
11:55	10	5.8	Reset	60	105
12:00	10	5.9		60	105
12:05	10	6.0		60	105
12:10	11	6.0	15	60	
12:15	11	6.0	10	55	Start
12:20	11	6.0	5	50	
12:25	12	6.2	5	50	
12:30	12	6.2	0	45	
12:30	12	6.2		45	90
12:35	12	6.2		40	85
12:35	12	6.2	35		80
12:40	13	6.4	30	75	
12:45	13	6.4	25	70	

Fig. 11 – Wind Graph and strategy for a Persistent Shift. This Wind Graph shows a persistent shift to the left. As the wind worked its way left it nearly ran off our graph. At 11:55 we had to reset the wind graph to re-center our numbers. By gathering wind information before the start we were able to form a sound race strategy to take advantage of the expected new wind. As always, we sailed toward the next shift. Challenge Question: Why does the wind often seem to shift faster or more often after the start? The answer is embedded in Chapter 10.

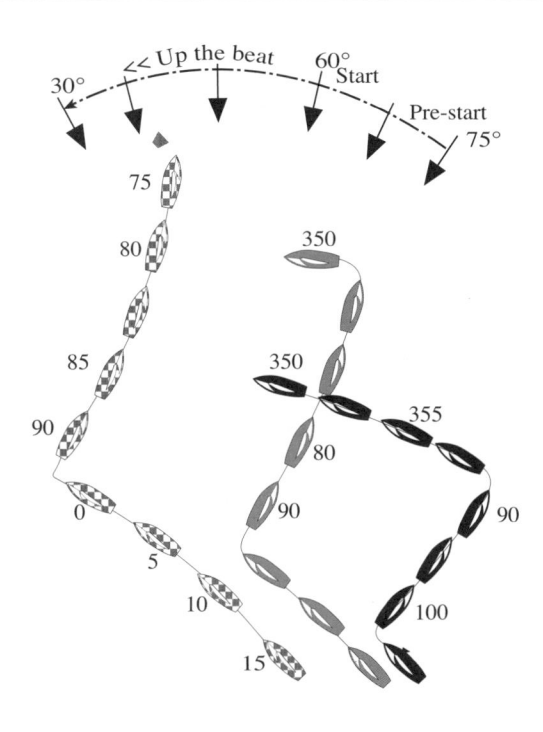

worse and worse. The port tack boats ended up sailing what is known as the *great circle route*, getting lifted around the outside of the mark.

Too Far Ahead?

If the fleet goes right and you think the wind is going left, then position yourself to the left of the fleet. Don't split completely with the fleet, for two reasons:

First, if you split and you are right, you will end up way ahead, and everyone will think you were just lucky. *You don't want to win by too much*; just a comfortable margin that will let everyone see who is out front.

Second, if you split with the fleet and happen to be wrong, you are sunk. (Somehow it is not unlucky to be half a mile behind – you are just bad.) Hedge your bets.

Oscillating Example
Pre-Race Data

In preparation for our 12:15 start we periodically record and plot our wind information. Using the close-hauled compass course on each tack, we are able to calculate the wind direction. The Wind Graph from our Race Planner shows the following (Fig. 12):

- An oscillating breeze, shifting back and forth.
- Starboard tack headings ranged from 170° to 185°.
- Port tack headings ranged from 260° to 275°.
- We tack through 90°; from 170° on starboard to 260° on port, or from 185° to 275°.
- The wind speed is a steady 8 to 9 knots.

Stay in Phase—Tack on the Headers

Coming off the starting line, we are sailing on starboard with a compass course of 180° to 185°. These are high numbers for starboard tack, which means we are lifted. Gradually our course drops to between 175° and 180°. This is an average course, neither headed or lifted, and we can sail on either tack.

Soon the crew reports that our course has dropped below 175°. Other boats are showing similar angles. We are headed. We tack. As we settle on port tack the compass reads 260°–265°, low numbers which mean we are lifted on port tack. As the numbers rise, we are getting headed. Remember: Port, Higher, Header. When our course falls below our average, we tack again and sail lifted on starboard.

As the plot shows, we continue tacking on the headers in the oscillating shifts. Gradually we find ourselves to the left of the middle of the course. We use the time when the wind is at the average direction to sail on port tack, which returns us to the middle. We sail on starboard only when lifted above 180°; we sail on port for any heading between 260° and 270°.

A New High!

Further up the leg, we are sailing lifted on starboard. Compass readings show a course between 180° and 185°. Gradually we are lifted to 190°. At this point lights should flash, bells should ring, and sirens should sound. 190° is beyond our range of oscillations. We are lifted higher than ever before.

We may have to reevaluate the conditions and modify our strategy. What is causing this new reading? Helmsman error? Changing weather? Are we closer to shore? Are there any new clouds? What is going on with the rest of the fleet?

Is this a momentary aberration, after which we will return to earlier conditions? Or is this the beginning of a persistent shift? Perhaps the wind will continue to oscillate, but over a new range or wider range.

The key is to first recognize that something new is happening. The next step is to evaluate the change and make plans accordingly. Ideally we would have seen it coming—either from wind on the water, an expected shift near shore, or by observing other boats (in an earlier class—we are leading our fleet, remember).

The Impact of Shifts – Don't Miss 'Em

Meanwhile, one of our competitors has sailed off the line on starboard tack and continued one third of the way up the leg before tacking. From there he sailed across the course on port tack, to the starboard tack layline. Ignoring the shifts has left our rival out of phase and sailing headed half the time. On the other hand, he has only had to tack twice! On a two mile beat with 10° oscillations, a boat which sails in phase will be *minutes* ahead of a boat which ignores the shifts. That's even after we throw in the cost of a couple of extra tacks!

A little later, we'll pull out our slide rules and find out just how big a deal wind shifts are, but for now, just remember: Track the shifts, and hit 'em!

Wind Graph

Time	Wind Spd	Boat Spd	Stbd	Wind	Port
11:15	8	5.2		220	265
11:18	8	5.1	180	225	
11:20	8	5.1	185	230	
11:21	9	5.6		230	275
11:25	9	5.5	175	220	265
11:30	9	5.5		220	265
11:35		5.6	170	215	260
11:43	8	5.0	180	225	270
11:45		5.2		225	270
11:50	9	5.5	185	230	275
11:55		5.6	175	220	265
12:01	9	5.5	170	215	260
12:07	8	5.2	175	220	265
12:12	9	5.5	180	225	270
12:15	9	5.5	185	230	(Start)
12:20	8	5.1	180	225	270
12:23	8	5.1		215	260
12:25	9	5.5		220	265
12:28	9	5.5	185	230	
12:30	8	5.1	180	225	
12:33	8	5.1		215	260
12:35	9	5.5		220	265
12:40	9	5.5	190	235	

Fig. 12 – The Wind Graph shows the plot of an oscillating wind over time. Using this information, the tactician is able to plan a strategy to take advantage of the shifts, shown by the checkered boat, above. The black boat ignores the shifts, and falls behind.

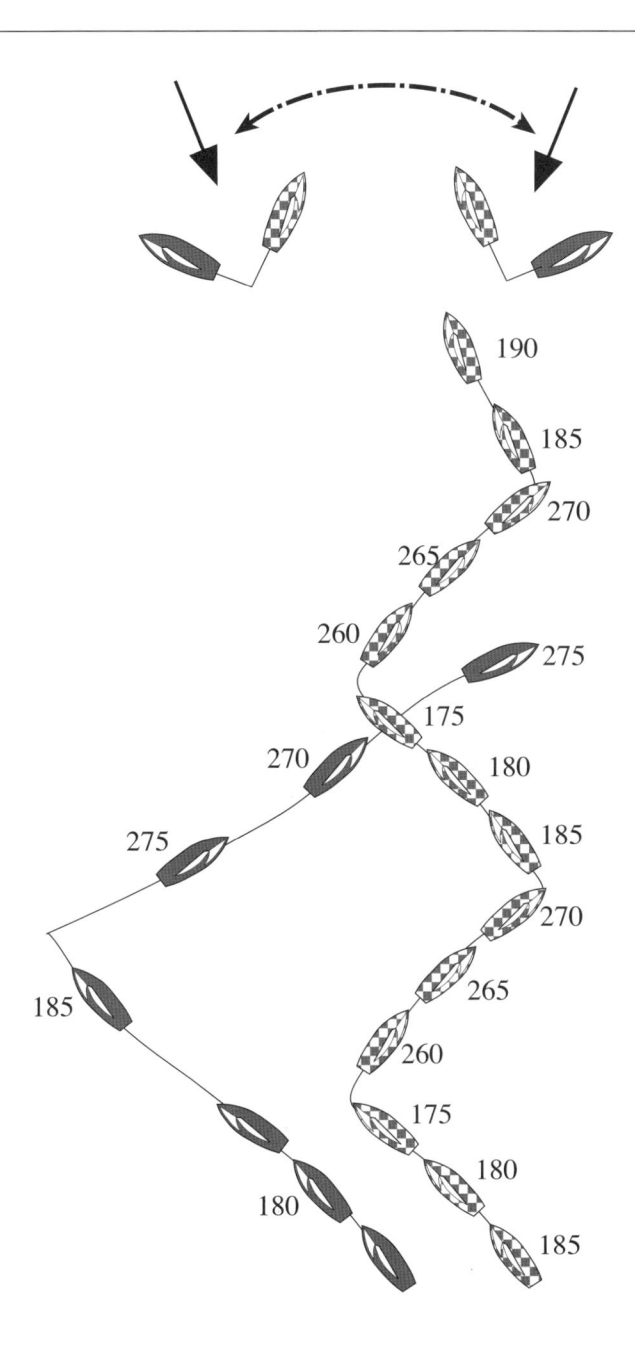

Chapter 7: Upwind Strategy

Other Types of Shifts

As we said above, pure persistent and pure oscillating wind shifts are quite rare. There are infinite variations.

One variation is a mix of persistent and oscillating shifts. This mixed condition is characterized by oscillating shifts gradually shifting one way or the other – veering or backing – over time.

Several other types of wind shifts occur. One is a major shift where a new wind completely replaces the existing wind. This can happen suddenly, or after a period of calm. Winds vary in other ways. There are geographic shifts caused by the configuration of land, and thermal wind shifts created by the heating of land. There are also differences in the wind due to differences in current (as we will see below), and there are shifts caused by the movement of weather systems.

Mixed Conditions

In mixed conditions, combining both oscillations and persistent characteristics, the strategy is to sail toward the persistent shift while still playing the embedded oscillations.

Part of the trick in coping with these mixed conditions is to realize that the range of oscillations is gradually changing. The high and low numbers on each tack will be increasing or decreasing. What was once a header may now be the median, with a new lower header on the way.

When conditions are too confusing to diagnose, the fall back strategy is to sail to the mark. Which ever tack takes you closer to the mark is preferred until there is reason to do otherwise.

MIXED CONDITIONS EXAMPLE

Here is an example of strategy in mixed conditions (Fig. 13).

Pre-Race Data

Our pre-race data is listed in the Wind Graph. It shows mixed conditions. The trend is veering, but we have oscillations as well. Our strategy will have to consider both; we will also have to keep a keen eye out for changes in conditions. One thing to look for is stronger breeze to one side. Is the trend shifting and building (as in this example) or shifting and fading.

. . . And They're Off

It is interesting to see the different strategies which emerge from these difficult conditions. Some of the fleet will treat the beat as though they were sailing a persistent shift. Others will tack on the headers. Some will try to balance the mix. And still others will be confused and uncertain of how to handle the conditions.

As the fleet moves up the beat in mixed conditions, the apparent leaders will change with each shift. Often it is unclear until the last shift of the leg who will come out ahead.

Keep Fighting

In mixed conditions you are never out of it. Keep working, keep trying to decipher the next shift. There are plenty of opportunities to catch up (and more than enough chances to get confused). If you find yourself baffled, try to regroup. Everyone will have their moments—if you can keep from going to pieces during your bad moments, you'll have another chance for good times.

Wind Graph

Time	Wind Spd	Boat Spd	Stbd	Wind	Port
11:15	8	5.0		285	330
11:18	8	5.1	240	285	
11:20	9	5.4	245	290	
11:21	9	5.4		290	335
11:25	9	5.5	245	290	
11:30	10	5.8		295	340
11:35	10	5.9	250	295	
11:36	9	5.6		290	335
11:43	8	5.1	245	290	
11:45	8	5.2	250	295	
11:50	9	5.4		295	340
11:51	9	5.5		300	345
11:55	10	5.8	255	300	
11:58	10	5.9		295	340
12:001	11	6.2		305	350
12:02	11	6.3	260	305	
12:07	11	6.3	255	300	
12:08	10	5.9		295	340
12:10	10	6.0		300	345
12:12	11	6.3		305	350
12:15	11	6.3	260	305	
12:20	12	6.3	265	310	
12:23	11	6.4	260	305	
12:25	11	6.4	265	310	
12:28	10	6.0		300	345
12:31	10	6.0	260	305	
12:33	11	6.2	265	310	
12:36	11	6.3	265	310	

Fig. 13 – The Wind Graph for mixed conditions shows oscillating winds gradually ratchetting to the right. Strategy in these conditions is to work toward the favored side while playing the oscillations.

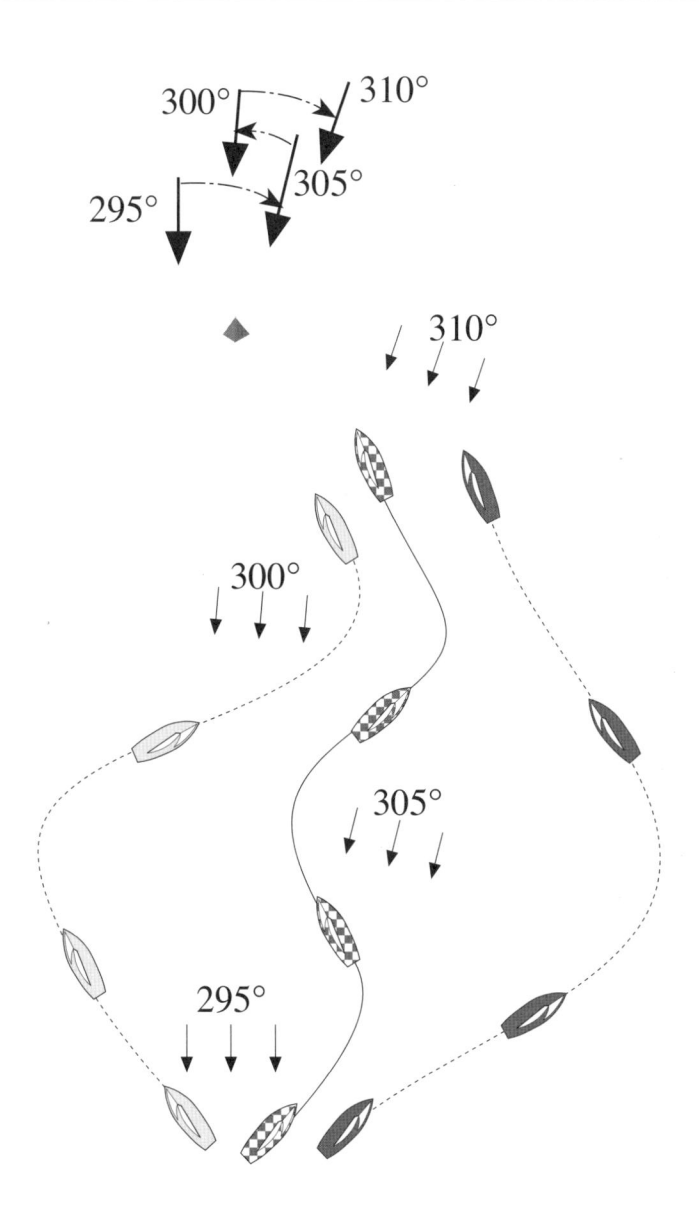

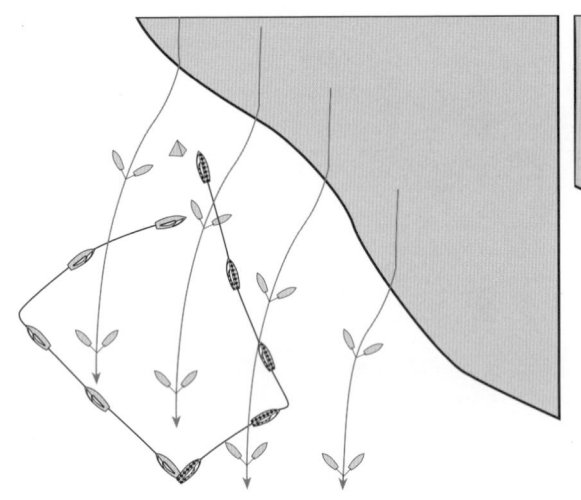

Fig. 14 – Offshore winds tend to shift more perpendicular to the shoreline.

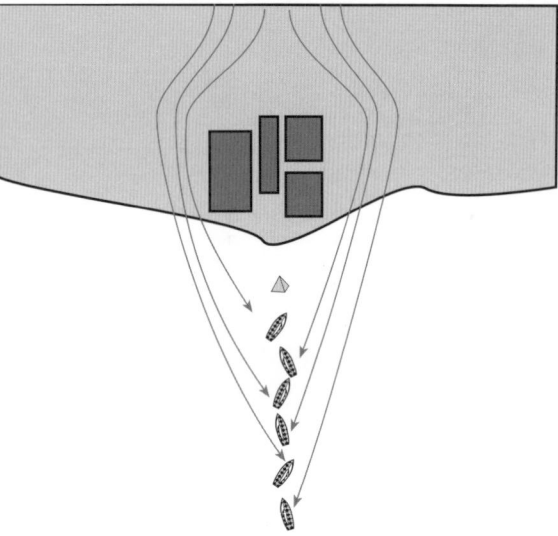

Fig. 15 – A city or hill can create oscillating shifts, with bigger shifts near shore.

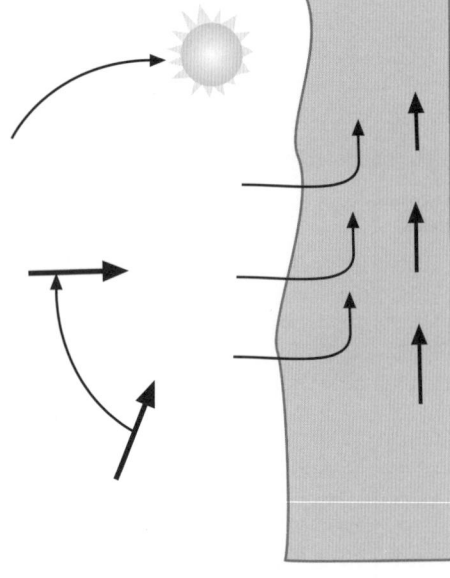

Fig. 16 – As the land heats up, you get a persistent shift as the prevailing wind shifts to the sea breeze direction.

Geographic Shifts

We do most of our racing near shore, where the interaction of the land and water affects our sailing wind. Further offshore conditions are more stable and predictable; but along the coast wind conditions are difficult to predict.

There are many ways the shoreline changes the wind. First, the shoreline funnels the wind. The wind shifts to follow the shoreline. Second, offshore winds tend to shift more perpendicular to the shoreline (Fig. 14). Third, winds shift around obstacles such as hills, buildings, and thermal domes in areas with lots of pavement (Fig. 15).

Fourth, the heating of the land creates thermal winds—sea breezes—which blow towards shore during the day.

Fifth, the thermals create turbulence and mixing which can pull the upper winds down to the surface. These upper winds are generally shifted to the right of the surface winds (at least in the northern hemisphere).

The effect of these geographic changes can be either persistent or oscillating. In offshore winds, there will commonly be a mixed effect—with puffs coming from shore lifting the tack which is parallel to shore, and with those lifts being stronger the closer you get to shore.

The thermal effects on an onshore wind usually create a persistent shift from the prevailing wind direction to the normal sea breeze direction (Fig 16).

For more on weather, see the *North U. Weather for Sailors* book and CD-ROM.

Weather System Wind Shifts
A Major Change
As weather systems move or weaken, one wind can replace another. A prevailing wind may be pushed aside by a thermal, or a new weather system wind may arrive. Whatever the cause, there are occasions where a new and different wind appears and all the earlier information becomes irrelevant.

If we can anticipate this change based on forecasts or observations (new clouds etc.) and be in position for it, there can be tremendous gains. But beware–There is a danger in chasing the predicted conditions and expecting a shift which does not arrive as scheduled. Summer weather systems often stall or even disappear as the get to the coast.

Squall Winds
Another type of weather system wind is a localized late afternoon squall. These can turn the entire fleet on its head. Squalls create two opportunities—one as the squall hits, and the other as the squall passes.

Be prepared. If you are ready to shorten sail and race through the squall while others scramble, huge gains are possible. Sail toward the new shift – usually the wind backs to the left – to avoid windward work once it arrives. A squall drill should be part of your crew training.

If the squall is localized, then after the squall passes conditions often return to the conditions which existed prior to the squall. If the squall is part of an advancing cold front, then conditions behind the front will be entirely different from earlier. By recognizing the type of squall you may be able to anticipate conditions during and after its passage.

Wind Shear
Wind shear is a condition where there are layers of wind—one at the surface, and the other aloft. Wind shear is uncommon. It occurs most often over smooth cold water early on a spring day, or at night.

Fig. 17 – Wind shear is the stacking of two winds, one on top of the other. The upper wind usually displaces the lower wind.

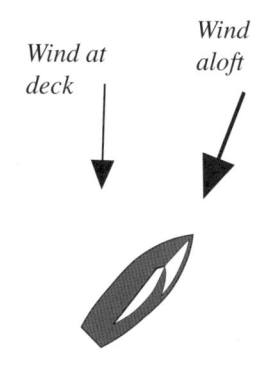

There is a boundary layer of cool air on the surface, and a different wind aloft. Sail trimming with the wind 30° or more different from the deck to masthead can be baffling, to say the least. Tactically it is a little more straightforward.

Generally the upper wind will become dominant. Fundamental wind strategy says sail toward the new wind—in this case sail toward the upper wind, as it will eventually displace the surface wind. If the upper wind is from the right, go right. Here's a trick if you are a small boat in a mixed fleet: Look at the mastheads of larger boats. Sometimes you will be able to find a wind shear (and a clue to the expected wind) which does not show at your masthead (Fig. 17).

Don't confuse wind shear with wind gradient. Wind gradient is the tendency for winds at the mast head to be stronger than those at deck level. It exists almost all the time, and is more dramatic in light air, less pronounced in heavy air.

Chapter 7: Upwind Strategy

7.5 The Impact of Wind Shifts

It is often difficult to predict the wind. Is it worth it to try to figure out what the wind is going to do next? How much difference does it make?

The Impact of Persistent Shifts

We'll assume here a course set to the wind at the start, with incremental shifts to the right. For the initial segments boats make equal progress upwind. Then the wind shifts 5° to the right.

The boat on port tack, going right, is headed. The tactician struggles with his own convictions, and resists the tide of sentiment to tack on the header. Meanwhile the boats on starboard are lifted up toward the mark – *Yippee*!

They sail on.

Another shift, further right. Finally, the tactician going right calls for a tack. Now they are lifted on starboard – higher than any lift they'd seen before the start.

The boats going left are in a quandary. They are lifted, but the wind is going right. The black boat bites the bullet, and tacks. It is very hard to tack when you are lifted – if you don't believe me, you've never tried it. But it is the right thing to do. If the wind continues right, then there is nothing to be gained by continuing to the left. Cut your loses, and sail to the shift.

The grey boat carries on, hoping for an oscillation. Its a gamble – if the persistent shift continues, his position will go from bad to worse. He's sailing the great circle route and will never get a good angle to sail to the mark. But, BUT, if the wind oscillates back, (oh please, oh please) even for just a short time, he can recover nicely. (Fig. 18)

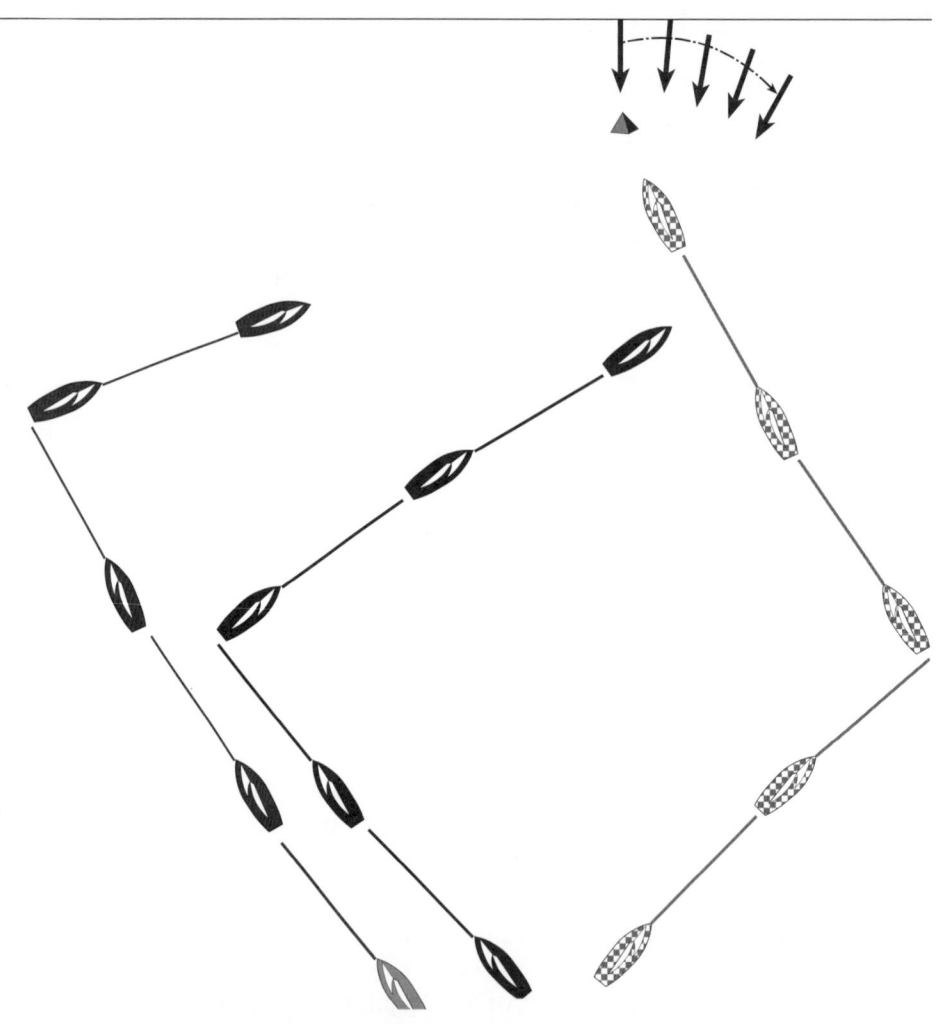

Fig 18 – Persistent shifts – sail to the new wind!
Here are some numbers, assuming a 5° shift every 5 minutes, with the boats sailing at 6 knots: After 20 minutes the checkered boat will be 1.5 miles upwind of the starting line, and over 1/4 mile ahead of the black boat. The checkered boat will be on just 1/8 mile ahead of the grey boat, but that lead will be growing quickly.
The black boat would be expected to cross the grey boat when he tacks.

The Impact of Oscillations

We'll start first with a boat sailing upwind, with a tacking angle of 90°. Using trigonometry (yikes), we find that the distance sailed is 1.42 times the straight-line distance. To sail to a mark one mile upwind, the boat will have to sail a total of .71 miles on port tack, and .71 miles on starboard tack.

If the wind is oscillating as little as 5° either side of the median, then performance improves significantly. To sail to a mark one mile upwind, the boat will have to sail a total of .65 miles on port tack, and .65 miles on starboard tack. By taking advantage of the shifts, the distance sailed is reduced to 1.30 times the straight-line distance. That's a savings of over a tenth of a mile – over 600 feet!

If the wind is oscillating 10° either side of the median, then performance improves dramatically. To sail to a mark one mile upwind, the boat will have to sail a total of .61 miles on port tack, and .61 miles on starboard tack. By taking advantage of the shifts, the distance sailed is reduced from 1.42 to 1.22 times the straight line distance. A savings of .20 miles, which is nearly 15%, or about 1200 feet! (Fig. 19)

At a boat speed of 6 knots this represents 120 seconds – or two minutes in one mile! These numbers are for big right or left shifts – not a gradual oscillation, and for a boat sailing the wind shifts perfectly. But *even at 25% efficiency, you'll still save 30 seconds per mile!*

Hit the shifts!

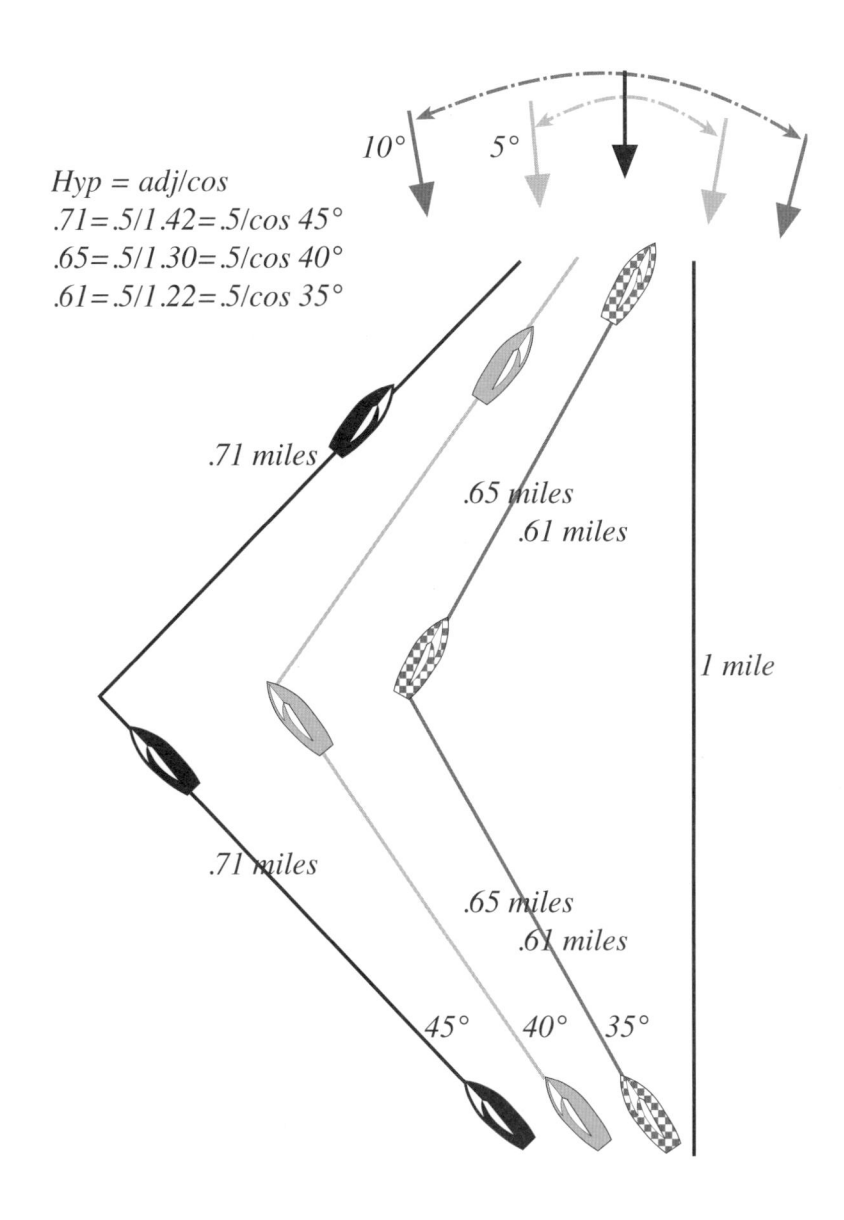

$Hyp = adj/cos$
$.71 = .5/1.42 = .5/cos\ 45°$
$.65 = .5/1.30 = .5/cos\ 40°$
$.61 = .5/1.22 = .5/cos\ 35°$

Fig. 19 – Conclusion on the impact of oscillations: BIG.

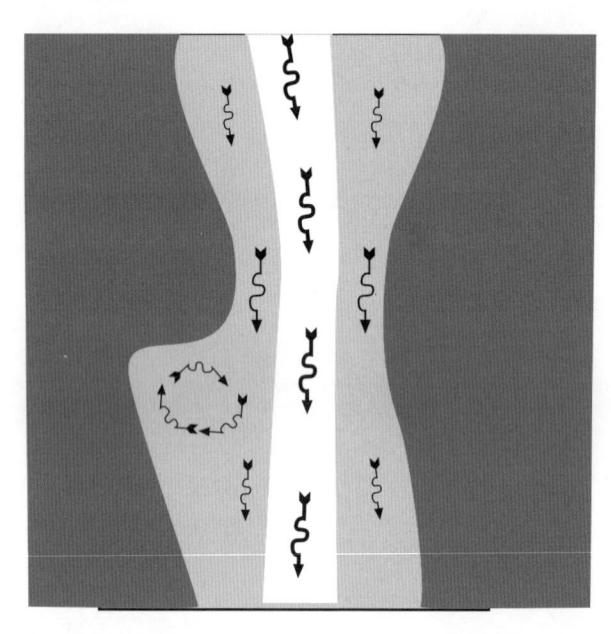

Fig. 20– Currents are created by tides and rivers. They run stronger in channels than in shallows, and can be a major strategic factor.

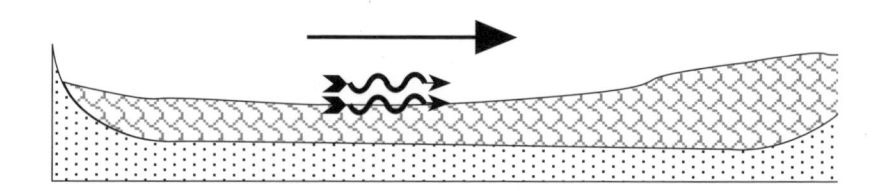

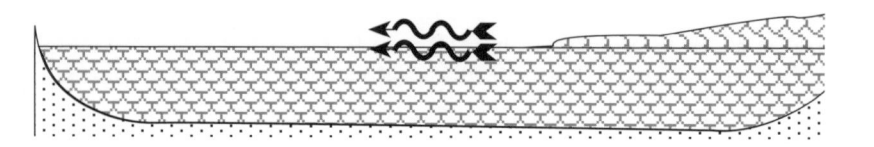

Fig. 21– Wind can create current. Wind driven current can exaggerate or reverse tidal currents in shallow bays. And it can create currents where there otherwise would be none. After the wind has pushed water to one end of a basin, the current will reverse when the wind subsides.

7.6 Current

Current adds complexity to strategic planning. The obvious, and primary, strategic concern is to seek out better (more favorable or less adverse) current. When the current is not uniform across the course, it can be an overriding strategic factor. Currents run stronger in deep water than in shallow, and faster in narrows than in open water. Below points and around bends, eddies can develop. They can race across flats. Adding further complexity is the fact that currents change. Correct strategy can change dramatically over a period of hours. Storms and strong winds can distort surface currents and delay tides, sometimes making tide tables useless (Fig. 20).

Wind Driven Current

Currents are not limited to rivers and tidal basins. In the Great Lakes, for example, currents of one full knot are possible. Currents build when strong winds drive the surface water. After the winds abate, the currents reverse as the water, which has been stacked up at one end of the lake, returns to level (Fig. 21).

Uniform Across the Course

When the current is uniform throughout the course, it affects the laylines and sailing angles to the mark. If it is running across the course, then it can also change the balance of time spent on each tack (Fig. 22).

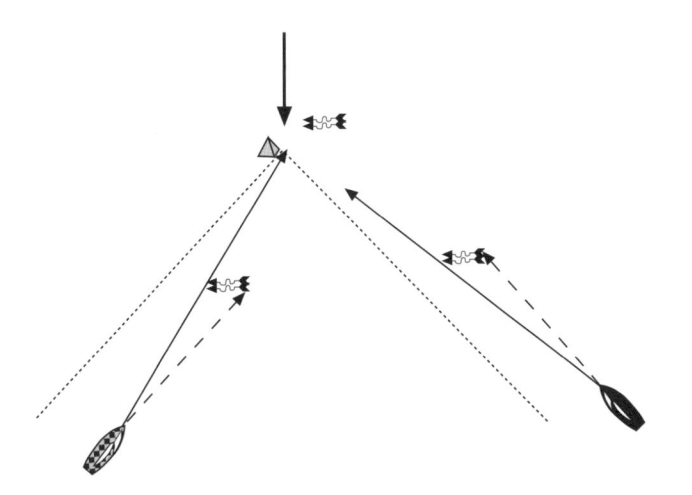

Fig. 23 – When there is stronger current to one side, go to it if favorable, sail away if adverse. The advantage can change with the tides.

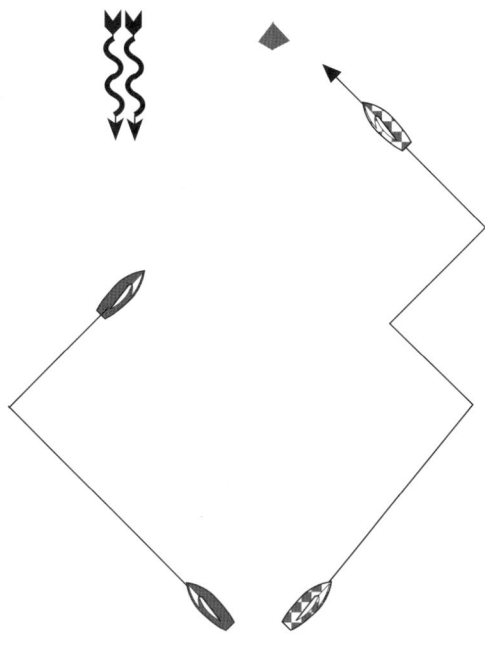

Fig. 22 – When the current is uniform throughout the leg, the biggest impact is on laylines into the mark. Current can also skew the course, changing the balance of time on each tack.

When Current is Not Uniform

When the current is not the same across the course area, then we must seek out the advantage. Differences across the course can shape our strategy. Unless there are dramatic differences in wind conditions a current advantage is key to strategic planning.

Current to one side

Obviously if the current is stronger to one side seek out that side if it is favorable, and avoid that side if it is adverse. A favorable current, running against the wind, can set up a pronounced chop. Look for this. Sail into the choppy water and ride the current upwind. Similarly, smooth water can indicate wind and current running together. Avoid this area upwind (Fig. 23).

Current across the course

When the current runs across the course and is stronger in one part of the leg, you want to take advantage of the change in sailing wind caused by the current. Sailing bow into the current, you will be lifted; sailing with the current astern, you will be headed. For example, in ten knots of wind and one knot of current the sailing wind is shifted 6°. With one tack lifted and the other headed, the effect is a 20% advantage in VMG (Fig. 24).

Predictable, to a Point

Current, whether tidal or river generated, is predictable. Tide tables and current charts should be studied, and their predictions compared with observation. When the current runs strong it is often more reliable and predictable than the wind; a small current advantage translates into big gains.

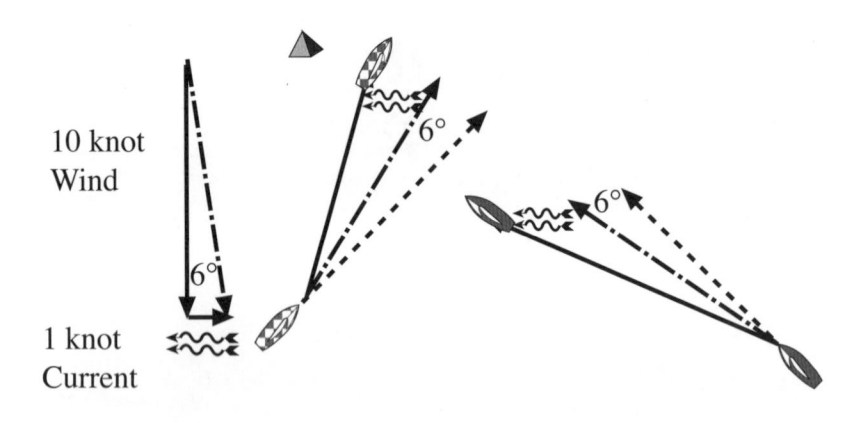

Fig. 24 – When current is not uniform, take advantage of the shift in sailing wind. In this example we have 10 knots of wind, 1 knot of current, and boats tacking through 90°. The current gives one boat a 6° lift, the other a 6° header. The lifted boat's VMG is 20% better than the headed boat's. (VMG is normally .71 of boat speed. The shift is 6° because arc-tan 6°=1/10. A 6° lift creates a VMG of .78, a 6° header creates a VMG of .63. .63/.78=.80. I'm glad you asked.)

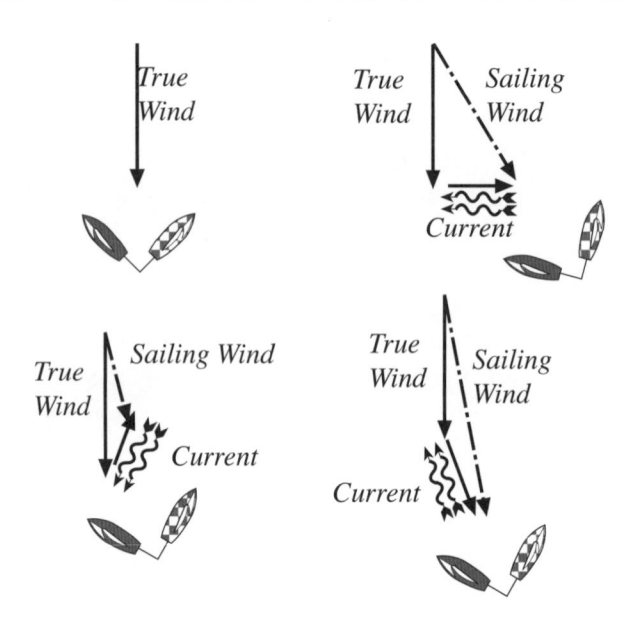

Fig. 25 – The vector of the current is added to the true wind to create our sailing wind.

In tidal areas the advantage can be fleeting—or reverse—over the course of a race. Obviously we need to pay attention to changes in the tide.

Changes with Wind Conditions

The wind can upset current predictions, particularly in shallow water. A strong wind blowing over a long period can overwhelm tidal effects, pushing surface water and delaying or reversing tides. When the winds abate, the current distortions will remain until the water has had a chance to return to level by flowing in the direction opposite the earlier wind. Winds can also create currents where there otherwise are none, as mentioned above.

Effects on Sailing Wind

Current changes the sailing wind for a boat. The sailing wind is the sum of the true wind over the bottom and the current. When sailing upwind, the net effect of current on the wind reinforces the effect or the current. A favorable current creates a favorable change in the sailing wind, and an adverse current makes for an unfavorable change in the sailing wind (Fig. 25). Details are explained in Chapter 13: Weather.

Develop Local Knowledge

One key to success in current is to develop local knowledge. Keep records of how the current runs in various wind and tide combinations. Our strategic plan is only as good as the information it is based on. Accurate current information is critical to good strategic planning.

7.7 Strategy vs. Rivals

While dealing with other boats is really a tactical issue, other boats can enter into our strategic planning. Late in a series we may be concerned with particular boats which are close to us in the standings.

It is good strategy to consider your close rivals, but do not let them distract you from sailing your own boat well. There is a danger in becoming preoccupied with the opponent. The rivals are but one strategic factor. If you sail your own boat well, the rest will fall into place. If you sail badly, then you stand a greater chance of losing your private war.

The basic strategy when ahead is to stay between the competition and the next mark (Fig. 26).

When behind the basic strategy is to split with the rival, but not simply for the sake of splitting. If you are behind and the rival is going the right way, splitting will leave you further behind. You have to be patient and look for your opportunities. For further discussion see Chapter 8: Upwind Tactics, next. There are times when you may be close enough behind in the race to be able to preserve a lead in the series. In this case the strategy is simply to follow the rival. You must, of course, consider handicap time differences when evaluating your position.

Fig. 26 – Cover your chief rivals. Stay between them and the next mark or the new wind.

7.8 The Land of Opportunity

It happens, even to the best of racers. You find yourself at the tail end of the fleet. Who knows how you got there—a third row start, a miserable first beat, a big shift, a boat handling disaster. I will not dwell on the ways to fall behind; at that, it seems, we are all uniquely qualified.

The Most Important Race

So, you're back in the pack. What should you do?

Before getting into details, recognize that in any regatta or series your worst race is often the most important. One astronomical score can shatter an otherwise competitive record. The ability to bring that astronomical finish down to earth is the mark of a champion, and success starts with attitude.

Don't Dwell

As a skipper you should take charge. Never mind how we got into this mess—let's focus on getting out of it. (Besides, more than likely it was your fault.) (Fig. 27).

Fig. 27– Sooner or later, you will find yourself in "The Land of Opportunity."

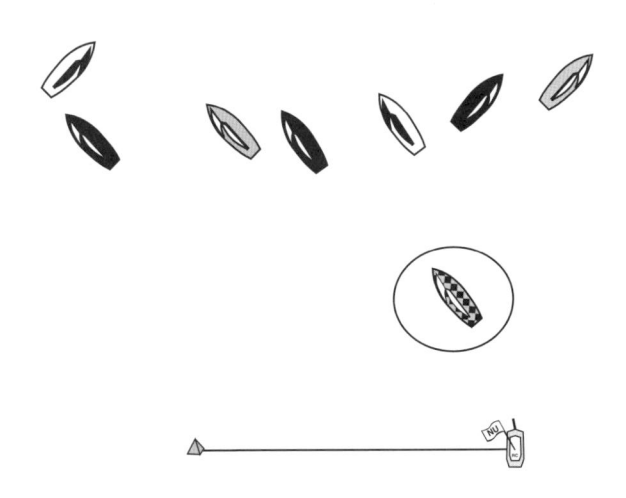

How Many Can We Pass?

When you find yourself at the wrong end of the fleet, don't get depressed. You are in The Land of Opportunity—there is a whole fleet of boats waiting to be passed! Don't wait for a miracle to save you. Get to work and grind 'em down, one at a time. You're not going to win this race; that is no longer the goal. Actually, winning is redefined for this race: Winning is passing as many boats as you can.

Sail Fast & Go the Right Way

Don't panic. Settle down and work on boat speed. You will not pass anyone without good speed. Concentrate on speed, and you should be able to knock off a few tail-enders easily.

Go the right way. In The Land of Opportunity you must concentrate more on your overall strategy than on immediate tactics with those nearby. Upwind, figure out which side of the course is favored and head that way. Back here it is hard to sail the middle; all that gets you is traffic and bad air. You must pick a side. Do it carefully – you can't afford another mistake. If you are not sure which way to go (maybe that's how you landed in the Land of Opportunity), look to the leaders for guidance. The leaders are probably doing what is right – hint: they're in the lead. Others will gamble against the odds in hopes of passing the leaders. Our goal is pass the gamblers.

Sail Clean, Fast, Smart

On the reaches, you can save distance by sailing the rhumb line while letting others waste distance sailing high and then low. Avoid luffing duels, plan well ahead for the inside position at roundings and, above all, keep sailing fast.

Running legs offer an opportunity to attack those ahead. For all you need to know about Running Strategy and Tactics, skip ahead a few chapters. There are real opportunities here.

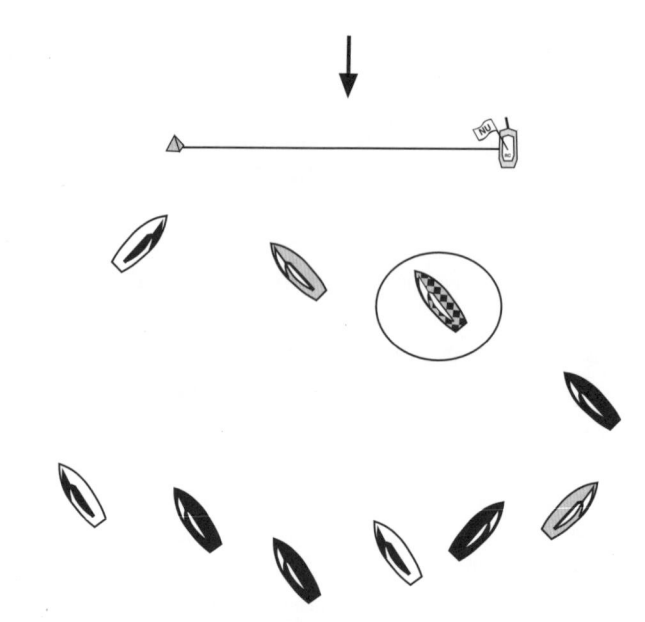

Fig. 28 – When you fall behind (as on the previous page) get to work. With grit, determination, and a little luck, you can reach The Promised Land.

The Promised Land

Hopefully you've fallen behind early, so you have plenty of time to catch up. Play the shifts and work the favored side; and keep sailing fast. Position yourself carefully to pick up a few boats at each mark rounding. Look ahead for changing conditions and be ready to respond.

Sometimes, late in a race you may need to gamble, split with the fleet, and hope to get lucky. But don't panic if you fall behind early. Don't count on luck. Get to work.

Every boat you pass is worth a point, and it is easier to move from 15th to 5th than it is from 5th to first. When you find yourself in The Land of Opportunity, keep cool, sail fast, go the right way, and avoid confrontations. You can reach The Promised Land. The End (Fig. 28).

7.9 Local Knowledge

Consistent success in a local area depends on local knowledge. You must learn to recognize local conditions and know the strategy which is called for.

When I raced collegiality at Yale, our team captain, Steve Benjamin, required us to complete a regatta report for every regatta we sailed. All the regatta reports were compiled into a notebook. Later, when I went racing on the Charles River in Boston, for example, I could refer to dozens of reports by my teammates covering the boats and sailing conditions I would face.

Local Knowledge: Racing in Annapolis

Each year it seems I race a regatta or two on Chesapeake Bay, out of Annapolis. The northern bay offers a challenging sailing venue. It is close enough to the ocean to be affected by sea breezes, and far enough north to be battered by cold fronts in early fall, when I seem to do most of my racing there. Winds come from all points and in all strengths. The currents run strong and vary widely across the bay. The winds have a big effect on the current, sometimes making a joke of the tide tables. (Refer to the chart on the next page.)

Disclaimer

Following are my impressions. God save you if you are foolish enough to follow my strategic advice when you go racing on Chesapeake Bay.

South East/South Sea Breeze

Comes in on top of prevailing southerly or when no other weather pattern is firmly in place. South East to South winds are generally shifty but not strong. Current is important, since this wind takes us diagonally across the bay. Beware of getting too far in toward the Eastern Shore. The breeze tends to run lighter and more southerly there, lifting starboard and making it painful to tack out onto port—and easy to take the great circle route.

Against the current you must get very close to the eastern shore to avoid the current in the main channel, and this often leads to great circle route just described. It seems better to stay right to avoid some current and still keep breeze. Tendency to clock also favors the right.

With an outbound current, sail to the main channel to get to the current but stay right once in the current. Avoid the left corner.

South/South West Sea Breeze

The sea breeze will fill and reinforce a South to South West wind. As the breeze builds, it does not back to the south as might be expected (since ocean lies to S.E.). Winds around 200°–210° roll straight up the bay. Winds tend to clock, and lift inshore between Tolly Point and Thomas Point.

Against the flood, the best tactic is to tack inside the line between Tolly and Thomas (don't forget to honor Tolly Pt. Buoy) to avoid the current. With the wind tending right, all signs lead inshore.

On the ebb, a more moderate strategy is called for; but the channel is often out of reach to the left, and there is rarely a strong ebb current against a southerly wind. The wind effectively blocks the current, and wind strategy prevails.

Westerlies

The prevailing westerlies can become blustery after a frontal passage. Most cold fronts take the wind N.W. or N., but a post-frontal westerly is not uncommon. The races are generally started near the Eastern Shore, with the windward mark set at the mouth of the Severn River. The wind tends to fan out of the Severn, particularly in the upper half of the beat. Boats sailing out to either side are lifted. They never get a favorable shift for a return tack, and boats come back from the corners headed. The wind also gets lighter off to the sides. Work the middle for the steadiest and strongest winds coming straight out of the Severn.

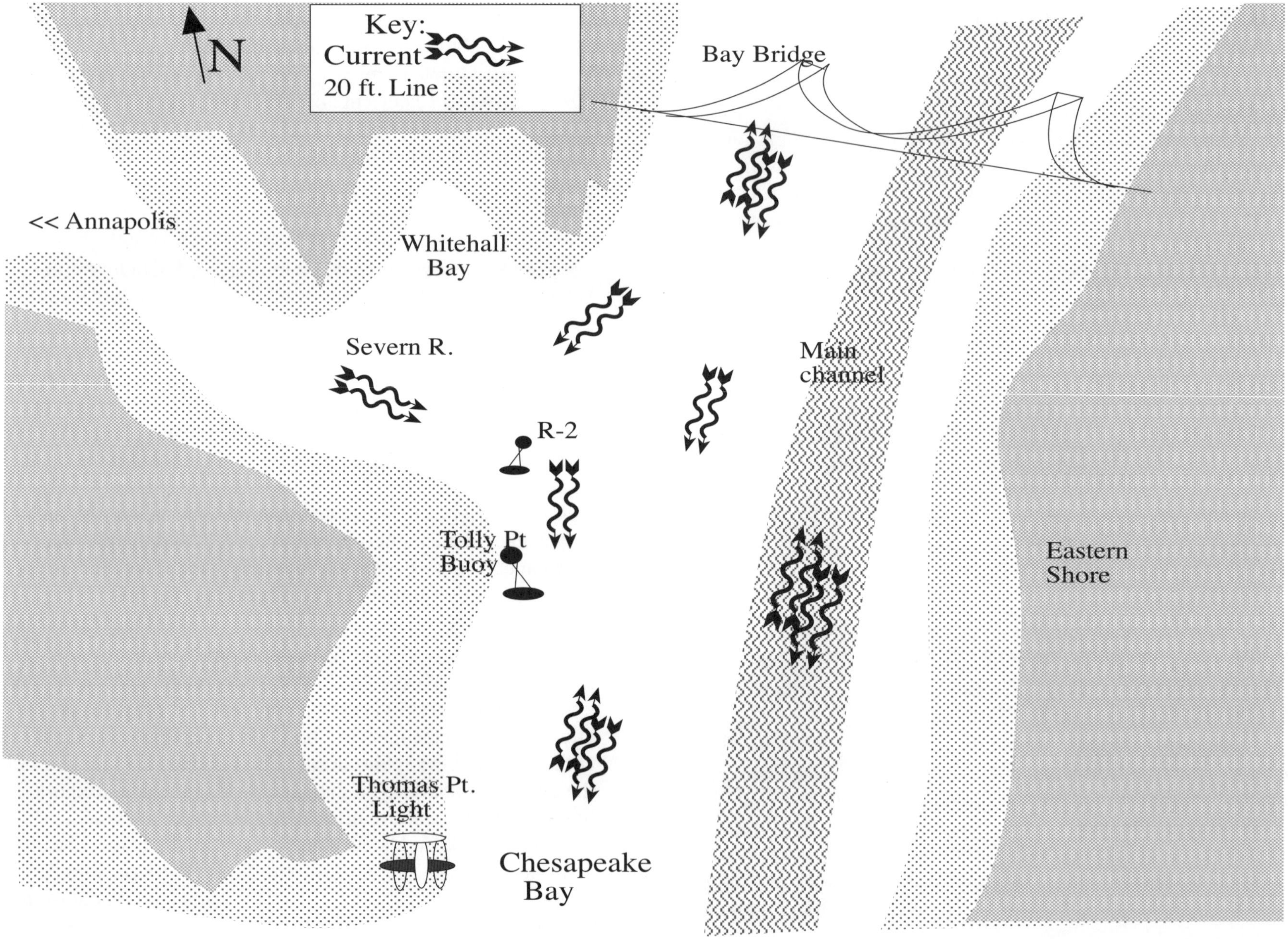
Key:
Current
20 ft. Line
N
Bay Bridge
<< Annapolis
Whitehall Bay
Severn R.
Main channel
R-2
Tolly Pt Buoy
Eastern Shore
Thomas Pt. Light
Chesapeake Bay

For triangle races, the reach mark is set in the middle of the bay, south and east of Tolly Point. After rounding the windward mark, particularly on the blustery days, the leg appears too tight for a spinnaker. Go ahead and set. Sail low on the early part of the leg, in the strong winds from the Severn. Later in the leg the breeze will lighten and fair, and it will be advantageous to be able to reach up from below.

WARNING: Things don't always work out this way on the first reach. Sometimes a S.W. puff will come off the shore inside Tolly Point and the boats inside will beam reach across, while those down low struggle to reach up. It depends on the wind direction (S. or N. of W.?) and the position of the mark (the closer under Tolly Point the more likely S.W. puffs are to be a factor).

The second reach across the bay is dominated by current. The same is true of the later part of any leeward leg. The current runs strongest near the mark. Overcorrect for the current early to make sure you are sailing with it late in the leg. (Work south on a flood, north on an ebb). The wind tends to be much lighter on the Eastern Shore and you don't want to have to fight the current in the main channel.

In the westerlies, the wind tends to be stronger by the river than on the eastern shore. Be ready for more breeze at the top of the leg.

If the frontal passage is weak the sea breeze may push the breeze to the S.W. in the afternoon. A strong front will tend to clock the breeze to the N.W.

Northwest Wind

After a frontal passage in the fall the strong N.W. winds provide some of the year's best sailing. From a start in mid-bay the windward mark is set at the mouth of Whitehall Bay or off Hackett Pt. to the east. Coming off the line there tend to be starboard tack lifts, with the boats up the line gaining an advantage. From there the race is often a sprint to the left in search of puffs from the Severn. The puffs are starboard headers, allowing a tack to port and a lifted track into the mark.

North Wind

In a northerly there is no fixed strategy. With the mark set below the bridge there may be some port lifts off Whitehall, but there may also be better breeze in the open part of the bay. If the wind is clocking then plan a strategy to take advantage of the persistent shift. Current can become a big factor. Stay left to avoid an ebb. Go right to take advantage of a flood, though the wind may diminish its strength.

Northeast Wind

As the frontal wind fades the breeze will clock to the northeast. The temptation is to go right, and that strategy may pay off early in the leg. But if the mark is set under the Eastern Shore the right will be a problem later on. In the second half of the beat boats coming in on port from the left hand side will be favored by more northerly puffs which roll down from the bridge, while those on the right suffer in fickle easterly puffs off the shore and big northerly headers.

The current can be a big factor, as you will have to cross the main channel on the way to the mark. After a strong northerly there will be little water left for an ebb, but beware the flood which may run longer and much stronger than usual as the bay refills.

Easterly Wind

The easterlies are among the most fickle and difficult of bay breezes. One thing is for sure. Rain is on the way. Stay home, stay dry; put in the storm windows until the rain starts, then watch football on TV. Have you noticed that the Redskins have been lousy since they closed Marmaduke's?

Local Knowledge: Racing In Chicago

Lake Michigan offers residents of Chicago some of the finest (though somewhat seasonal) sailing in the country. Conditions vary through the full spectrum—from shifty westerlies in smooth water to tremendous northerlies with jaw-breaking waves. The 300 mile long lake is capable of dishing up anything at anytime. And it is all fresh water!

Southwest Winds
Sail in toward the city for better breeze and a starboard lift.

West Winds
Look for dark patches coming off the city bringing breeze and big shifts. If you fall behind don't split – sail to the next shift.

Northwest Wind
With a passing cold front, the N.W. wind will blow cool and strong. Though the breeze tends to clock to the north, you find better breeze and port lifts inshore. Once the wind gets to the north, the left no longer pays. Watch for the wind to clock further.

North Wind
Sail fast and bring your foul weather gear. Even in mid-summer, the waves can stir up cold water. Try the right.

Northeast & East Wind
Get out into the lake for better breeze.

Southeast Wind
Go left, into the lake to fresher breeze and left shift.

South Wind
South wind bends near shore, for a SW shift near shore. But the breeze may back as the south wind may be due to a passing low or due to a building thermal blowing on shore. If it is cloudy, go in. Clear? Sail Fast!

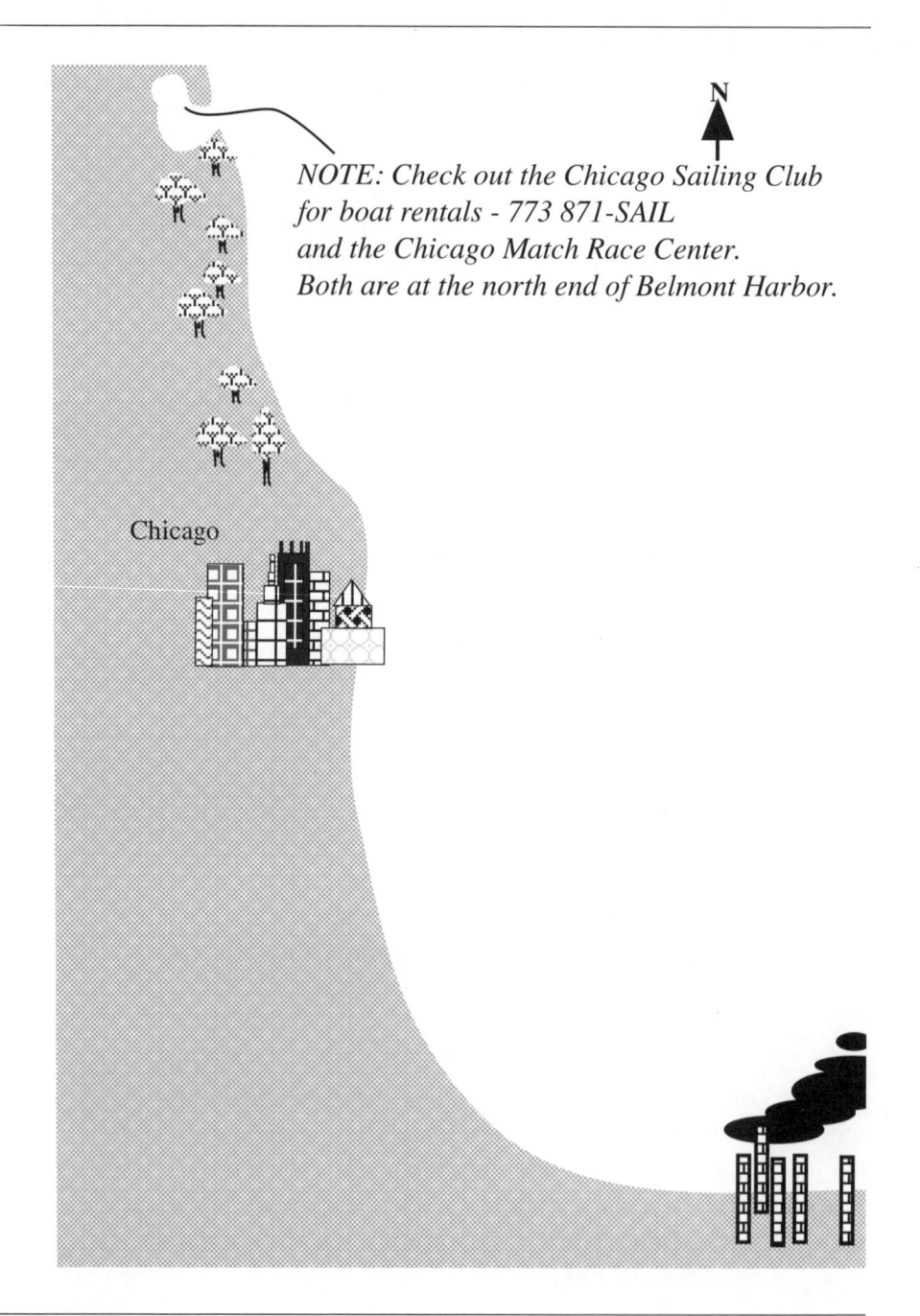

NOTE: Check out the Chicago Sailing Club for boat rentals - 773 871-SAIL and the Chicago Match Race Center. Both are at the north end of Belmont Harbor.

Homework

Make Your Own Local Knowledge Chart

Make a copy of your local sailing area and create a local knowledge chart of your own. List the prevailing wind conditions and strategies for each condition.
What clues help you pick your strategy?
Is a cloudy northerly different from a clear one?
You will be surprised at how often conditions repeat.

If you create your own race planner (or use ours from Chapter 2), print your local knowledge chart on the back. Keep a record of wind and current conditions, and strategies that worked (and didn't work). Also, after each race, write down what you learned about boat handling, and trim, as well as weather and strategy.

You can start by making a few notes here.

When you create your local knowledge chart and written analysis please send a copy to me. Really. I collect them.
Bill Gladstone
North U.
29 High Field Ln.
Madison CT 06443-2516

Quiz

Newport Rhode Island Strategy Quiz:

See the Chart at Right

We are part of a crew racing in Newport, just outside the harbor, adjacent to Goat Island. The course is Windward Leeward — 5 legs. We are getting ready to race. Our skipper wants to know what our strategy should be; which way should we go?

Looking upwind here is what we see:
The sea breeze is blowing steadily across the course, about 15 knots true, and very steady everywhere.

On the right hand side of the course there are waves rolling in with the sea breeze. To the left, under the headland, smooth water, but the same wind; strong and steady.

Which way should we go?

Upwind: Against the waves to the right,

or in the smooth water to the left? _____.

Downwind: With the waves,

or in the smooth water?_____.

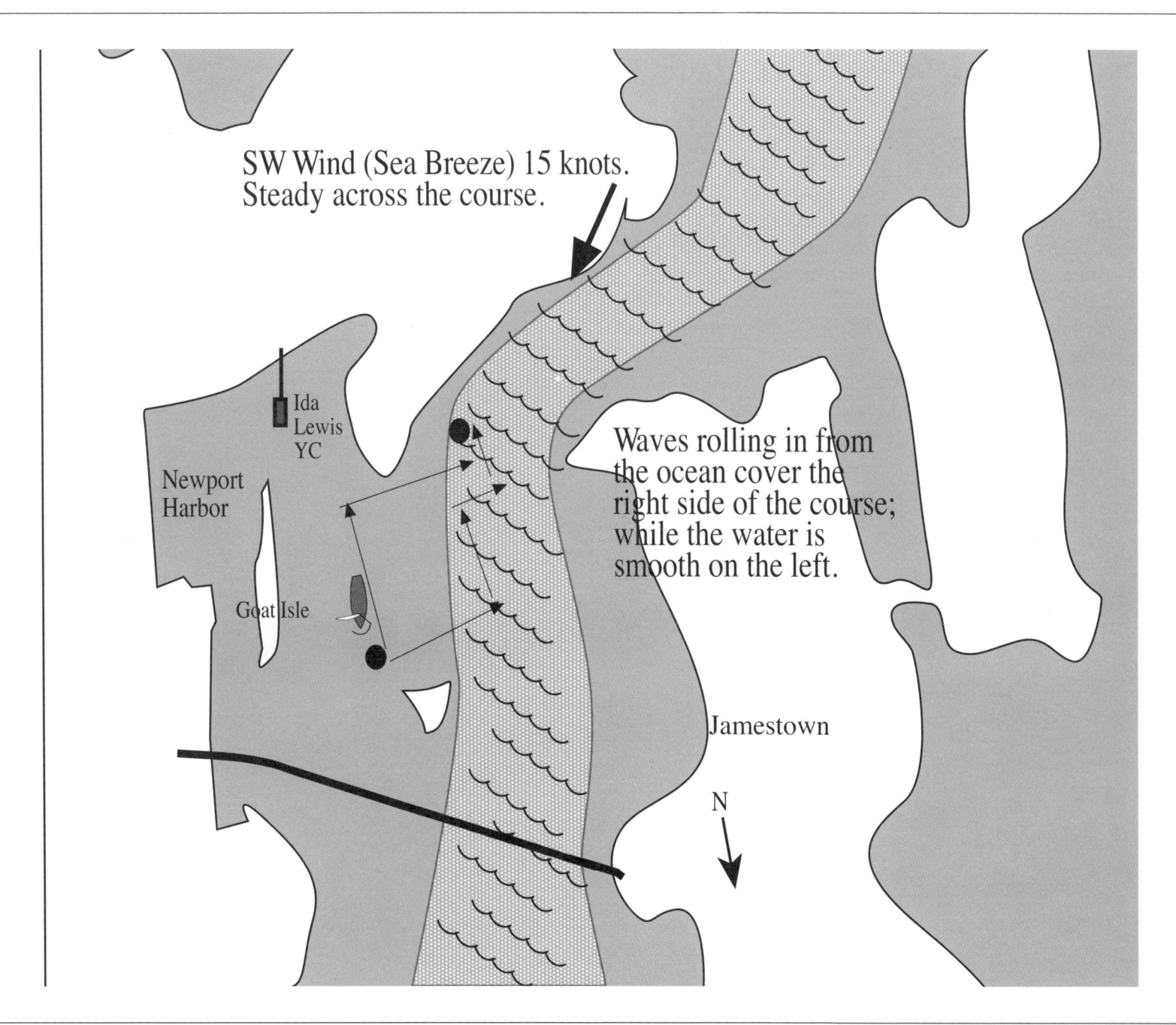

SW Wind (Sea Breeze) 15 knots.
Steady across the course.

Ida Lewis YC

Newport Harbor

Waves rolling in from the ocean cover the right side of the course; while the water is smooth on the left.

Goat Isle

Jamestown

N

Chapter 7: Upwind Strategy

Page 83

Newport Rhode Island Strategy Quiz Answer

Which way did you go?

The obvious answer is to go upwind in smooth water, and downwind with the waves. That's exactly what we did—this is a true story—and we were wrong. People sailing in the waves passed us while going upwind; and downwind we got passed by boats sailing the smooth water while we surfed the waves.

Finally I realized the key factor was current. The tide was going out, and it was creating the chop in the channel as it was opposed to the wind. The correct strategy was to ride the current upwind and avoid it downwind.

By the start of the next race I understood what was going on, and sailed into the channel to go upwind. Of course, by then the tide had turned…

Chapter 8: Upwind Tactics

8.1 Introduction
8.2 The Impact of Wind Shifts
8.3 Tactical principles
8.4 Tactics Up the Beat
8.5 Tactical Weapons
8.6 Rules Upwind
8.7 A Tactician's Nightmare
8.8 No More Tactics
8.9 Quiz and Skill Building Tips

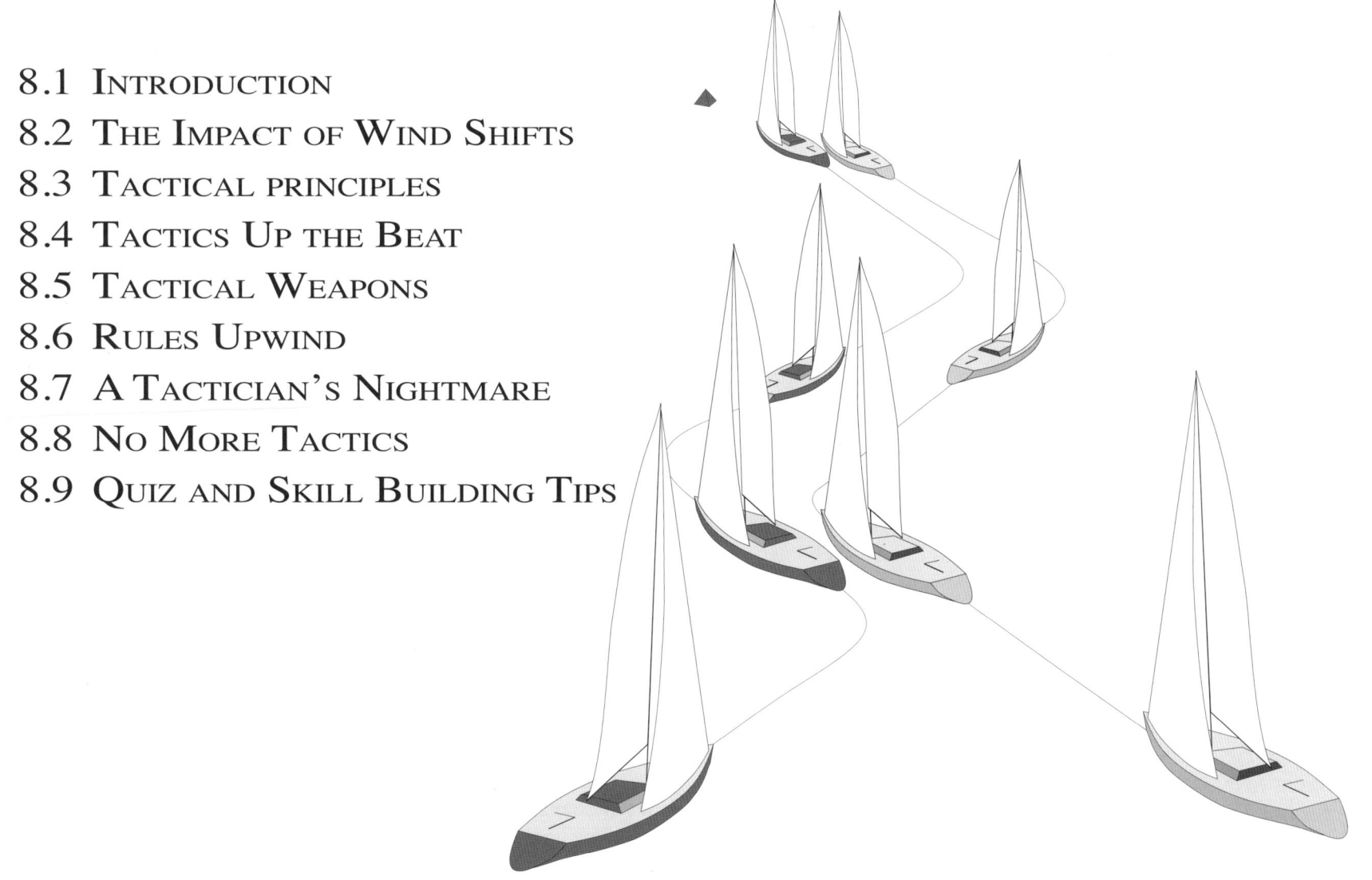

Chapter 8: Upwind Tactics

8.1 Introduction

Tactics to Win

We work for years to develop competitive boat handling and boat speed skills. Why? So we can enter the tactical game in a position to win. With the foundation of our performance pyramid taken care of, we can pick our head up out of the boat and enter the world of tactics

Upwind tactics involve positioning against individuals or groups of boats (Fig. 1) to take advantage of strategic conditions (i.e. wind, shifts, and current), or to control tactical situations (crossings and mark roundings). Over the course of a leg or race, tactics become increasingly important. Early in a leg or race, it is best to avoid confrontations and concentrate on a strategy that will put you near the top. At the end of a leg, you battle tactically to round ahead of those nearby. Toward the later stages of a race, your general position is relatively fixed, and your efforts focus on boats just ahead and just behind.

Tactics are relatively unimportant in mixed fleet races, where you are racing the clock. In one-design or level rated racing tactics predominate—as your closest rivals are the boats nearby.

This chapter covers Upwind Tactics in nine sections. Following this introduction, Section Two looks at the impact of wind shifts. Next, we consider tactical principles used for positioning and control, followed by an explanation of how tactics change over the course of a windward leg. Section Five looks at the tactical weapons, and Section Six covers rules and their tactical application. Section Seven describes one tacticians nightmare while Section Eight tells why and how to eliminate tactics from your racing! Finally, we offer a Quiz, and Tactics and Strategy Skillbuilding ideas.

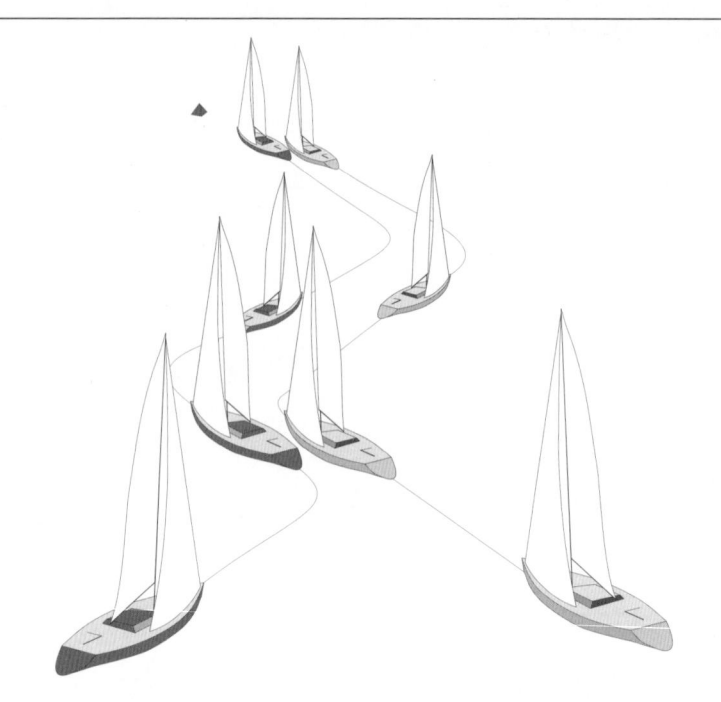

Fig. 1 - Upwind tactics involves positioning against other boats to take advantage of conditions and control situations.

8.2 The Impact of Wind Shifts

Our strategy forms the framework for our tactics. We use tactics to fulfill our strategic goals. One key element of strategy is wind shifts, which we discussed in the previous chapter. As we work to take advantage of shifts, we need to know their tactical impact: How should we position ourselves against our rivals in order to take advantage of the shifts, and what impact do the shifts have?

LEP: Climb the Ladder

Sailing upwind is like climbing a ladder. The rungs of the ladder hang perpendicular to the wind, and boats on the same rung are equally far upwind. Each rung is called a line of equal position—an LEP (Fig. 2a).

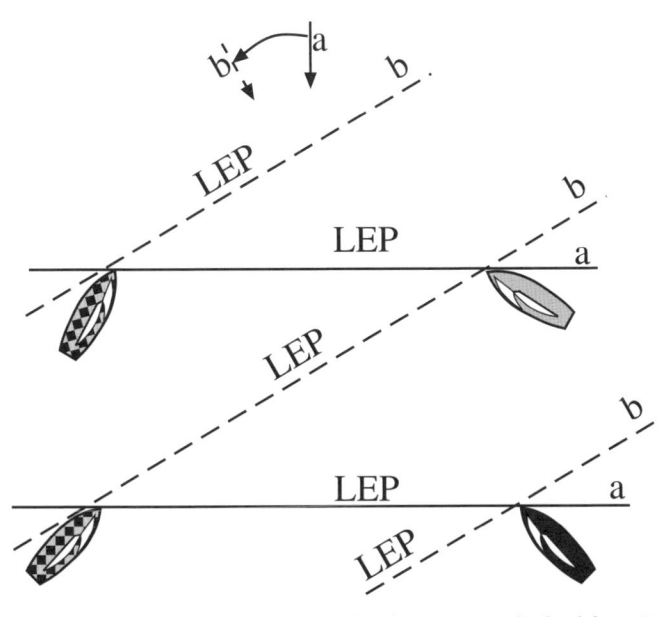

Fig. 2a - Sailing upwind is like climbing a wide ladder. Boats which are equally far upwind are on the same rung.

Fig. 2b - When the wind shifts, the ladder rotates. The boat closet to the shift ends up on the top rung, and is ahead.

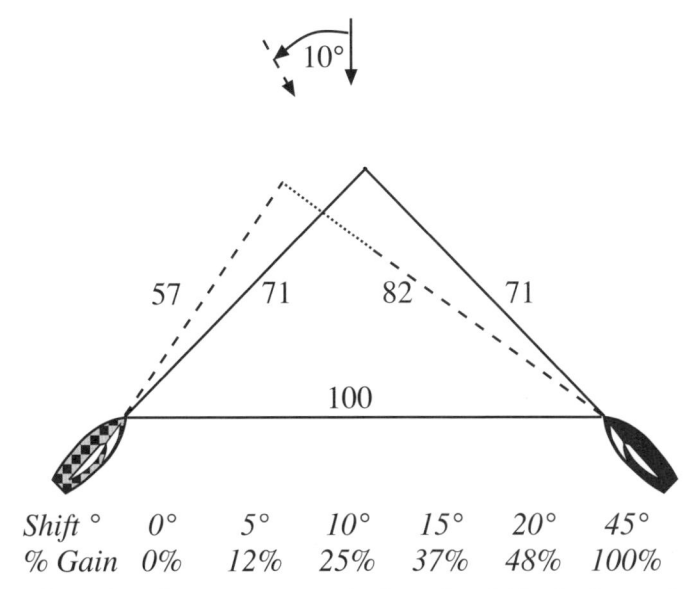

Shift °	0°	5°	10°	15°	20°	45°
% Gain	0%	12%	25%	37%	48%	100%

Fig. 3 - When boats are even before the shift, the boat closer to the shift gains. In a 10° shift the gain (loss) is 25% of the distance between the boats. Wow!

Strategy in Brief: Be Near the Shift

When the wind shifts, the ladder rotates. A boat closer to the new wind gains—he is on a higher rung, and boats further from the shift end up on a lower rung. The closer to the shift you are, the further you are up the ladder and the less distance you have to sail to get to the mark. Sail to the next shift. Where have I heard that before? (Fig. 2b).

How Much do you Gain (or Lose) in a Shift?

The distances are staggering. When the wind shifts 10° the boat closer to the shift gains 25% of the lateral distance separating the boats.* For boats on the same LEP, and separated by 100 yards the gain is 25 yards. For boats separated by a greater distance the gains/losses are greater** (Fig. 3).

For example, if two boats are separated by 848 feet the gain/loss would be 212 feet. 848 feet of separation may seem like a lot but consider……

---

* Trigonometric analysis of shifts first appeared in Dave Perry's <u>Winning in One Designs</u> - US Sailing

** Note: Assumes boats tack 90°, though the numbers change little for narrower tacking angles.

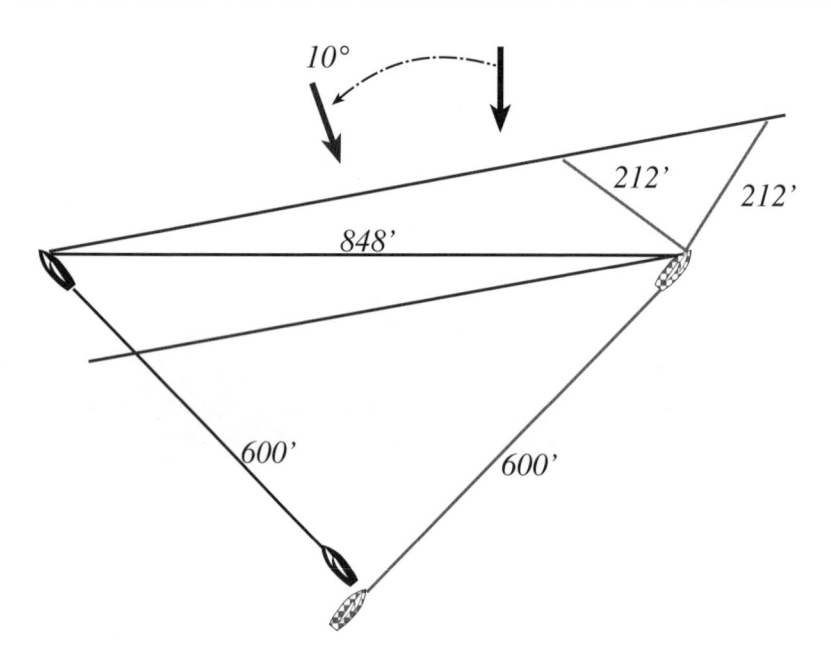

Fig. 4 - After one minute of sailing time at six knots, boats are separated by 848 feet. 212 feet will be gained or lost in a 10° shift. It takes 21 seconds to sail 212 feet at six knots.

......How Quickly it Happens

Imagine two boats sailing close hauled at a boat speed of 6 knots and tacking through 90°. They cross tacks, with the port boat ducking. Each boat sails for one minute—you know, sixty seconds. After one minute of sailing time, they will be 848 feet apart. A 10° shift will put one boat 212 feet ahead. At six knots, that distance represents 21 seconds of sailing time. Separating for 60 seconds creates a 20+ second gain/loss. Your risk/reward on a 10° shift is one-third the time you spend splitting tacks with another boat (Fig. 4).

So, we were caught to the right when the wind shifted 10° left. What should we do? And what about the boat that went left, what should they do?

Well, we've missed that shift. The question is: What will

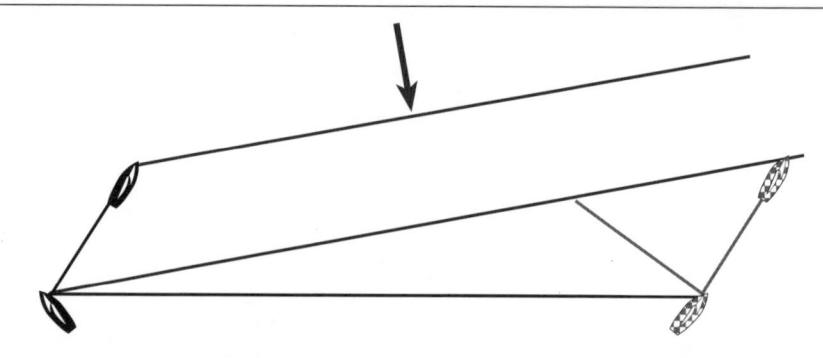

Fig. 5 - Being unsure of what will happen next, the boat on the right would most likely keep going, rather than tack on the lift, and hope the wind would shift right, and erase the loss. The boat on the left would likely tack to try to consolidate the gain.

happen next? Strategically, we want to sail to the next shift, so if the wind is going to go further left, we'd tack and go to it. If the next shift is going to return to the right, then we'd keep going. That's what strategy tells us. (Fig. 5)

Tactically, if we tack, we have given up these 212'. If we hang on, and keep our 848' of separation, then we can gain it all back just as quickly as we lost it... just as quickly as the wind returns where it was. We could even pull ahead if the wind goes further right. What will the wind do?

If we tack we will be 212' plus 2 boat lengths behind. If we are one tenth of a knot faster, we'll gain 10 feet per minute. We could catch up in about 25 minutes, or gain back half the loss in 12, and be close enough to get the rest on a small shift.

Assuming our rival tacks on the shift, continuing parallel puts us no further behind – as long as the breeze doesn't shift further left. Let's hang here, and look for a little righty to tack on, or maybe a big righty. That would help.

Looking back, maybe we shouldn't have separated so far. But tacking would have cost us too, about two boat lengths, and no way to recover those – they are spent.

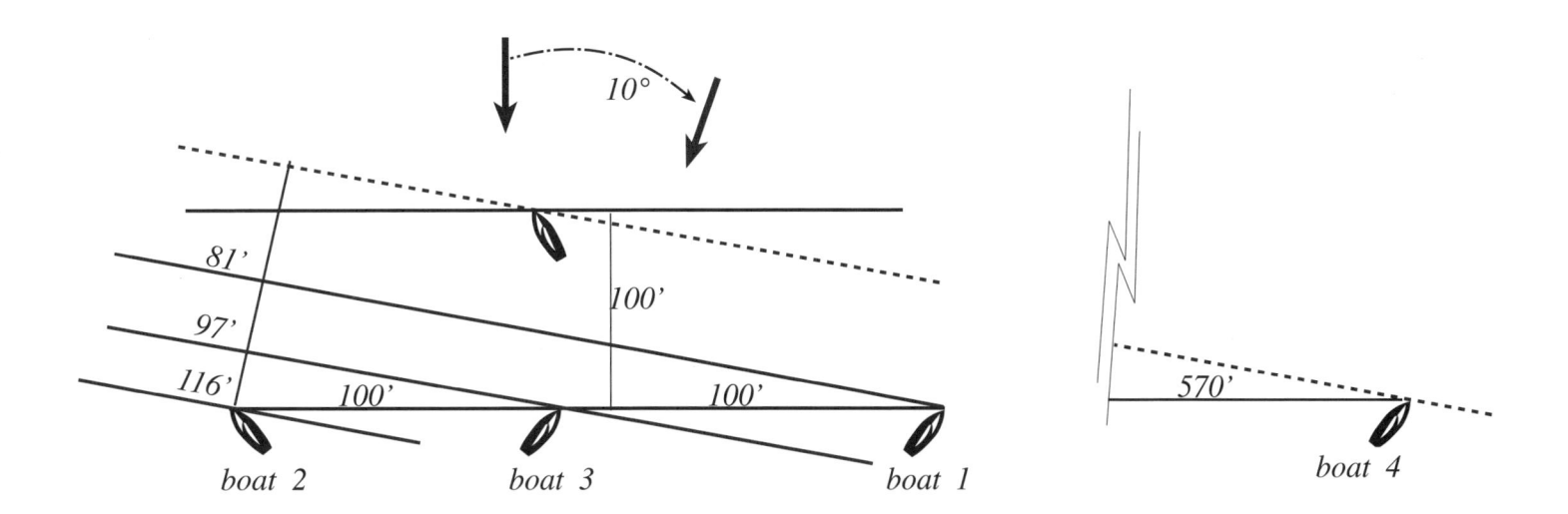

Fig. 6a - When one boat is ahead and the wind shifts right boats to the right of the leader gain; boats to the left lose. If your leverage equals your distance behind, then you gain 19% or lose 16% in a 10° shift.

Fig. 6b - If your leverage is 5.7 times your distance behind, you would draw even on a 10° shift in your direction. It deserves mentioning that a 10° shift the other way would put you twice as far behind. A bigger shift would have a bigger impact.

When One Boat is Ahead

When one boat is ahead of another, results are similar. Consider gains and losses as a percent of distance behind, from LEP to LEP. We will consider three cases: the boat behind will have leverage equal to the distance behind either toward the shift (boat 1), or away from the shift (boat 2); or will be straight downwind, with no leverage (boat 3). When the wind shifts 10°, the boat closer to the shift gains 19%, the boat away from the shift loses 16%, and surprisingly, the boat straight downwind gains slightly—about 2% (Fig 6a).

When the boats are further separated, the gains and losses increase. We use the term leverage to describe this lateral separation. The further apart boats are, the more leverage they have, and the more they stand to gain or lose in a shift. A boat which is behind will pull even with the leader in a 10° shift if his leverage is 5.7 times the distance behind (boat 4) (and if the shift is to his side). That may seem like a lot of separation, but as we saw earlier, leverage builds fast when you split tacks. In a bigger shift less leverage is needed to catch up, or to fall twice as far behind! (Fig. 6b).

WOW!

Through all numbers and examples, one point stands out: wind shifts are a big deal. As I said before, the potential gains/losses are staggering.

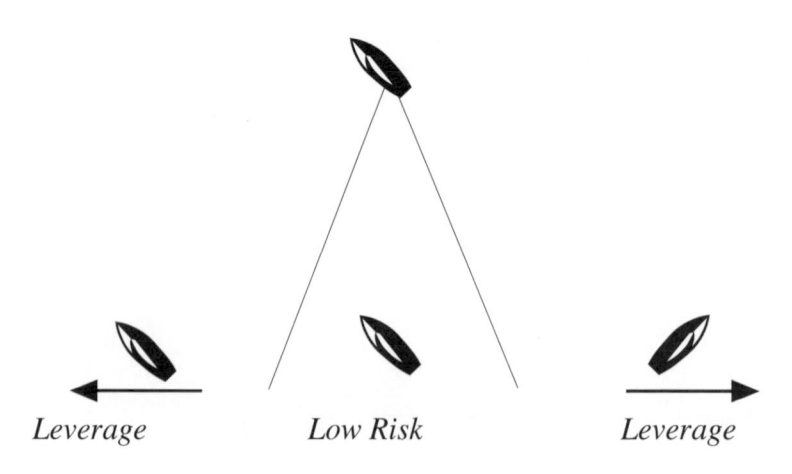

Fig. 7 – The greater your leverage, the more you stand to gain (or lose) on a wind shift. If you can predict the next shift, sail to it. When in doubt, minimize leverage.

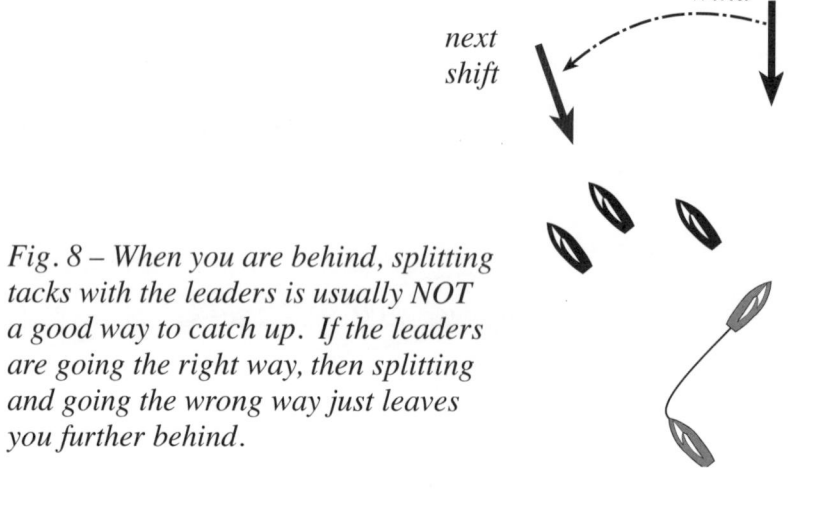

Fig. 8 – When you are behind, splitting tacks with the leaders is usually NOT a good way to catch up. If the leaders are going the right way, then splitting and going the wrong way just leaves you further behind.

The Message

Wind shifts are a big deal. We got that message.
Two corollaries follow:
First, if you can predict the next shift, sail to it.
Second, if you don't know what to expect, then minimize leverage to minimize the impact of shifts. (Have you ever been unable to anticipate the next shift? Me neither, and the check is in the mail.) (Fig. 7).

We'll look at these two corollaries from two perspectives: catching up when you are behind, and protecting a lead when you are ahead.

Catching Up

When you're unsure of the next shift, minimize leverage by staying in the low risk zone. Try to nibble away at the leaders with speed while eliminating the risk due to shifts. By minimizing leverage, you deny the leaders the chance to stretch the lead, and you stay within striking distance. Then, when you can predict an upcoming shift, go to it. Remember how quickly leverage grows; you don't need to split for long if you've stayed within striking distance.

Splitting with the leaders just for the sake of splitting is a bad risk. Since the leaders are usually going the right way (Hint: they are in the lead), you are more likely to fall further behind than to catch up. Stay close and wait for an opportunity. Split only when the odds are in your favor. (Fig. 8).

Staying Ahead

You hear this said about champions: He gets ahead, and he is gone. How do they do it?

About other racers you may hear: Don't worry about him, eventually he'll go to pieces. Why?

Tactical dogma when in the lead is stay between the competition and the next mark. Cover 'em and you can't lose.

When you're in the lead, it is not enough to simply stay between the competition and the mark. If you are looking back, and just reacting, then those behind can get leverage and eat away at your lead.

Fig. 9 – To stay in front, you can't just cover. You have to keep doing the things that got you there. Lead to the shifts; don't simply tack in response to the trailing boat's tack.

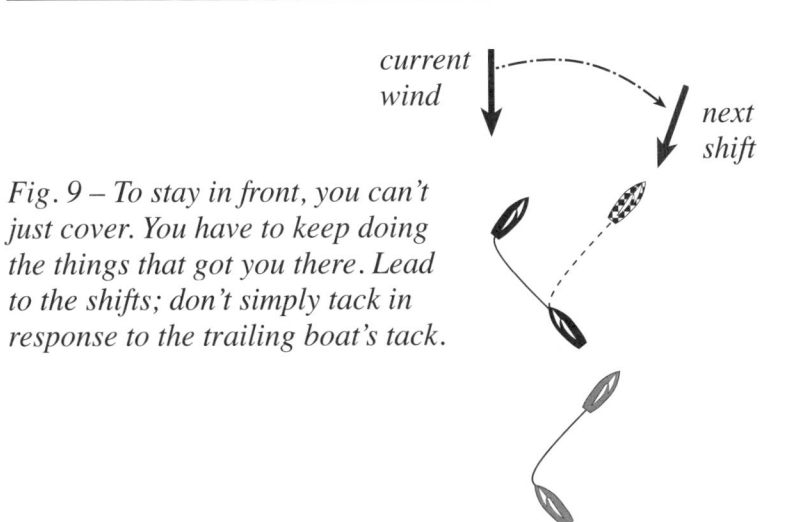

Keep the Initiative

Real leaders continue to lead. To keep the lead, you must keep the initiative. Sail fast, hit the shifts, and do the things you did to get the lead. Pay attention to those behind you, yes; but think in terms of stretching the lead and adding a cushion rather than simply going into a defensive shell and sitting on the lead you've got. You certainly don't want to split with the fleet, but you have to do more than look back and cover. The true champions pay attention to the fleet behind them; but they keep working, keep hitting the shifts, keep looking ahead. (I've yet to test this myself, but I'm ready to give it a try). (Fig. 9).

All too often, sailors change their tactics once in the lead, and lose the initiative. Maybe you've experienced this. You kick and scratch and fight your way to the lead. Once you get there, you start to shake, you feel queasy, and your look back instead of ahead. Take a deep breath, and keep plugging.

When you're sailing with a comfortable lead, proper positioning can help protect it. If the next shift or the mark is to the left, then position yourself to protect your left. Use a loose cover (details below) and don't let trailing boats get enough leverage to threaten your lead.

Wind Shift Prospectus

Playing shifts carries inherent risks. While much can be gained, one should not lose sight of the risks involved. Be aware that past shift performance is not a guarantee of future shifts. Read the prospectus in full before leveraging.

The gains made on shifts can be fleeting. While you may gain on the shift, the gain is not realized until you tack on the shift and cross between the wind and your rivals. Until the gain is realized, it can vanish as quickly as it appeared. Tacking to consolidate your gains is a transaction cost – think of a good tack as a form of discount brokerage.

When behind, splitting tacks with the leaders is not always sound strategy. While you may gain on a wind shift, you are at least as likely to lose, as the leaders are (more often than not) going the right way. They are, after all, in the lead.

The prudent tactician will not split tacks on a whim in hope of getting lucky; but will sail fast, and go the same way as the leaders when the leaders are going the right way in order to stay within striking distance. Then, when an opportunity arises to catch a shift the leaders miss, the prudent tactician will still be close enough to catch up. Remember, you can get plenty of leverage in a hurry (if you are not too far behind), so stay close, sail fast, be patient, and look for your opportunity.

When you do get a chance to split or lead to a shift, don't get greedy. Rather than try to catch up all at once, sometimes it is better to just get closer. Gain back half the distance, rather than push too far and suffer a reversal as the shift dissolves.

Boatspeed, while offering less immediate rewards, can provide a more consistent and reliable return with less risk. Boatspeed remains entirely within your control, unlike wind shifts, which are subject to the vagaries of the weather.

A mixed portfolio of competitive tools has historically provided the most consistent results.

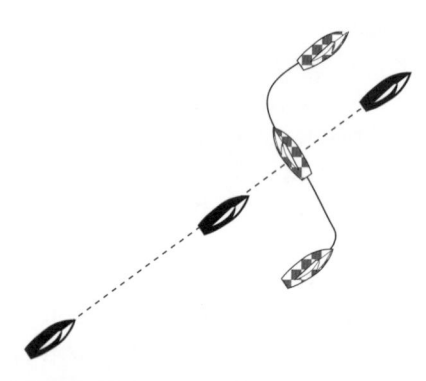

Fig. 10 – Cross when you can. If you don't, the wind may shift and you may lose the opportunity.

8.3 Tactical Principles

There are a number of general tactical principles to keep in mind as you sail upwind. The overall objective—your upwind strategy—should remain the priority. Use tactics to help you achieve that goal.

Keep Clear Air & Freedom

Keep control of your own destiny. Avoid situations where other boats can control you. You need to look ahead and position yourself clear of crowds.

Cross When You Can

This is also called consolidating your lead. If you wait, conditions may change, and you may lose your opportunity (Fig. 10).

Don't Let Others Cross You

When the wind shifts, don't let those who gain consolidate. Go to the next shift and recoup. By staying off to the side, ahead and to leeward, a favorable shift will help you (Fig. 11). The catch is that you have to be going the right way. If the shifts are large and difficult to anticipate, you run the risk of

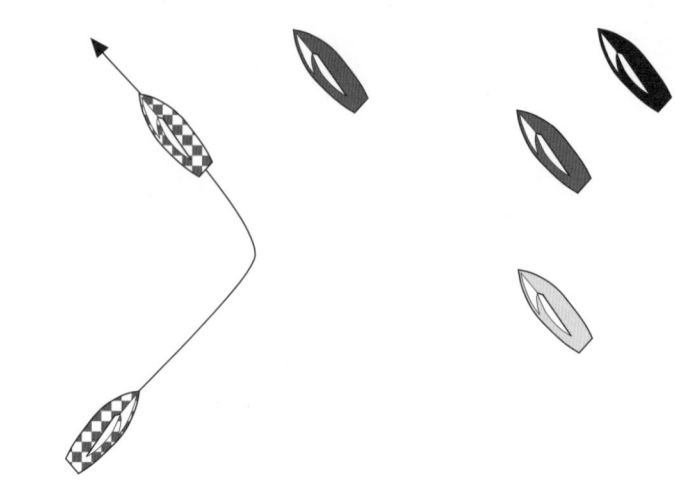

Fig. 11 – Don't let others cross you. Once you let others cross, you have conceded your position. Stay to the (favored) side, and catch up on the next shift.

being buried if the shift works against you. When things get weird, it may be best to position yourself with the leaders until you can sort things out; then use the Catching Up ideas from the previous section.

Stay Toward the Middle

A championship tactic, which sometimes doesn't work for the rest of us who spend most of our time in the middle of the fleet. When you are in the lead, or near it, adhere to this rule, as it minimizes leverage for those behind and gives you the ability to go either way to protect your position, to clear your air when attacked, and to pursue shifts. (Fig. 12).

Back where most of the fleet does most of their sailing, the traffic and disturbed air of the middle can be devastating. Yes, sail the middle when you can; but balance this with concerns for clear air and the search for favorable shifts.

When one side of the course is heavily favored, then the middle moves with the fleet. The middle is the middle of the

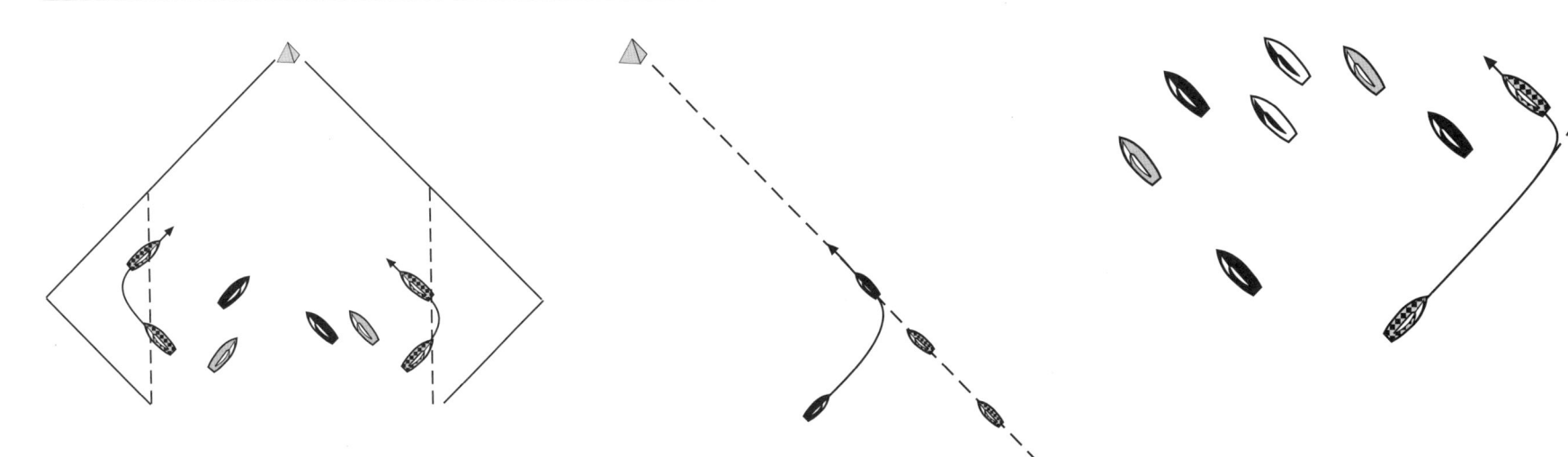

Fig. 12 – Sailing up the middle allows you to play the shifts and cover the fleet; but the middle can be pretty messy if you aren't near the front. Then you might have to pick a side.

Fig. 13 – Once you reach the layline, you run out of options. You are vulnerable to attack, and the shifts no longer help you.

Fig. 14 – Don't split with the fleet. If the fleet is going the right way, then splitting only leaves you further behind.

fleet, really. When the entire fleet goes left, the middle goes left with the fleet.

Avoid the Laylines

Once you hit the layline, you are out of options. You are subject to attack, and you are hurt by any shift (Fig. 13).

Avoiding the laylines is a good principle, with few exceptions. The most notable exception is in the middle of a huge fleet. First, you will be forced out of the middle by traffic. Then, as you approach the mark, the turbulence and disturbed air between the laylines must be avoided; often by sailing a few boat lengths beyond the layline to get clear air. Until you have approached the windward mark 52nd in a fleet of 63, you don't know how bad bad air can be.

Stay With the Fleet

When you are ahead, stay with those behind you. No surprise here. Sail the same breeze as those around you; just sail it better. When you are on the favored side, there is no need to split. Just stay on the favored side of the fleet.

The real application for this principle is sailing to a favored side when you are behind. It is true that you can't win by following, but tacking away will only make matters worse. Until the leaders make a mistake, you won't catch 'em. Hang on even if it hurts, and stay close. Tacking away from the favored side or a persistent shift is not the answer. You'll get a chance to fight back if you stay close, and you'll get hammered if you go the wrong way. Rather than tack and follow, lead the fleet to the next shift – if you can find it. (Fig. 14).

Chapter 8: Upwind Tactics

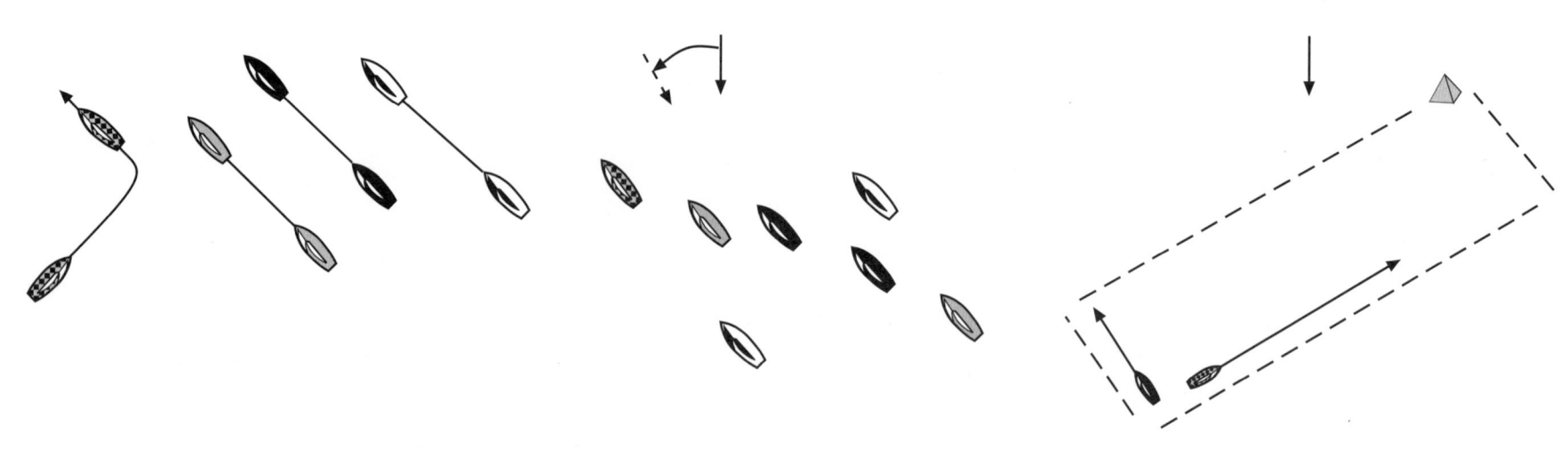

Fig. 15 – Lead the crowd by tacking ahead and to leeward.

Fig. 16 – When in front, cover by staying between the fleet and the next shift.

Fig. 17 – On a one-legged beat sail the long leg first.

Lead the Crowd

As you approach a crowd of boats, tack ahead and to leeward, rather than sail through the crowd to their hip. There are a number of reasons why this works. First, it is best to stay with the fleet, as mentioned above. Second, if the crowd is sailing toward the next shift, then you will be the first to get it. Third, once you sail into a crowd you may have trouble finding clear air or a tacking lane. Fourth, if you decide you want to get across to the outside, you can tack again and exercise that option later. Once you cross the crowd, you can't reconsider and return to the ahead and to leeward position.

This principle is particularly powerful if you can lead the crowd toward the middle of the course. On the other hand, you may want to abandon this principle if crossing the crowd will get you to the inside of the group, closer to the middle. From a position on the inside hip, you are ready to lead the fleet to the middle as they tack that way (Fig. 15).

Cover When Ahead

Stay between the fleet and the next shift. If you are ahead and can anticipate the next shift, sail to it. If you are ahead, you have to hit the shifts to stay ahead. Your lead won't last long if you follow the fleet into the shifts (Fig. 16).

Stay between the fleet and the next mark. If you can't find the next shift, find the mark and protect your position that way. Lead the fleet toward the mark or shift.

Sometimes you can't cover. There are times when it simply does not pay to cover. When conditions become dramatically shifty, the impulse is to cover tightly. But in these conditions it can prove impossible to cover an opponent. Concentrate on sailing your own race. Try to keep your cool when things get weird.

One-Legged Beats

When the course is skewed by a major wind shift so you can nearly fetch the windward mark, you are sailing a one-legged beat. Tactically, the best position is ahead and to lee-

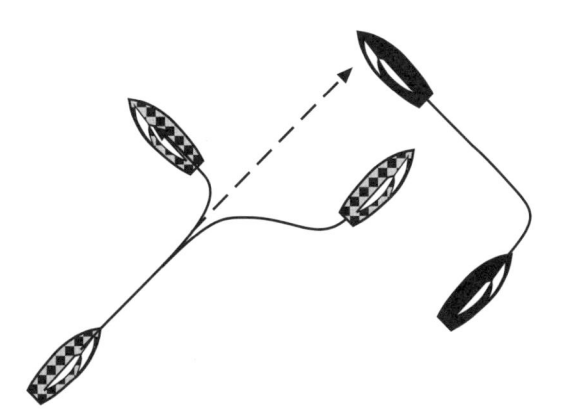

Fig. 18 – When on the hip of a port tacker, anticipate his tack. Will you tack, cross, lee-bow or duck?

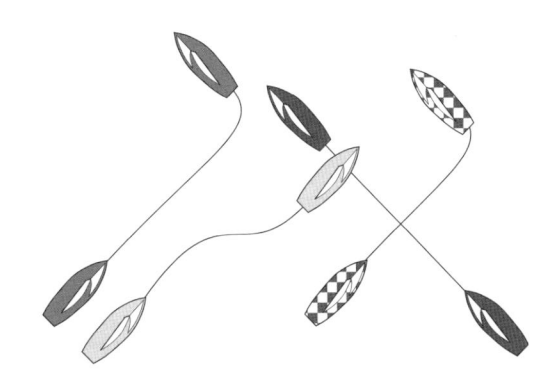

Fig. 19 – When tacking toward a crowd, get a blocker. Cross him and tack. Others will have to deal with him first, leaving you free.

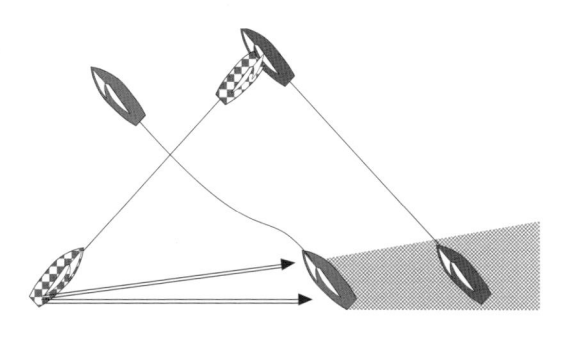

Fig. 20 – When a starboard boat waves you by, watch out for a second starboard boat previously hidden from view!

ward. If the leg is a port fetch, try to avoid a clearing tack to starboard when you round the leeward mark. On a starboard fetch, try to tack immediately at the mark.

From the ahead and to leeward position, you have greater control and better opportunities in wind shifts. If you are lifted you may fetch; and if you are headed, you will be able to tack and cross those on your hip.

If you sail the short leg first, then you will quickly find yourself in the corner with few options (Fig. 17).

More Tactical Ideas

Anticipate

When you're on port tack, sailing on the hip of another port-tack boat, plan how you will react if he tacks. Will you tack or duck? Your response depends on a number of tactical and strategic factors. Don't wait for the other boat to tack to decide your response (Fig. 18).

Get Blockers To Protect You

You're on port, and you're getting ready to tack. You look over your shoulder and see a crowd on your hip. You need a blocker (a boat ahead and to leeward) to shield you from the crowd (Fig. 19). A blocker will take all the heat (lee bows etc.) as you sail into the crowd. A boat you can just cross makes an excellent blocker. After you cross, sail two lengths and tack. Now your blocker will lead you through. Anyone who can cross the blocker can cross you. Boats which might normally create a problem for you run into the blocker first. You sail on without interference.

Hidden boat trick!

Watch for this: Two starboard-tack boats are approaching a port-tack boat. The leeward starboard boat waves the port tacker by, "Go ahead." Imagine the port tack boat's surprise when he sees another starboard tacker previously hidden from view! (Fig. 20).

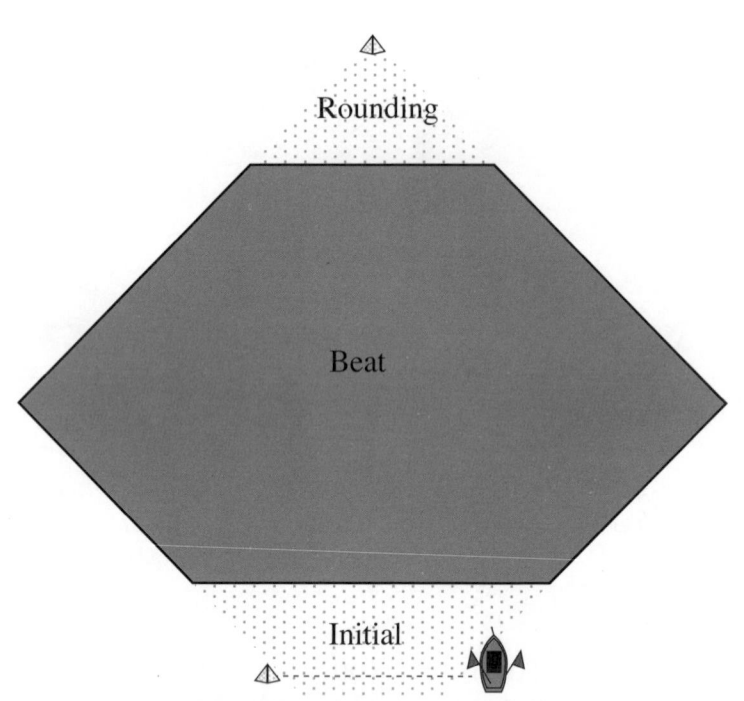

Fig. 21 – The windward leg can be divided into three tactical segments: the initial segment, the beat, and the rounding.

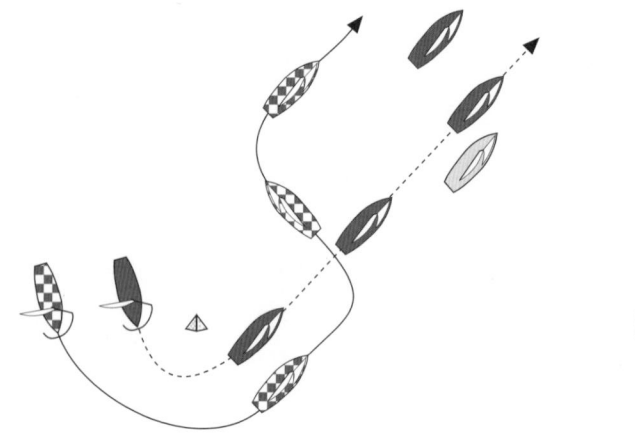

Fig. 22 – A short tack to the left may be needed to find a lane going right. You may be able to foot around a crowd.

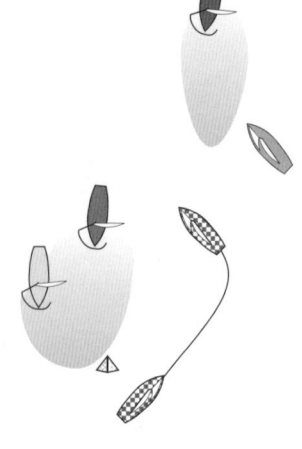

Fig. 23 – To go left, tack into an open lane, clear of traffic.

8.4 Up the Beat in 3 Stages

Tactics upwind is a matter of positioning for wind shifts and positioning for control. We can divide the beat into three segments. The initial segment is the period after the start or leeward mark rounding when we are sailing in a crowd and fighting for clear air. The middle segment starts when we break out of the crowd and are free to pursue strategy. The final segment is the battle for position approaching the windward mark. Boat-to-boat battles predominate at the beginning and end of the leg, while wind shifts are the focus in the middle segment (Fig. 21).

The Initial Segment: Positioning for Freedom

The priorities during the first part of any beat are to keep clear air and to have the freedom to pursue your strategy. The first few minutes after a start, as discussed earlier, are critical; any advantage gained there will be magnified.

At the beginning of subsequent beats, the goal is to catch the first shift and get to work on strategy. If the goal is to work to the right, it may be necessary to tack shortly after rounding and then tack back when a clear lane to the right is available. If you are outside at the rounding, you may be able to reach through for clear air and save two tacks (Fig. 22).

If the strategy is to go left, then you must work to be free to tack after the rounding. Beware the wind shadow and turbulence of boats which have yet to round and are still on the previous leg. While you will have right of way close hauled

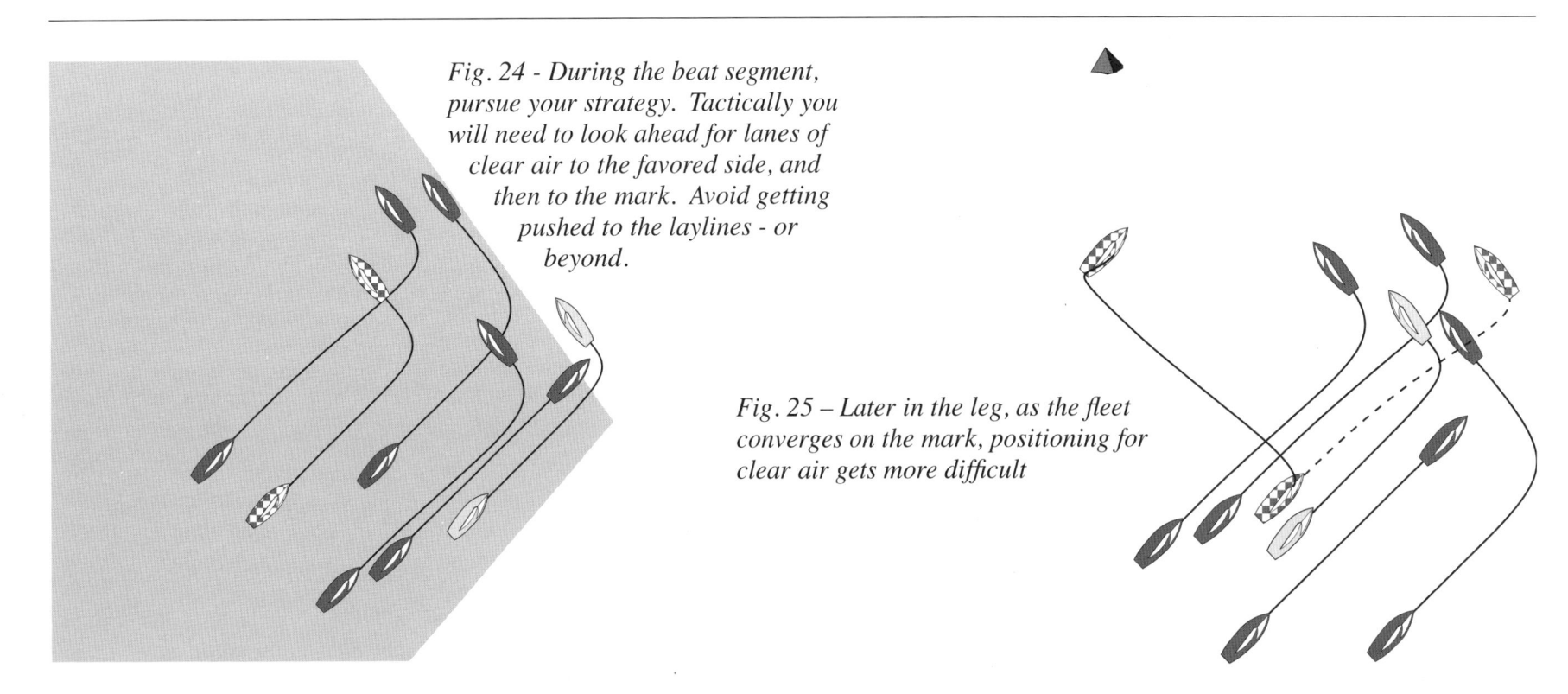

Fig. 24 - During the beat segment, pursue your strategy. Tactically you will need to look ahead for lanes of clear air to the favored side, and then to the mark. Avoid getting pushed to the laylines - or beyond.

Fig. 25 – Later in the leg, as the fleet converges on the mark, positioning for clear air gets more difficult

on starboard, there may still be reason to delay a tack until you can clear that hazard (Fig. 23).

The Beat: Strategy Reigns

The middle segment starts once you are clear of the crowds at the start or leeward mark and continues until you start working for position at the windward mark. Tactics on this segment focus on the freedom to pursue your strategy.

The tactical principles discussed above come into play during this segment. The overall objective—your upwind strategy—should remain the priority. Use tactics to help you achieve that goal.

Course Management is the term used to summarize your efforts up the beat. The challenge is to look ahead, and anticipate developments. When your strategy suggests one side is favored, good course management means finding a lane of clear air so you can get to the favored side with good speed.

Course management comes in to play as you get to the favored side, and must once again find a clear lane from the favored side to the mark. Looking ahead, work the favored side as hard as you can, but tack before you are forced all the way to the outside of the crowd. Better to tack early – you can tack out again later if you want – than to get pushed to the outside (Fig. 24).

As the fleet converges on the mark clear air is harder to come by. Coming in on port provides clear air – at the risk on being frozen out on the layline (Fig. 25).

The rounding segment is next.

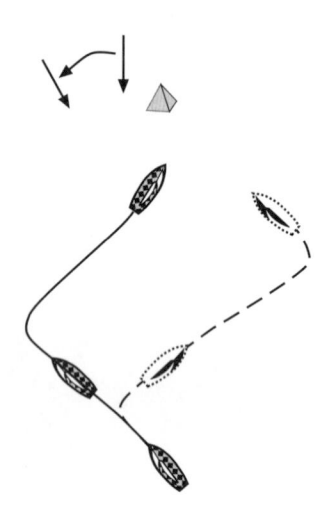

Fig. 26 – Sail into the last oscillation going into the mark as though it were a persistent shift.

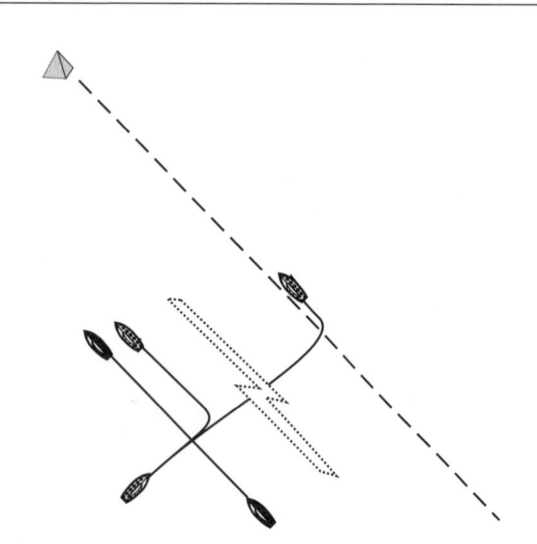

Fig. 27 – If a port tacker can cross, he can then tack and pin a starboard boat or sail on to the layline.

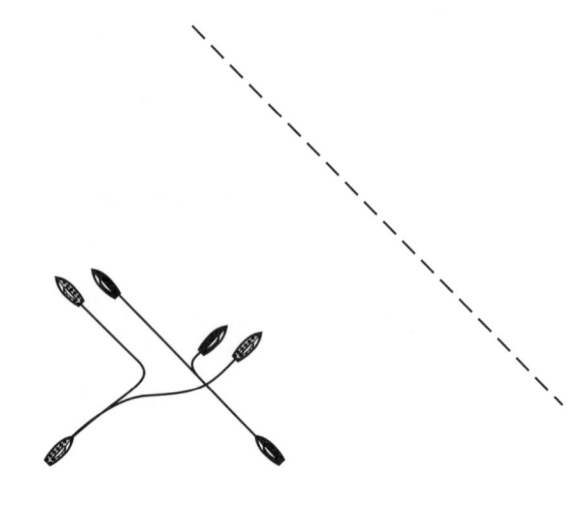

Fig. 28 – If the port tacker can't cross, he can tack (into a pin) or duck—and get pinned to the right.

The Rounding: Positioning for Control

Approaching the weather mark, work for control of those nearby. Keep clear air, and try to keep from being pinned by others. With marks to port, the left side is inside at the rounding, but a boat on the right controls the last starboard crossing. Starboard roundings put a premium on controlling the right, as the right owns both the inside position and the last starboard crossing.

The Last Oscillation Is A Persistent Shift

In an oscillating breeze, treat the last shift before the mark as a persistent shift. That is, sail the header to the layline, then tack for the lift. Any leg which has just one shift should be sailed as you would in a persistent shift. Think of the last part of the leg as a very short leg with just one shift (Fig. 26).

Inside the Laylines

Inside the laylines, a weather quarter position gives control, as a boat on the lee bow is pinned and not free to tack. This position must be carried all the way to the layline or it will be reversed if both boats tack.

A port-starboard crossing near the layline is a common situation which offers many options and counter options.

If the port-tack boat can cross, he has several choices. He can cross and continue on port tack toward the starboard layline; he can tack to lee bow or cover the starboard tacker, giving the starboard tacker incentive to tack away; or he can tack to pin the starboard tacker and carry out to the port layline (Fig. 27).

If the port tacker cannot cross, then he can tack or duck. If he chooses to tack, he may be pinned out until the starboard boat tacks. A well-executed duck creates an opportunity for a reversal at the next crossing. To prevent a reversal, the starboard tack boat can tack and pin the port boat. If the starboard

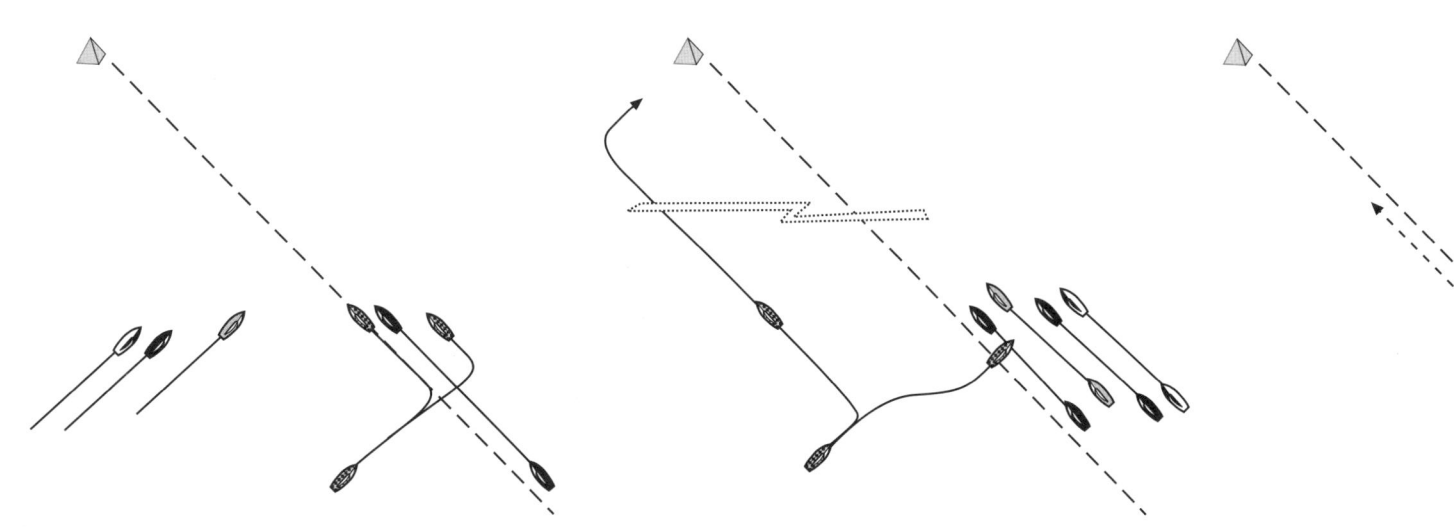

Fig. 29 – A port tacker can lee bow a starboard boat on the layline, or cross and use the starboard boat as a blocker.

Fig. 30 – Tack short of the layline if the layline is crowded. Clear air and a small shift could put you ahead.

Fig. 31 - If you find yourself in bad air just below the layline, bail out. You cannot pinch in bad air.

tacker is not prepared or fails to execute properly, then he will not be able to prevent a reversal (Fig. 28)

If the port-tack boat sails to the starboard tack layline, then the starboard tacker (now coming in on port) may be able to lee bow and lead to the mark. If the port tacker tacks short of the layline, then we have a reversal of our earlier situation. Go back one paragraph. Do not round the mark. Do not collect $200.

On the Laylines

On the layline, a lee bow position is preferred; just don't fail to fetch the mark.

If the starboard tacker is on the layline, a port tacker can tack ahead, or on the lee bow, to round ahead of the starboard tacker. If there is doubt about whether or not the starboard tacker will fetch, it is best to cross and tack to weather, using the starboard tacker as a blocker against those coming into the layline later (Fig. 29).

If there is a crowd on the layline, tack away and come back later, rather than sail extra distance or in bad air at the layline. Once you go to the layline and duck the crowd, you concede (for that leg). By tacking out, you give yourself one more chance—at the risk of losing others if the layline fills (Fig. 30).

Bail Out Early

You're on the layline. Almost. Just a little shy of the layline maybe, but you can pinch up and make it. Maybe. Stop kidding yourself and bail out now.

If you bail out early, there may still be room on the layline to get back in line. If you wait until later to flop to port, it may be too late. You will end up ducking the entire fleet before you find a space on the layline.

If you are approaching the mark in clear air and no turbulence, you might be able to pinch up and make it; but if there are other boats on your air then bail out early (Fig. 31).

Chapter 8: Upwind Tactics

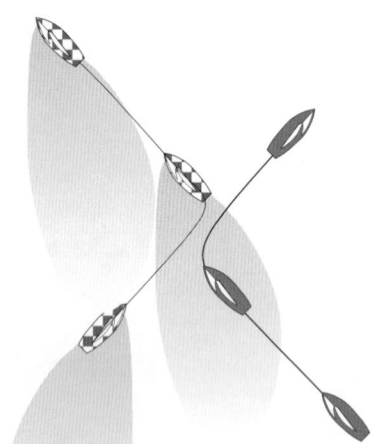

Fig. 32 – A tight cover puts your rival in your wind shadow and forces a response.

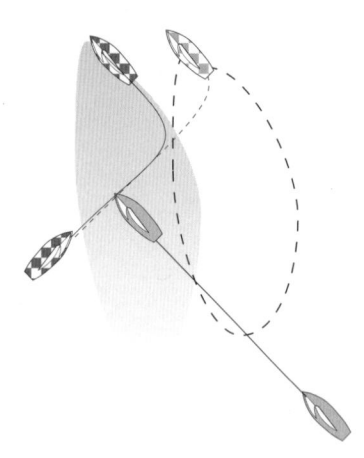

Fig. 33 – Tack so you end up upwind; don't tack when you are upwind.

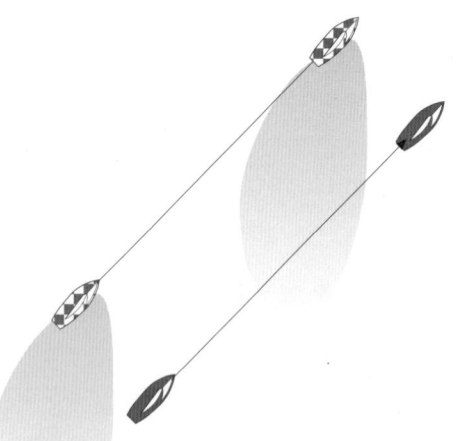

Fig. 34 – A loose cover does not impede the progress of your opponent. It keeps you sailing in the same conditions as your rival.

8.5 Tactical Weapons

Our upwind strategy gives us the big picture, and our tactical principles guide us as we confront groups of boats. Tactical weapons are the tools we use to put the principles into practice and achieve our strategic goals. Broadly speaking, there are two general categories: Those that allow us to control and influence others, and those which allow us to prevent others from doing the same to us.

As we look at tactical weapons, we will discuss what each does and how it is used.

Controlling other Boats
Tight Cover

A tight cover is a an aggressive move which slows an adversary by putting the him in your wind shadow. A tight cover necessitates a response. Use a tight cover when you want to force another boat away (Fig. 32).

To put it another way: You should tack and cover only if it would be time to tack anyhow, even if the other boat weren't there. You use a tight cover when you want to go the way they were going, and want to force them to go the way you were going, which suggests that maybe you were going the wrong way to begin with...

Tack so you are directly upwind after accelerating or the rival may escape your shadow (Fig. 33).

Loose Cover

A loose cover is a course parallel to the opponent(s) which does not put the other boat(s) in our wind shadow. A loose cover is more defensive than a tight cover. A loose cover does not impede the progress of the other boat(s). It puts you in a position where you can protect your lead (Fig. 34).

Your intent with a loose cover is to deny your opponent the opportunity to sail different conditions than you are sailing. A tight cover, on the other hand, often forces your opponent to tack away. The danger with a tight cover is that your opponent then separates from you, and may find more favorable conditions.

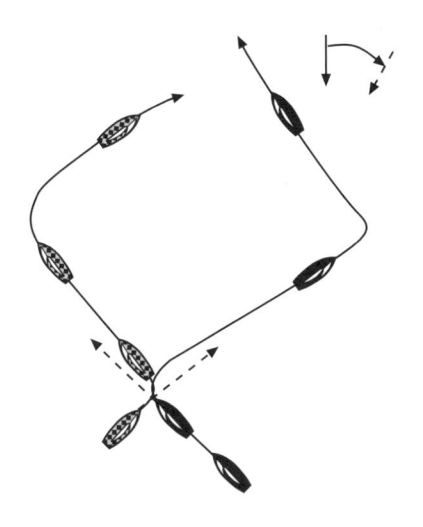

< Fig. 35 – Do Not tack and cover someone when you are going the right way and they are going the wrong way.

> Fig. 36 – You can herd a boat with a tight cover on one tack and a loose cover on the other tack.

>> Fig. 37 – A pin prevents the outside boat from tacking until the inside boat tacks.

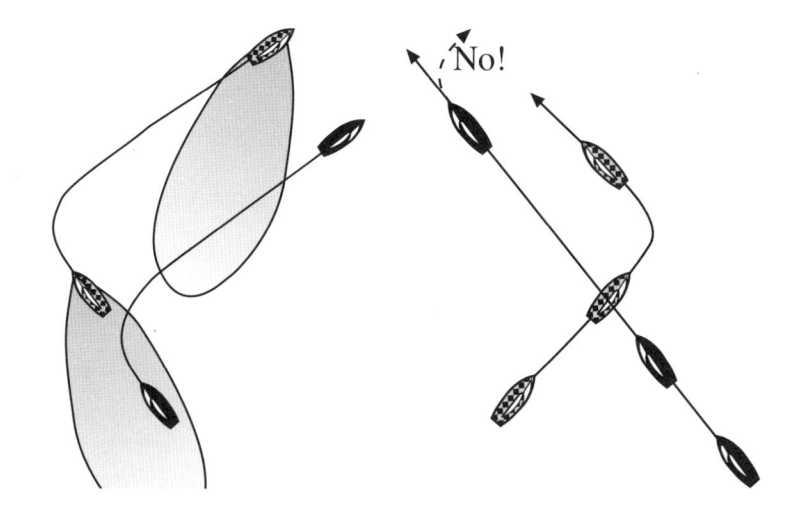

When you are unsure of what to expect next with the wind, a loose cover lets you sail near your opponent.

Go Ahead and Cover

If you are ready to tack but delay for a moment, you can dump bad air on an opponent close behind. This frustrates the opponent, as he must now tack away or sail in bad air. Given the chance, you can be sure he will return the favor.

The assumption is that you would be tacking anyhow, for strategic reasons, and take the opportunity to force the rival to sail the wrong way.

The Sucker Cover

You are crossing a close rival and tack on his air. You hadn't planned to tack, but couldn't pass up the opportunity to face on your rival. Trouble is, you were going the right way, towards a shift perhaps. Now you have traded places. You are going the wrong way, and you have forced your rival to go where you wanted to go. Sucker.

Don't lose sight of your strategy as you play tactical games (Fig. 35).

Herding

Herding is any technique which encourages other boats to go the same way you are going. Hmm. Why would you want to do that? And how would you do it?

You herd other boats along when you are fearful of what may happen if they get away. If you are uncertain of what the wind shifts will do, you want to stay near others to minimize your risk.

There are two basic ways to herd another boat. The first uses a series of tight covers on one tack and loose covers on the other tack. This encourages the opponent to sail the loosely covered tack (Fig. 36). The second is with a pin, which is described below.

Pin

A pin is a tack into position on another boat's hip which prevents the opponent from tacking away. It is used approaching a layline, where you can prevent your opponent from tacking to the mark until you do. It is also useful when herding one boat back toward a pack you want to cover (Fig. 37).

Chapter 8: Upwind Tactics

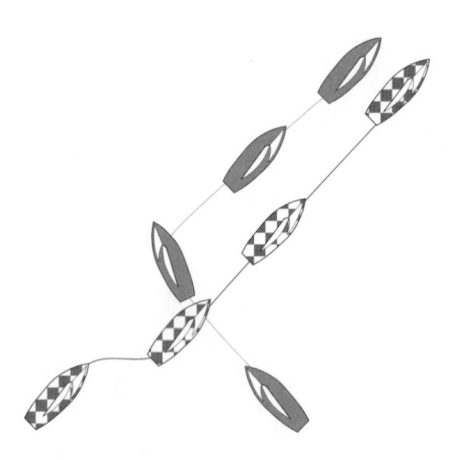

Fig. 38 – A Slam Dunk is used by a starboard-tack boat to pin a port tacker. It doesn't always work.

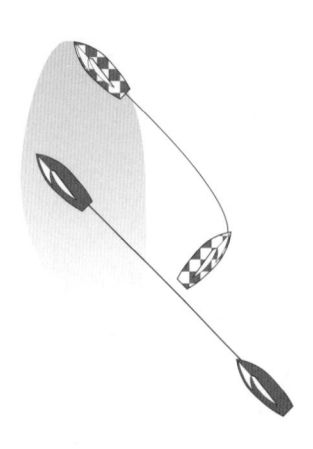

Fig. 39 – Tack into a position on top of another boat to put them in your wind shadow.

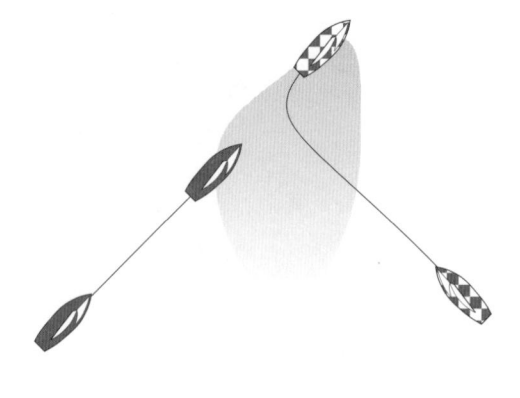

Fig. 40 – A tack directly in front of another boat will push the rival back.

Slam Dunk

The Slam Dunk is a technique for pinning a port-tack boat after he ducks a starboard-tack boat. Immediately after the port tacker ducks, the starboard boat tacks.

The Slam Duck often does not work. The Slam Dunk is a good way to pin a rival out to the starboard tack layline if it is not too far away, but over time the leeward boat can often gas off the windward boat (Fig. 38).

Using Your Wind Shadow

You can slow another boat by positioning your wind shadow on him. Once in your wind shadow, the opponent can either sail slowly or tack away.

From Directly Upwind

The simplest way to attack another boat is to position yourself directly upwind. This is the epitome of a tight cover. When tacking into this position, remember that you want to be directly upwind after you finish your tack and regain speed. It is common for attacking boats to tack too late and let the target boat break through (Fig. 39).

From Ahead

Another effective position for attack is directly in line with the opponent. The turbulence off your sails will foul the air for a several boat lengths off your stern. To assure that your opponent cannot escape your wind shadow without tacking, aim for a position between directly upwind and ahead (Fig. 40).

From the Lee Bow

As the name suggests, a lee bow position is on the leeward bow of an opponent. Boats create a surprising amount of turbulence to windward. Tacking ahead and to leeward can have a devastating effect (Fig. 41).

When you tack on a lee bow, be sure you have proper position. You must be nearly a full boat length ahead in order to lee bow properly; otherwise the opponent will squeeze up and put you in a pin; or worse, he may even roll you and force you to tack again (Fig. 42).

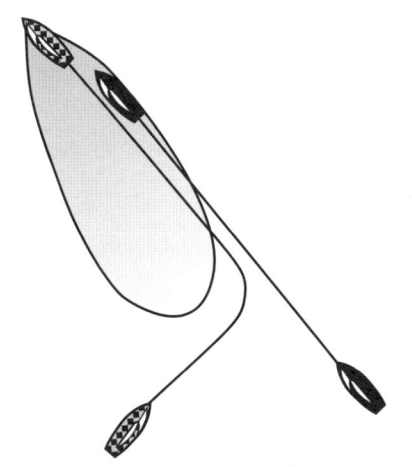

Fig. 41 – A tack on a rival's lee bow necessitates a response.

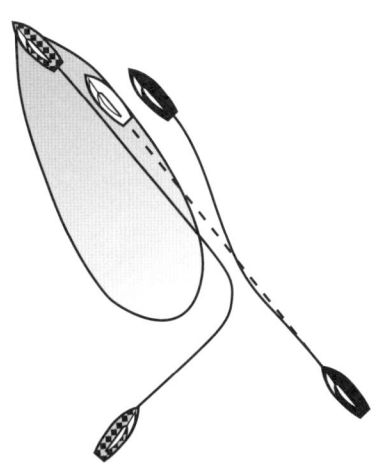

Fig. 42 – If the weather boat can squeeze up, the lee bow boat will be pinned.

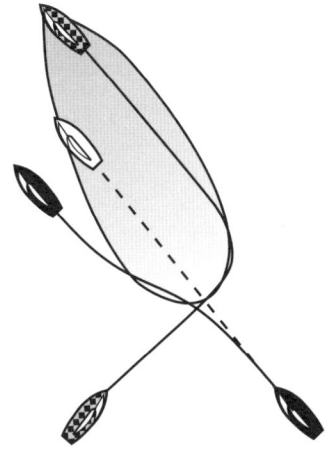

Fig. 43 – When you are attacked, you can try to keep clear air by driving off to leeward.

Defending Yourself

The defence from attack is anticipation and quick response. In order to survive an attack, you must break through to clear air before the attacker has reached full speed. Once the attacker is up to speed, it is nearly impossible to break clear.

Squeeze Up to Windward

If an opponent tacks on your lee bow, you may be able to escape by pinching up into clear air. React as soon as you are attacked. Once you fall into the attacker's exhaust, performance will suffer and you will not be able escape (Fig. 42).

If the attacker's position is strong, tack out as soon as possible, before the attack impacts your ability to tack and escape smoothly.

Drive Through to Leeward

If a boat tacks on your air, you can either tack away immediately or try to drive through to leeward to clear air. If you anticipate the attack, you can prepare to respond. If you want to stay on your present tack, then reach off slightly as soon as the attacker crosses your bow. With a little extra speed and a slightly late tack by the opponent, you may be able to break through in front of his wind shadow (Fig. 43).

If you plan to tack away, then do so immediately. Start your clearing tack while you still have full speed to minimize the hurt.

Don't Tack into a Pin

When tacking to leeward of a boat or boats, do so with enough room to be free to tack back should the need arise. Don't hand a rival boat the power to decide when you will next be free to tack.

Sucker Cover

If you are preparing to tack and see a rival coming, you may want to delay your tack for two reasons. One is to avoid tacking into a pin. The other is to tempt the rival to tack on you (and presumably sail off in the wrong direction) while you tack as planned (presumably going the right way). See earlier Figure 35 for Sucker Cover, but now you are the other guy!

Fig. 44 – If you are going the right way, wave a port tacker by, even if you have to duck a little.

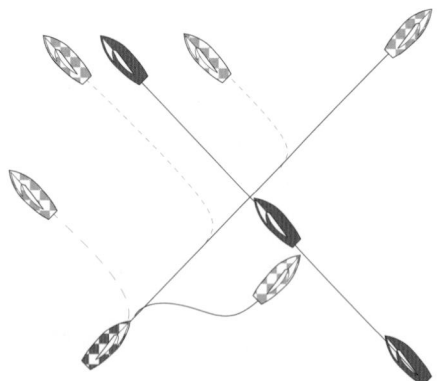

Fig. 45 – When in doubt, duck.

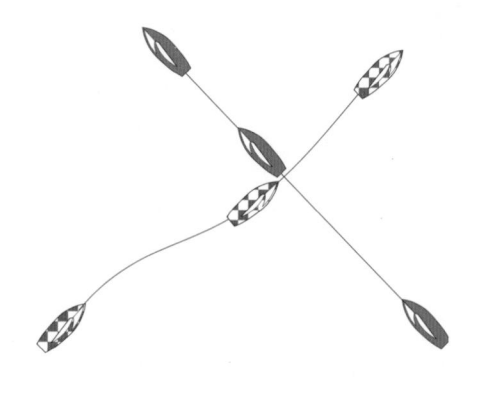

Fig. 46 – Make a smooth turn and carry speed as you trim up.

Wave 'em By

A port tacker who may or may not cross you can become a real nuisance if he throws in a last second lee bow tack. If you want to continue on starboard, wave 'em by, even if you have to duck a little bit. Anything to encourage him to keep going the wrong way and stay out of your way (Fig. 44).

Ducking and Reversal

You're on port tack, and you are approaching a starboard-tack boat. You have five options: Cross, lee bow, cross and tack, tack, or duck (Fig. 45). Your selection depends on whether or not you can cross, and which way you want to go. If you can cross, go ahead. Or lee bow, as detailed in Figure 41. If you can cross, and you are unsure which way to go, then cross and tack to put your opponent in a loose cover. If you can't cross, then tack or duck–what would you do in the absence of the other boat? If you decide to tack, try not to tack into a pin. Otherwise, duck.

Take a Bearing

You can tell if you will cross by taking a bearing from your stern to the starboard boat's bow. If the bearing is increasing, you will cross.

If there is doubt about crossing, then duck. Don't forfeit the race with a protest. And don't wait for the last instant to decide. A good smooth duck costs little. A poor duck or a crash tack can be a disaster.

Here's How it Works: As you approach it looks close. "Let's duck." Wave to the starboard tack boat so they know you see them. No need to yell. From a few lengths, ease your main and jib slightly and bear off. Aim for the spot where the starboard boat will be as you pass. A boat length away, your bow will be pointed at his. He'll sail a boat length, and you'll pass smartly under his stern. Well, maybe don't aim exactly at his bow, but you get my drift.

As you pass under his stern you want to be going faster than your close-hauled speed (after reaching off), but you want to be trimmed up to close hauled again. You must ease to

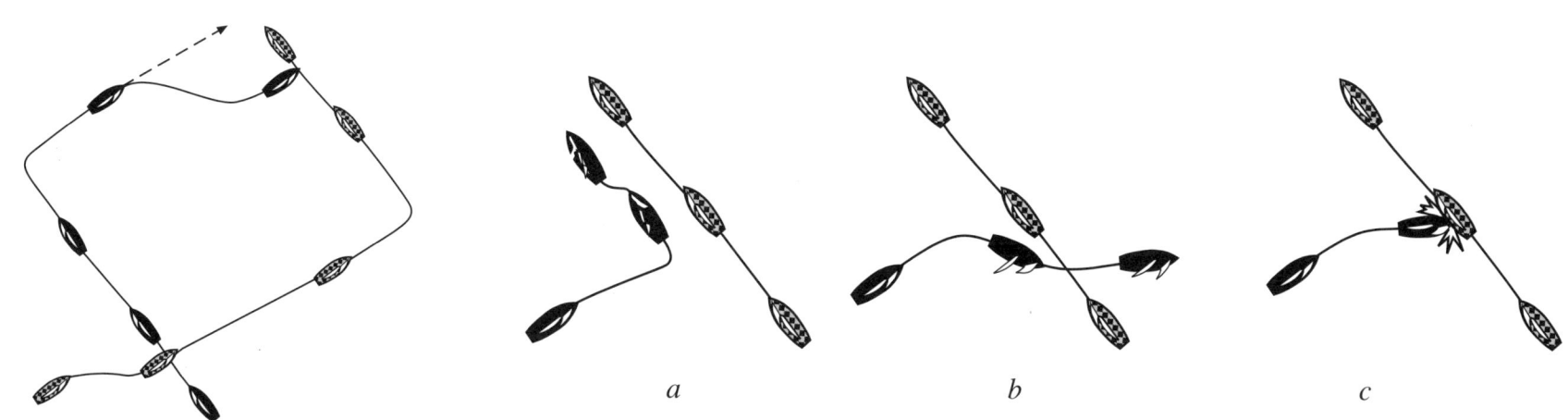

Fig. 47 – With a good duck, when you tack the next time you will be on starboard—and ahead!

Fig. 48a,b,c - Three things to avoid: The crash tack, The "OH! My God" duck, and The Starboard Tack Boat's Cockpit.

build speed when you bear off, but don't wait until you have passed to trim up again. Repeat: faster than close-hauled and trimmed all the way as you pass under his stern. You get a lift from the air off his sails. Pinch up in it and work to weather. If you're lucky, you'll even be able to surf out on his stern wave (Fig. 46).

You sail fast, and eventually you tack. Your opponent tacks too. You come together; only this time you're on starboard. You give him a wave. Theoretically he will cross you by the margin of your duck. Too close to call. Not only that, but you were going faster than full speed as you passed under his stern. You made up some of the distance. He can't cross. He'll duck … no, tack …. he can't decide (Fig. 47).

Here's how it doesn't work #1: He may cross. No, he can't. He decides to duck, no, tack. He throws the helm down. The crew are caught by surprise. The jib backs before it is finally released. It luffs on the new tack. No one was ready. There was no warning. Finally the jib is trimmed. As the sails fill the old foe is safely behind, in your wind shadow, unnerved, confused, and sailing badly (Fig. 48a).

Or #2: He may cross. No, he can't. He decides to duck, no, tack. Yes, duck. He pulls the helm up under his chin, but the boat hardly responds. The jib sheet is thrown off. "I thought you said tack." After a nervous moment the rudder grabs and the boat pivots down to a broad reach, sailing nearly parallel to you. Passing under your stern on a reciprocal course, they head the wrong way, finally coming to course about 2 boat lengths to leeward. The jib comes in slowly (Fig. 48b).

Or #3: He may cross. No, he can't. He decides to duck, no, tack. Yes, duck. He pulls the helm up under his chin, but the boat hardly responds. The main has not been eased and the boat won't bear off. He hits you amidships, just behind the shrouds, and takes a big chunk out of your port rail. The only thing bigger than the hole in your rail are their eyes (Fig. 48c).

In order to achieve a reversal, you must duck properly. Look ahead and be ready to react.

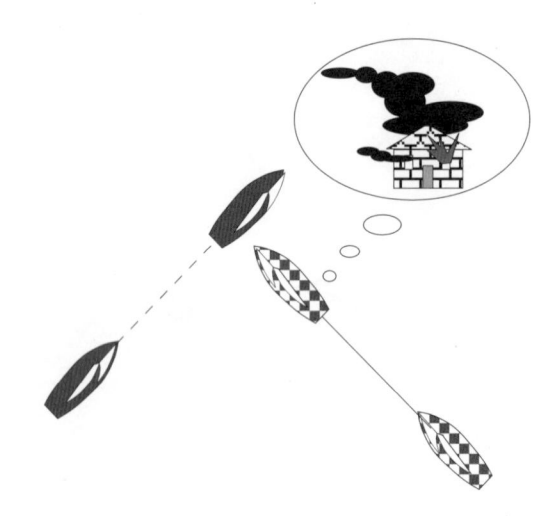

Fig. 49 – When on port, don't expect a starboard tacker to risk crashing his boat!

Fig. 50 – Rule 10 gives starboard the right of way. Rule 16.1 requires that if Starboard changes course, she give Port room to keep clear. Furthermore, under Rule 16.2, if Port is ducking then Starboard cannot change course in a way that requires an immediate change of course by Port.

8.6 Rules Upwind

There are only four Right of Way Rules in the entire Rule Book: Rule 10 – On Opposite Tacks, Rule 11 – Same Tack, Overlapped, Rule 12 – Same Tack, Not Overlapped, and Rule 13 – While Tacking . The Mark Room and Obstruction rules of Section C also come into play upwind.

It is difficult to survive a protest. If you scare someone and raise their blood pressure when tacking or crossing, they can protest you and throw you out. The same applies if you get someone angry.

There are two common ways to get in trouble: Greed and surprise, both of which can cloud good judgment. Don't be greedy (wishing you could cross is not sufficient) and look ahead to avoid surprises.

Opposite Tacks (Rule 10)

The next time you are on port tack in a close crossing consider this: Racing sailors would rather have their house burn down than crash their boat. After all, the family can always sleep on the boat; but if they crash their boat, they can't race the house. The guy on starboard is not going to risk crashing his boat to prove that you could cross. If it is close, he will bear off and protest. Don't risk it. Duck instead (Fig. 49).

While Rule 10 gives Starboard the Right of Way, Rule 16.1 limits the right of way boat to require that if she changes course she must provide the keep clear boat with room to keep clear. Furthermore, Rule 16.2 provides that if a Port boat is ducking then the Starboard boat cannot change course is a way that requires an immediate change so course by Port. (Fig. 50).

Fig. 51 – You have tacked too close if the trailing boat must start evasive maneuvers before you finish your turn.

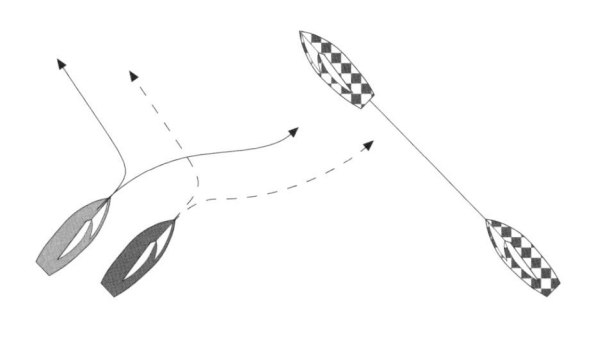

Fig. 52 – Two port boats must stay clear of a starboard obstruction.

Same Tack, Overlapped (Rule 11)

Windward boats must stay clear. With everyone sailing close hauled, the windward/ leeward rules are not as volatile upwind as they are downwind; but windward boats must still be careful. Even if your boat is not as close winded (doesn't point as high) as a leeward boat, you must stay clear.

While Tacking (Rule 13) and Same Tack, Not Overlapped (Rule 12)

After crossing head to wind, the tacking boat must complete her tack (finish turning and be on course) before the right-of-way boat initiates an evasive maneuver, or she has tacked too close. If it comes to a protest, then not only must you tack legally, you must also be able to prove it. Be careful (Fig. 51).

If a rival tacks in front of you then you must avoid hitting them from astern. Alter course to avoid a collision. If you must alter course before the tacking boat has completed her tack, she has fouled you. Avoid a collision and protest.

Obstructions (Rules 19 and 20)

When two (or more) port tack boats approach a starboard-tack boat, the port tackers must stay clear. The starboard-tack boat ranks as an obstruction. The port-tack boats may duck or tack in order to keep clear. The leeward port tacker may choose to duck and give others room to duck as well, or he may choose to tack (Fig. 52).

If the leeward boat chooses to tack, Rule 20 requires that he hail the boat) to windward. The windward boat must tack, or hail "You tack," and stay clear. The leeward boat must tack as soon as he gets a response (either action or words).

Windward Mark Roundings

The mark rounding rules at the windward mark differ from those on a free leg of the course. There are three basic situations:

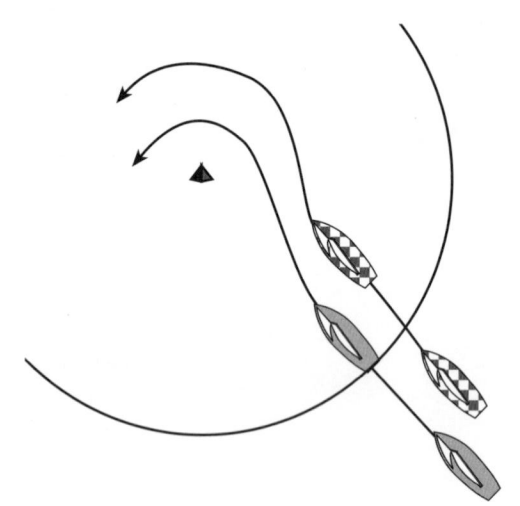

Fig. 53 – The inside, leeward boat is entitled to room and has right of way.

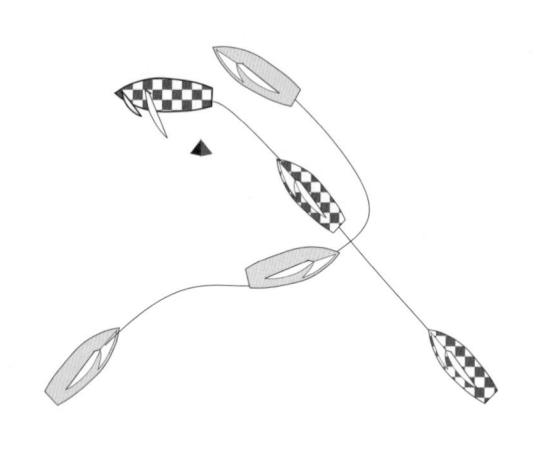

Fig. 54 – The starboard boat has right of way. There is no buoy room.

Fig. 55 – Rule 18.3 burdens a boat tacking inside the zone.

1) Both boats on starboard tack, leaving the mark to port, (or both on port, mark to starboard).

This is both a windward/ leeward or clear ahead/ clear astern and a Mark Room situation. The boat to leeward or ahead has right of way, and also receives Mark Room. She may luff to round the mark (this is proper course). The other boat must keep clear (Fig. 53).

2) One boat on starboard, one on port. Regular Right of Way rules apply. There is no Mark Room for boats on opposite tacks at a windward mark (See Rule 18.1 b). At a port rounding, the port tacker must stay clear (Fig. 54).

If a port-tack boat tacks to starboard inside the three boat length zone, then Rule 18.3 applies. If the starboard boat must head up above close hauled to avoid the tacking boat, the tacking boat has violated the rule. Furthermore, if the starboard boat overlaps the tacking boat to the inside, the tacking boat must give room. (Fig. 55).

The burdens on a boat tacking inside the zone are so onerous that I suggest you don't do it, and consider one of three options:
- Come in right on the layline and tack around the mark, minimizing your exposure. (Fig. 56 – option 1).
- Don't tack – Cross the starboard boat (if you can) and then tack. (Fig. 56 – option 2).
- Come in more than three lengths from the mark and complete your tack outside the zone. (Fig. 56 – option 3).

3) Two boats on port tack. When two port tackers approach a mark to be left to port, (or two starboard tackers for a starboard rounding), the Mark Room rules apply. The outside boat must give the inside boat room, including room to tack. (Fig.57a)

If the boats are *not* overlapped then the clear ahead boat gets Mark Room, but this does *not* include room to tack. A boat clear ahead must obey Rule 13: While Tacking when she tacks around the mark. (See Definition of *Mark Room*). (Fig. 57b).

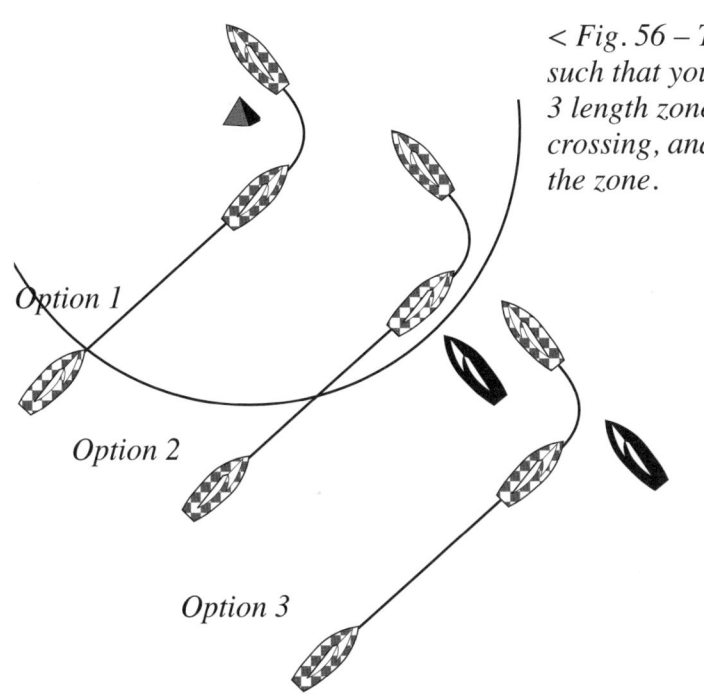

< Fig. 56 – The burdens of Rule 18.3 are such that you should avoid tacking inside the 3 length zone. Try tacking around the mark, crossing, and then tacking, or tacking outside the zone.

Option 1

Option 2

Option 3

Fig. 57a – An inside boat gets Mark-Room, including room to tack.

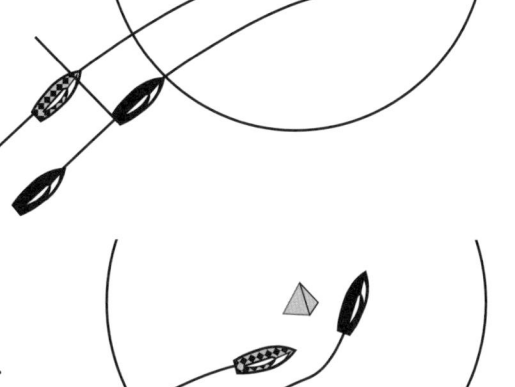

Fig. 57b – A boat clear ahead gets Mark-Room, but NOT room to tack.

Marks To Starboard

The mark rounding rules are the same when marks are to starboard, but they do not work as cleanly. At a starboard rounding, the starboard tacker has right of way while on course, but is not entitled to tack in a port tacker's path. The port tacker must stall, duck, or tack away while the starboard tack boat crosses ahead. The situation gets unruly during a crowded starboard rounding (Fig. 58).

Hitting The Mark (Rule 31)

A boat which hits a mark must immediately get clear of other boats and do a One-Turn Penalty before proceeding. While doing a penalty turn, a boat has no rights and must stay clear of all other boats. If the boat was wrongfully pushed into the mark, she may proceed, but she must protest the offending boat (Fig. 59).

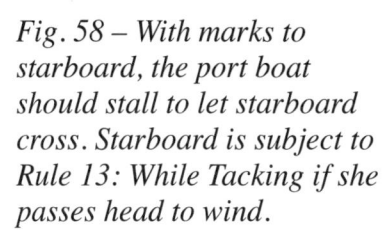

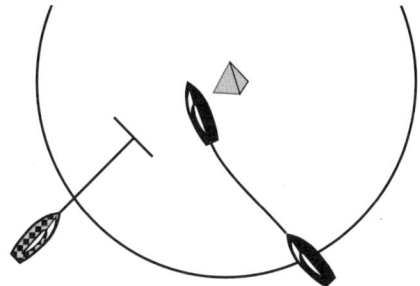

Fig. 58 – With marks to starboard, the port boat should stall to let starboard cross. Starboard is subject to Rule 13: While Tacking if she passes head to wind.

Fig. 59 – A boat which hits the mark must do a 1 Turn Penalty.

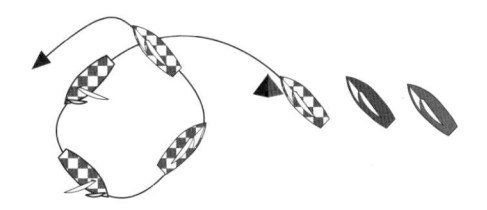

Rules, Ethics, and Self Interest

The rules upwind are straightforward, much more so than at starts or offwind marks. Protests are usually the result of greed or surprise which cloud your judgment. Don't get greedy—be ready to duck if you can't cross cleanly, and look ahead to avoid surprises.

And when you foul someone, acknowledge the foul and take your penalty.

When you have the right of way, you need not protest every offense. You can protest a close port/starboard; but you can also hail the offender, "You owe me one." In the long run, your own interests will be better served if you don't protest unless your performance suffers. If you protest even when the port boat might have made it, you will probably win the protest. He will be thrown out, and he will doubtless look for a chance to return the favor.

By the same token, you have an obligation to protest a gross offense. If you are badly fouled by a port tack boat, you owe it to the rest of the fleet to protest. Otherwise you are condoning cheating. Ideally the port boat will withdraw or take a penalty without forcing you to follow through with a protest.

But if people don't play by the rules then they are not playing the game.

8.7 A Tactician's Nightmare

There are a number of classic situations which make tacticians toss and turn. Here's one example:

Persistent or Oscillating

We were out early before the start, and got great data. The wind graph shows oscillations, and we've been playing them like a fiddle. Up the first beat we hit every shift. We held the lead downwind, and now we've turned upwind again.

Pretty much the same numbers as the first beat, so we're hitting the shifts as before. On starboard now, and lifted. Stretching out our advantage. A little more lift now, and we are beaming. We've hit the big one. More big gains while some out-of-phase rivals sail off headed.

More lift, and the first hints of paranoid fear infect our glee. The big lift holds, and we start to wonder if it will ever go back. A slight header, and we start to think about tacking, even though we are still lifted compared to average for the day, but before we can act the big lift returns.

Genuine concern now. Have conditions changed? Are we now on the outside of a persistent shift – sailing away from the shift on the Great Circle Route? Or will the oscillations return?

What should we do? Tack and take our medicine? Hang on and look for at least a bit of a header to go back on? (Fig. 60).

I wish I had the answer for this one. The best I can offer are ideas:

- Look ahead, and look at the sky. Have things heated up? Clouds moved in or out? Any clues from boats further upwind, or to the sides?
- Review the forecast. What did we expect?
- Where's the fleet? Our risk is measured in leverage. If our rivals are going our way, then the risk is small. If they've split, then the risk is great. If they are going both ways...

Fig. 60 – When conditions change mid-race, tacticians have to scramble to revise strategy. When oscillating shifts turn into persistent shifts (or is it just a longer oscillations – who knows?) you can be left scratching your head.

- One option is to tack and talk. Rather than continue, tack over and see how the other tack feels while we assess long term strategy.
- Focus on speed and tactics. Reduce risk by consolidating with the fleet, and sail fast.
- **Tack!** Face it – conditions have changed, and this is a persistent shift. Bail out now. As bad as things seem now, it will only get worse.
- **Don't tack!** Hang on. Don't panic. The wind will come back. The only thing more painful than being caught on the outside of a persistent shift is tacking, sailing headed, and then having the wind (finally) shift back so we have to tack and sail headed again. Not only are we in the tank, but our old neighbors who stuck it out on the original lift are far ahead. Aarrrgh.

There is no easy answer here, but a strategic theme bears repeating: When unsure of what the wind will do, then minimize the impact of shifts by minimizing leverage. Another theme: While we sort things out, sail the tack that takes us closer to the mark.

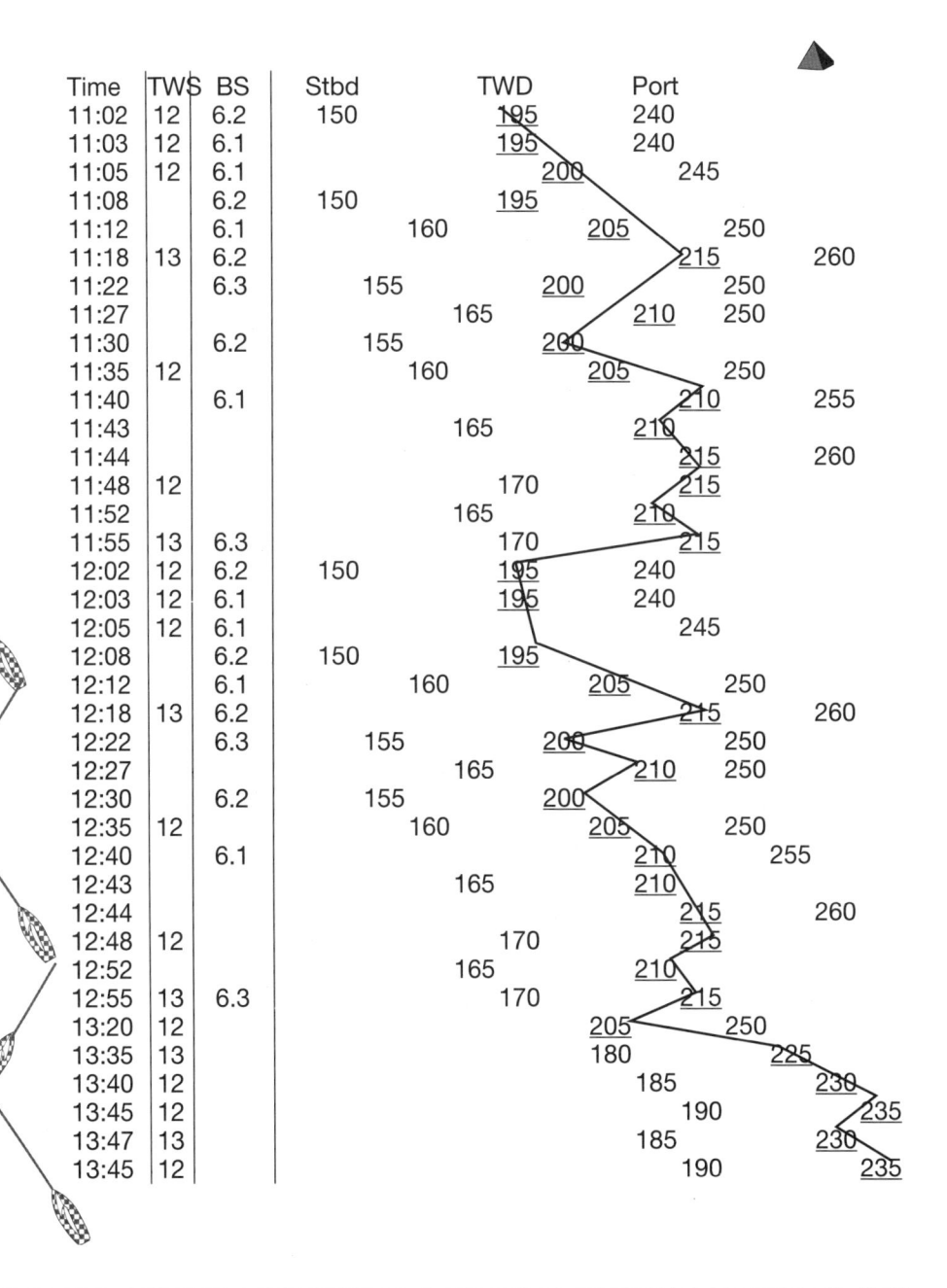

Time	TWS	BS	Stbd	TWD	Port
11:02	12	6.2	150	195	240
11:03	12	6.1		195	240
11:05	12	6.1		200	245
11:08		6.2	150	195	
11:12		6.1	160	205	250
11:18	13	6.2		215	260
11:22		6.3	155	200	250
11:27			165	210	250
11:30		6.2	155	200	
11:35	12		160	205	250
11:40		6.1		210	255
11:43			165	210	
11:44				215	260
11:48	12		170	215	
11:52			165	210	
11:55	13	6.3	170	215	
12:02	12	6.2	150	195	240
12:03	12	6.1		195	240
12:05	12	6.1			245
12:08		6.2	150	195	
12:12		6.1	160	205	250
12:18	13	6.2		215	260
12:22		6.3	155	200	250
12:27			165	210	250
12:30		6.2	155	200	
12:35	12		160	205	250
12:40		6.1		210	255
12:43			165	210	
12:44				215	260
12:48	12		170	215	
12:52			165	210	
12:55	13	6.3	170	215	
13:20	12			205	250
13:35	13			180	225
13:40	12			185	230
13:45	12			190	235
13:47	13			185	230
13:45	12			190	235

Chapter 8: Upwind Tactics

8.8 No More Tactics!

Tactics provide the thrill of direct confrontation with our rivals. The interaction of attack and response challenges our skills to react as situations evolve. We must consider not only the boats at hand, but also the rest of the fleet and our overall race strategy as we make split second decisions. This is hard!

Not only that, but if the wind is shifty we can lose hundreds of yards in a matter is minutes. This is scary!

Maybe we'd be better off eliminating tactics from our racing, or at least minimizing their impact, but how?

No More Tactics

The trick is to rely on things you can control: boat handling and boat speed. Then you can minimize the impact of things you can't control: the wind and other boats. Do this by positonong the boat clear of traffic, in lanes of clear air that allow you to sail your boat at full speed. (You can find clear air by sailing off to the sides of the course, but that leaves you at the mercy of the shifts. The trick is to control leverage while maintaining clear air – no mean feat.)

The more you can rely on things you can control, the less you will have to rely on things you can't (Fig. 61).

Fig. 61 - Tactics and Strategy require us to make the most of the unknown. The more we can rely on our boat handling and boat speed, the less we will have to rely on things we can't control.

Finally, we're around the windward mark and we can turn downwind. What's for lunch?

8.9 Upwind Strategy and Tactics: Quiz Questions

1. You are on port tack in a close crossing with a starboard boat and are unsure where the next shift is coming from. What should you do?

2. Sailing out to the start area before the race, you are broad reaching on starboard. You gradually got headed as you got away from shore. What should your strategy be going upwind?

3. A bigger, faster boat just tacked on your wind 200 yards from the finish line. What should you do?

4. The current is better to the right, but the wind is shifting to the left. Which way should you go?

5. You are on port tack and another port tacker is on your hip, two lengths to weather and two and a half back. You are 400 yards from the mark, and 100 yards from the starboard tack layline. What should you do?

6. Your boat is fast in a breeze—unfortunately today there is very little. How might this affect your strategy?

7. How much distance do you lose by tacking? How much do you lose if you miss a 10° shift?

8. How does a port/ starboard reversal work?

Skill Building: Upwind Strategy and Tactics

1. *Learning to see the wind:*
   Sure, good sunglasses help, but there's no magic beyond paying attention. Here's what to look for:
   See the wind on the water – dark patches are puffs.
   But which way will it shift?
   You may be able to see how it is moving – but that is tough. Your experience with the previous puffs is your best guide. Some days they are all right shifts, some days the puffs oscillate, some times it seems random.
   Another guide is other boats. See what is going on there.
   Finally, don't let sun sparkle and cloud shadows trick you. On a clear day the sun sparkle makes the sunny side look windy, and on partly cloudy days cloud shadows can look like puffs.

2. *Where are we?*
   Describing your position on the course and in relation to other boats is essential to tactical decision making. One helpful description of position is the ratio of each tack remaining. When you are exactly in the middle of the course you will spend equal time on each tack. As you move toward the laylines the ratios change. A position described as having "twice as much port as starboard" remaining helps the whole team understand the constraint on sailing starboard, and the desire to find a good lane and favorable shift for sailing on port.

3. *What's going on?*
   As a driver it is imperative that you focus your attention on sailing fast. At the same time, you may want to know what is going on with other boats. Rather than look yourself, you need to ask specific questions to help your crew know what kind of information you are after. Over time your crew will learn what sort of information you need, but with new or inexperienced crew some information training will be necessary.
   Some of the questions you might ask:
   How is (a nearby boat) doing compared to us: What is his distance ahead/ behind, to weather/ leeward? How does his speed/ pointing compare to ours?

4. *Using a hand bearing compass upwind:*
   Often it is hard to tell if you are ahead of or behind another boat, or if you are gaining or losing versus another boat. Your hand bearing compass can tell you.
   To measure your position sight perpendicular to the wind direction. This is your LEP. Any boat on this line is even with you. Boats above are ahead, boats below are behind.
   If you are behind another boat you can compare your bearing to the LEP bearing. This tells you how big a wind shift you'll need to catch up (assuming speeds are equal).
   Your hand bearing compass is also great for calling laylines. Practice to perfect your technique, and beware deviation between the ships compass and your hand bearing compass.
   (NOTE: A hand bearing compass makes a great gift. Give one to your skipper or tactician!)

Upwind Strategy and Tactics: Quiz Answers

1. You are on port tack in a close crossing with a starboard boat and are unsure where the next shift is coming from. What should you do?

Are you headed toward the middle of the course, or out to the sides? Where is the balance of the fleet? When you are unsure of the next shift, sail toward the mark and avoid the sides, and stay near the bulk of your rivals to minimize leverage.

2. Sailing out to the start area before the race, you were broad reaching on starboard. You gradually got headed as you got away from shore. What should your strategy be going upwind?

If the condition holds then you would gradually get headed going back toward shore on the opposite tack – a persistent shift. As long as the wind strength is as good (or better) near shore then sail to that side going upwind. If the wind strength is even across the course then downwind the opposite side would be favored.

3. A bigger, faster boat just tacked on your wind 200 yards from the finish line. What should you do?

Cheer. If boats which owe you time are tacking on your air a minute before the finish, then you're in pretty good shape.

Still, you might want to clear your air, though two extra tacks in the last minute might cost more than sailing in bad air. Depends on how badly you're being hurt.

4. The current is better to the right, but the wind is shifting to the left. Which way should you go?

Tough call. A compromise up the middle might be the worst choice. A knot of upwind current improves VMG about as much as a 10° shift. How much and for how long would you expect to have better current or the shift?

5. You are on port tack and another port tacker is on your hip, two lengths to weather and two and a half back. You are 400 yards from the mark, and 100 yards from the starboard tack layline. What should you do?

Go into point mode and work to close the gap. Being bow out does you no good. If you get to the layline first and tack then the rival will tack and give you bad air. Delaying the tack means wasted distance overstanding. Pinch up, close the gap, and simul-tack close on the rival's hip. Stay within two lengths and you can attack him on the run.

6. Your boat is fast in a breeze—unfortunately today there is very little. How might this affect your strategy?

When you can count on your boat speed then you want to minimize the impact of strategic factors. When your speed is suspect, more aggressive strategy is called for.

7. How much distance do you lose by tacking?
How much do you lose if you miss a 10° shift?

Tacks cost about 2 boat lengths – perhaps a little less in smooth water, a little more in chop. A 10° lift reduces sailing distance by about 15%. So, if you tack and sail 400 yards to weather, you'll save 60 yards of sailing distance – 180 feet. You'd break even if your boat was 90 feet long, and come out ahead with a shorter boat.

8. How does a port/starboard reversal work?

If you're on port and duck well with good speed then when you and your rival tack, the rival will not be able to cross. It is the last starboard tack up the beat which matters most – not the early ones.

Chapter 9: Reaching Strategy and Tactics

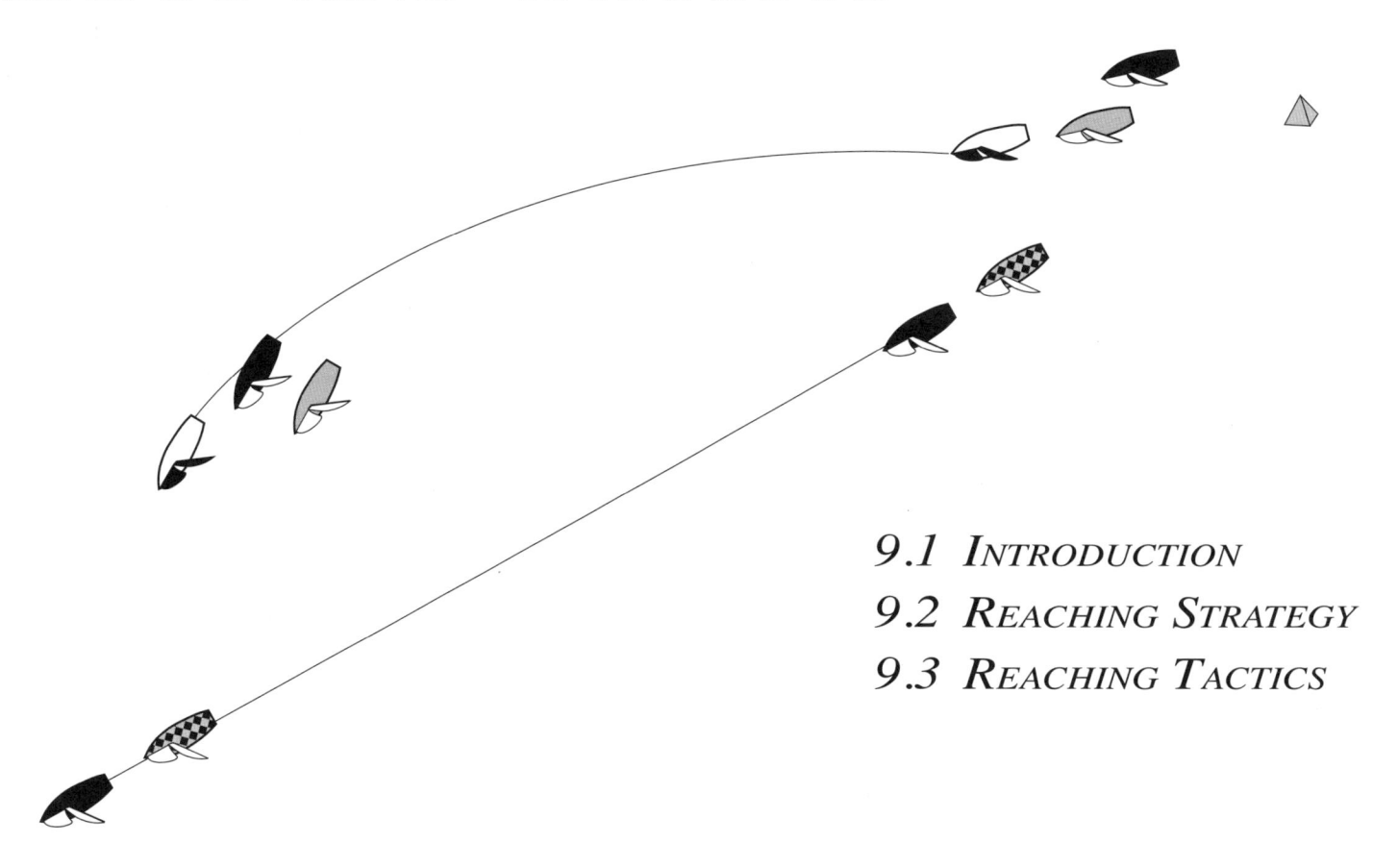

9.1 Introduction
9.2 Reaching Strategy
9.3 Reaching Tactics

Chapter 9: Reaching Strategy and Tactics

9.1 Introduction

This is not the time to have lunch. It is time to get to work. Have half your crew eat lunch sitting on the rail going up wind. Let the other half go hungry. Sailing downwind, we need the entire crew's efforts. There is much to do: Trim the spinnaker sheet, guy and pole, trim the main, call tactics, look back for shifts (and the competition, hopefully), find the mark, and more.

This chapter will cover *Reaching Strategy and Tactics*. We will look first at reaching strategy, and then tactics, in a variety of conditions. We will consider how tactics change with the type of fleet you are racing in, and where you fit into the crowd. *Running Strategy and Tactics* is an entirely different animal, and has a chapter all its own. Rules for reaching and running are covered in *Chapter 11: Downwind Rules, Mark Roundings and Finishing*.

General Strategy

I'd like to open this section with a couple of revelations: First, the shortest distance between two points is a straight line. (Until your boat speed approaches the speed of light this will remain essentially true.) Second, you will not pass anyone until you are going faster than they are. Add also the corollary: If you can sail faster than the boats behind you, you'll never have to look back (Fig. 1).

Reaching strategy can be built on these two fundamentals:
- *Sail the Rhumb Line*.
- *Sail Fast!*

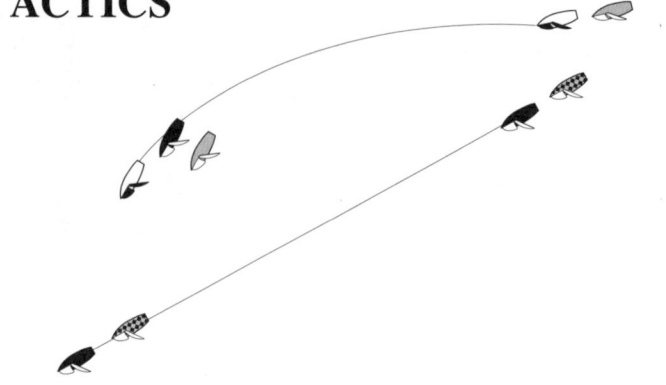

Fig. 1 - Reaching Strategy starts with two fundamentals: Sail the Rhumb Line and Sail Fast.

9.2 Reaching Strategy

Wind, Wind Shifts, and Current

With the two fundamentals of reaching strategy forming our framework, we can now apply the elements of strategy: Wind, wind shifts, and current. As with our earlier discussion of upwind strategy, we will first look at the strategic factors to analyze how we would sail around the course in the absence of other boats. Then we will add other boats and consider tactical issues.

Wind

The first deviation from our fundamental rhumb line strategy revolves around changing wind conditions.

"Off in the Puffs, Up in the Lulls"

The phrase is repeated so often that it is clichéd. It is also good strategy. In fluctuating winds, bear off below the rhumb line in a puff to stay in the puff longer. In a lull, reach up to

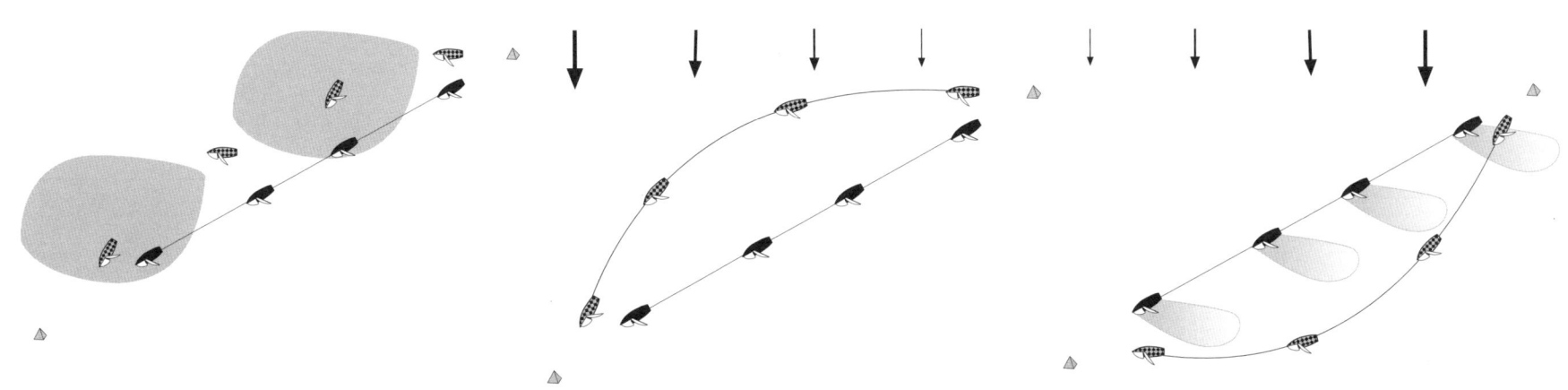

Fig 2 - Bear off in the puffs and head up in the lulls.

Fig 3 - In a building breeze reach up to the new wind and drive off with the stronger breeze.

Fig. 4 - In a fading wind reach off first if you can still keep clear air. Head up later for a faster reaching angle in the lighter wind.

hold speed, and to reach the next puff sooner. We all tend to sail down to—but not below—the rhumb line in puffs, and above it in lulls. This is both to protect clear air, and because it feels fast to reach up a little higher. Trouble is, it leaves you above the rhumb line and forces you to reach off later. Avoid this if you can. Sail below the rhumb line in puffs, so you can preserve your fast reaching angle later in the leg (Fig. 2).

Off in puffs, up in the lulls is sound reaching strategy. It is not always true on runs, as we will see in the next chapter.

Building Breeze / Fading Breeze

Don't wait for a building breeze to come to you—go up and get it. Think of a building breeze as one long lull followed by one long puff. Go up in the lull and off in the puff to get the best overall performance. You make big gains by aggressively pursuing a new wind. Be bold (Fig. 3).

In a fading breeze, the same strategy applies in reverse. The existing wind is a relative puff—sail low in it and reach up as the breeze fades (Fig. 4). This is a difficult strategy to pursue as tactical considerations often overwhelm it. Sailing low invites those behind to sail over you and to steal what wind you have. If you can hold low and keep clear air, your dividends will be big. Reaching up in the lighter air will give you a real boost. It will also push your apparent wind angle forward so your air will be more difficult to steal.

Wind Shifts
Oscillating Wind Shifts

Oscillating conditions will often feel like puff and lull conditions and should be treated that way. As the wind shifts aft (a lift), the apparent wind will decrease. Head up to maintain apparent wind strength and boat speed. Similarly, as the wind shifts forward, drive off. Use the favorable wind angle to push down, below the rhumb line course (Fig. 5).

You should not head up one degree for each degree of lift, nor should you drive off as many degrees as the wind

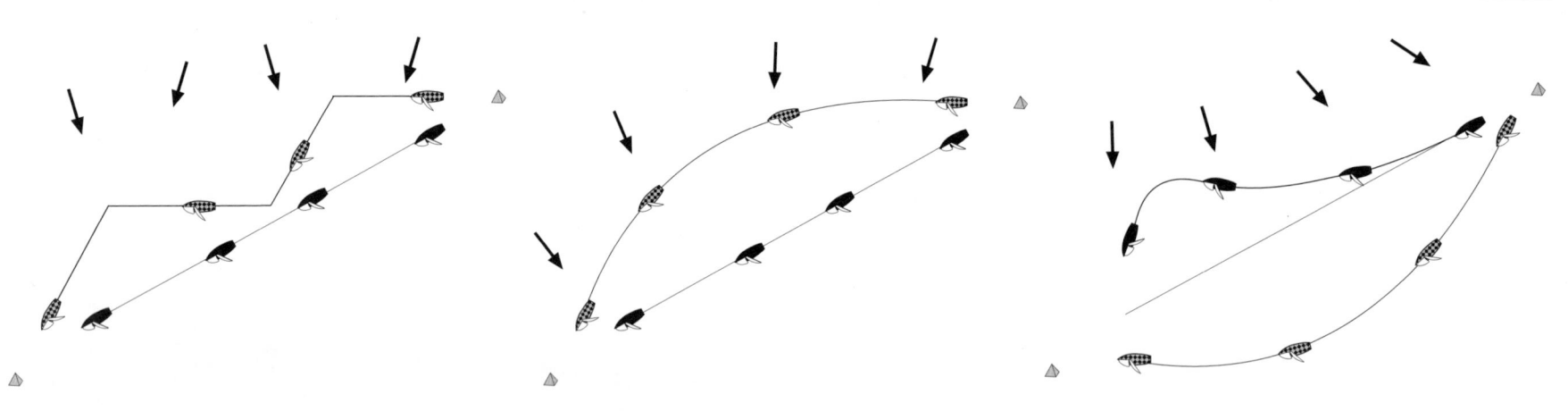

Fig. 5 - In oscillating winds head up in the lifts and off with the headers to keep more consistent apparent wind and boat speed.

Fig. 6 - In a persistent header sail up initially and drive off as the wind moves ahead.

Fig. 7 - In a persistent lift try to hold a low course initially so you can head up later with the lift.

shifts forward. You must balance the extra speed with the extra sailing distance to arrive at the optimum course and speed. A change of course roughly half the angle of the shift seems a good place to start.

Persistent Wind Shifts

In a persistent, gradual header, sail above the rhumb line initially and let the shift push you down to the mark (Fig. 6). In a gradual lift, the correct strategy is to sail low initially, and then reach up to the mark as the wind shifts aft (Fig. 7).

Sailing low in anticipation of a lift is a difficult strategy to follow. Sailing lower and slower is not a performance choice we make easily—and the reality of tactics makes it hard to do, as other boats may sail over us as we pursue the strategy. If you have the discipline to work low in the early part of a reach in a persistent lift, *and if you can keep clear air,* then you will reap big gains later in the leg, as you approach the mark with a favorable wind angle.

In persistent shifts, as with oscillations, you must balance the speed versus distance trade-offs to determine how far off the rhumb line to sail.

Current

Current creates great strategic opportunity on reaches. The first trick, of course, is to know what the current is going to do. In this section we'll take a look at strategy for current which is consistent over the leg, and also for current which varies in strength down the leg. For a discussion of current forecasting, see *Chapter 13: Weather,* later in this book.

Steady Current

When current strength and direction are consistent over the length of the leg, the strategic goal is to correct for it by steering a course which holds you on the rhumb line.

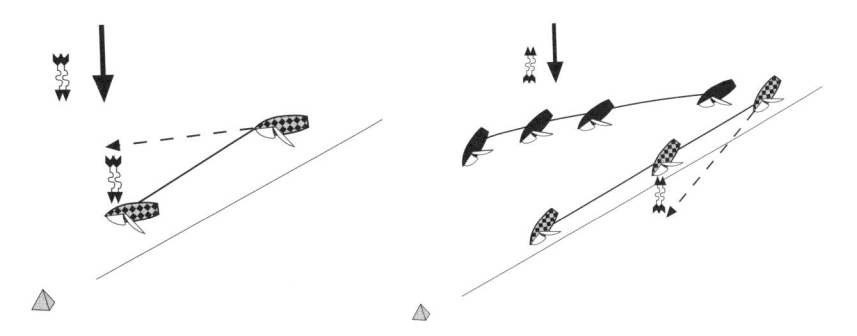

Fig. 8 - When the current is pushing to leeward, head up to compensate.

Fig. 9 - When it pushes to weather, drive off. Failure to compensate for the current can leave you sailing a low, slow course later in the leg.

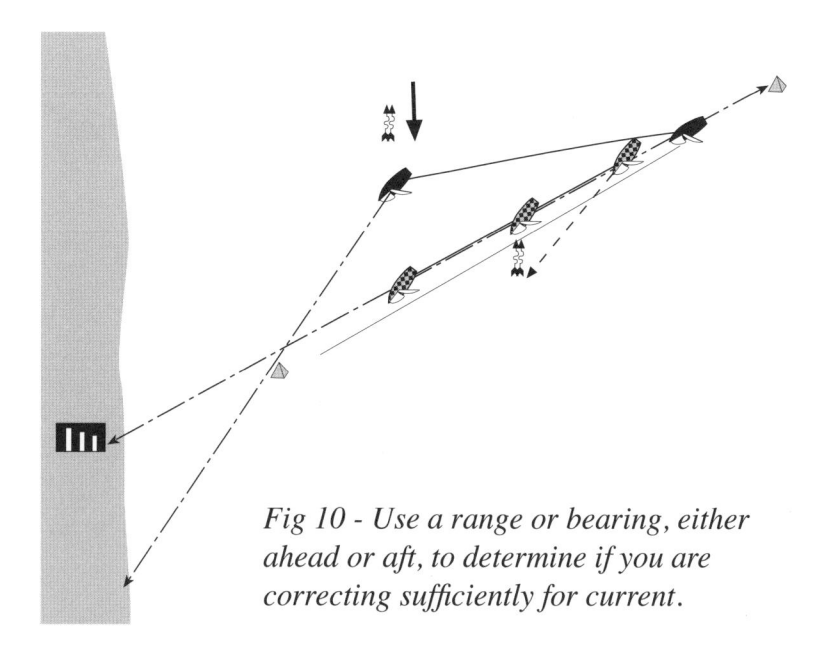

Fig 10 - Use a range or bearing, either ahead or aft, to determine if you are correcting sufficiently for current.

If the current is pushing you to leeward you can head up and sail a faster reaching angle. The current will then push you down to the mark (Fig. 8).

Conversely, if the current is pushing you to windward, you must drive off to compensate. It is in these conditions that your efforts to correct for the current are particularly important. If you fail to correct for current as it pushes you to windward, you will eventually have to sail down into it at an increasingly unfavorable reaching angle (Fig. 9).

Correcting for Current

How can you tell if the course you are steering is compensating fully for the current? There are several ways (Fig. 10):

- Use a *range*, or *transit*. Sight through the mark to shore. As long as the mark remains aligned to the same spot on the shore, you are steering the correct angle to compensate for the current. Note that the course you steer may vary as your boat speed changes with changing wind conditions.
- Use a *bearing, back bearing,* or *back range*. If you cannot establish a range ahead, try a bearing to the mark ahead, a back bearing to the mark you just rounded, or a back range through that mark to shore. You will be able to see if you are being pushed off your rhumb line course.
- Use the *Course Over Ground* (also know as *Course Made Good*) function on your GPS. If you do not have any objects to sight, then COG can give you course information. This information is not sound until you have been on course for some time. The averaging and sampling time varies from brand to brand.

The current rarely pushes you either directly to windward or leeward. Usually there is a component of the current aligned with the course. The current may be from your weather quarter, or leeward bow, or whatever...

Chapter 9: Reaching Strategy and Tactics

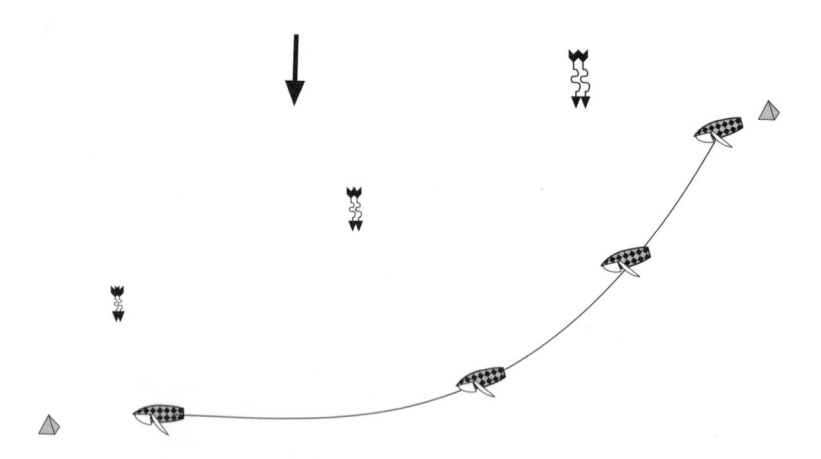

Fig. 11 - When current is strongest early in the leg and is pushing to leeward, don't worry if you can't hold the rhumb line. You will be able to make up ground later.

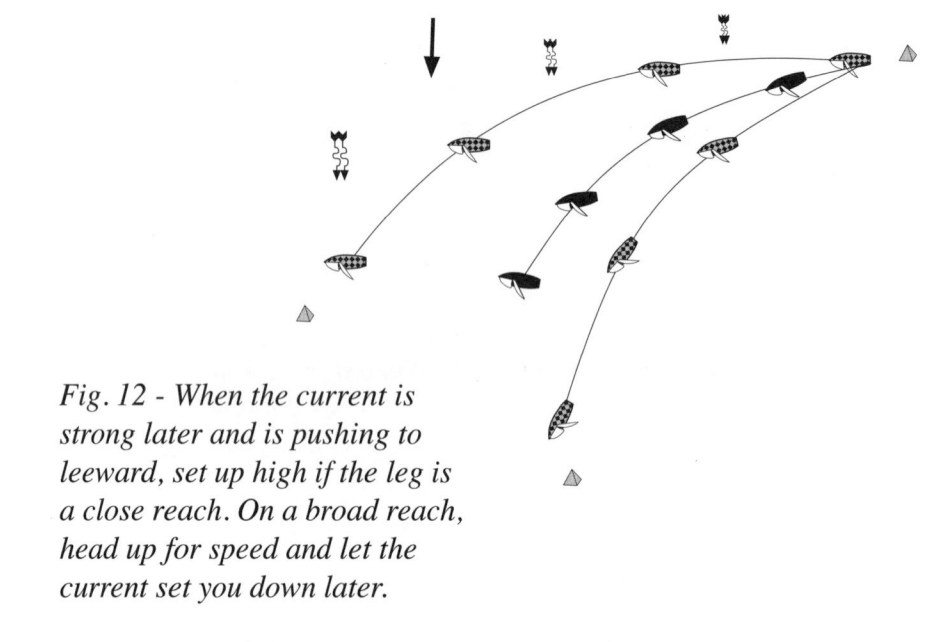

Fig. 12 - When the current is strong later and is pushing to leeward, set up high if the leg is a close reach. On a broad reach, head up for speed and let the current set you down later.

The component of the current which is aligned with the course, either on the bow or on the stern, effectively lengthens or shortens the leg. The case where the current is at your stern is the more interesting, as it tends to exaggerate the impact of any distance you are pushed laterally. Boats which are high of course will have to bear off even more to get down to the mark, compounding their difficulties (as in fig 9 on the previous page). If they fail to compensate sufficiently, they may be swept past the mark. This is particularly true in lighter winds, where performance suffers most on broader reaches.

Variable Current

When current varies down the leg, it can become a key strategic factor. We'll look at four permutations, though countless other scenarios are possible.

• *Current pushing to leeward and strongest at the outset:*
If you are on a close reach and having difficulty holding the rhumb line, fear not. As the current abates, you will not have to sail such a high compass course to make the mark. Furthermore, less current will shift your apparent wind aft, allowing you to sail a higher compass course with the same apparent wind angle (Fig. 11). For further discussion of the current's impact on sailing wind, see *Chapter 13: Weather*.

• *Current pushing to leeward and strongest at the end:*
On a close reach you will want to set up by sailing a high line early to assure a fetch. On a broader reach don't hesitate to sail a higher, faster reaching angle early on, with the knowledge that the current will set you down to the mark later in the leg (Fig. 12).

• *Current pushing to weather and strongest at the outset:*
Reach up to get across the current quickly, and you'll spend less time fighting it. But beware: the higher you go

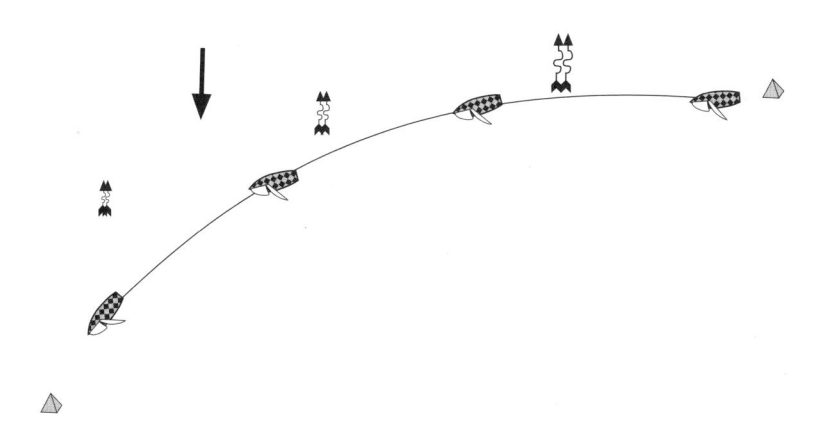

Fig. 13 - With the current running upwind and strongest early in the leg the fastest course is to reach up and get across the current quickly, then sail a broader, slower angle later.

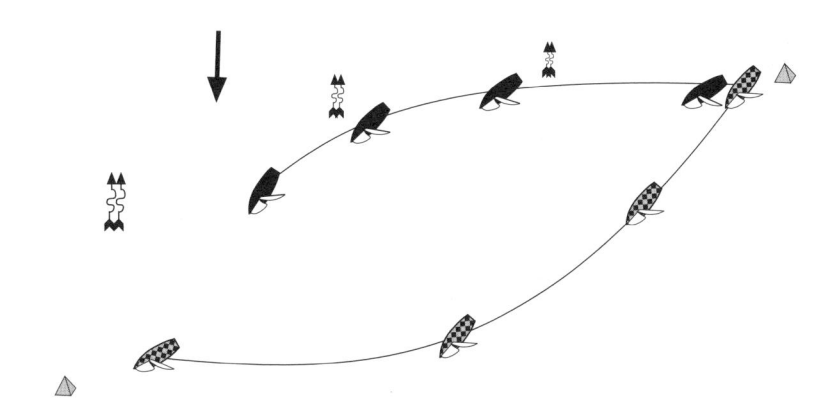

Fig. 14 - With current pushing to weather and strong later in the leg it is best to sail low early or you will have to fight the strongest current at a poor reaching angle later.

early, the lower you will have to sail later, once you are out of the current (Fig. 13).

- *Current pushing to weather and strongest at the end:* This case holds the greatest opportunities, as those who do not anticipate the current's set are at a distinct disadvantage. As boats are pushed to weather, they are forced to sail a lower and slower reaching angle to compensate. This slower course increases the relative strength of the current and compounds the error. Those who anticipate the current's push and set up low of the rhumb line will gain. Of course, sailing low early in the leg is not possible if there are rivals in hot pursuit looking to sail over you and steal your air. That said, the lighter the wind and stronger the current the more important it is to get low early. A diminishing wind and strengthening current can create devastating results (Fig. 14).

Reaching Strategy Conclusion

Sail Fast, Sail the Rhumb Line. Sometimes strategy is just that simple. Variables of wind, wind shifts, and current can add some complexity, but the real excitement comes with tactics— or lots of wind. The tactical battle for clear air and for position at roundings or in passing lanes is where the action is.

Reaches can become parades. In similar size boats, passing can be difficult. Leaders tend to stretch out their advantage by following the *sail fast, sail straight* principles, while the rest of the fleet struggles. In mixed fleets, big boats which have failed to round ahead roll up through the fleet, with the smaller boats unable to stop them. It is no wonder that, to avoid reaching parades, more and more races are being run on windward-leeward courses.

Onward to *Reaching Tactics*, where we will battle for clear air and work to achieve our strategic goals.

9.3 Reaching Tactics

Reaching tactics depend on our goals for the leg and the conditions in which they are sailed. In boats of similar size and speed passing other boats can be a difficult (and risky) undertaking. You must decide if your primary goal is to pass boats, or to simply stretch out your lead on those behind while closing the gap on those ahead. That decision depends on your current position in the race and the opportunities you expect down the road. Sometimes the status quo is just fine—sometimes it is best to wait until the next leg to pursue a more aggressive strategy.

Much of reaching tactics revolves around keeping clear air. Without clear air there is little chance for success. The struggle for clear air can tear us away from our strategy. Much of the tactical discussion will revolve around how to keep clear air, and how to balance that effort with our wind and current strategy for the leg. The battle to preserve clear air tends to push the fleet above the rhumb line on reaches. The higher course early in the leg, and lower course later in the leg, makes the second half of the reach slower than the first half. As the pack compresses later in the leg, tactical opportunities increase. Careful positioning early in the leg can bring rewards later on, and careless positioning can lead to disaster.

Often the first few boats to round are able to hold to the rhumb line, while the pack sails extra distance in the struggle to preserve clear air. Consequently, the leaders tend to get away – leaving the pack behind (Fig. 15).

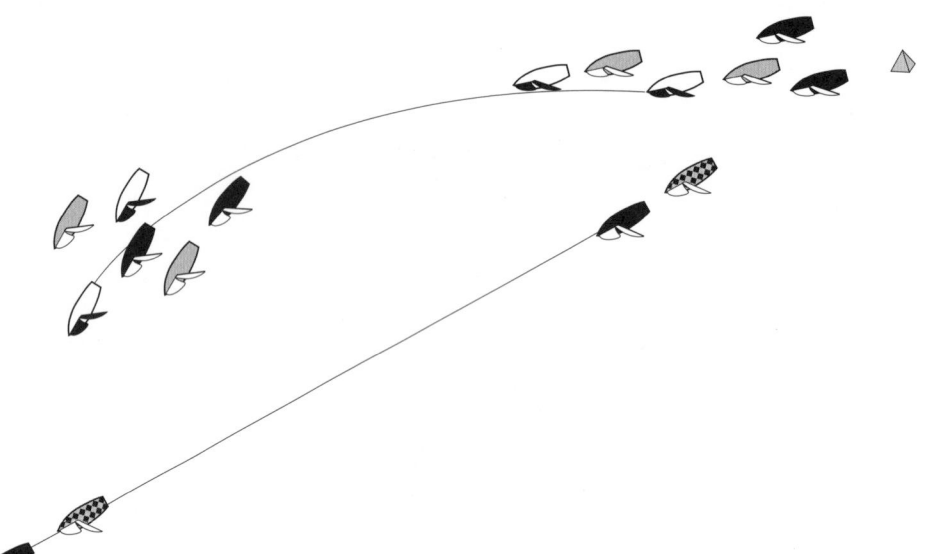

Fig. 15 - Only the first few boats can follow the Sail Fast, Sail Straight *strategy. The rest of the fleet must wrestle with other boats and battle for clear air.*

Passing Other Boats

The most obvious tactical goal on a reach is to pass those ahead of you; the obvious first step in that tactic is to sail faster than those ahead. You'll have a hard time passing them if you don't catch them first. Sail fast. (WOW, really?)

Sail fast, but don't sail high. The easiest way to build speed is to reach up. But it is also risky. As you sail up, the boats ahead will reach up too. You will be adding mileage to the leg without closing in on those ahead; and you will lose to other boats which sail less distance.

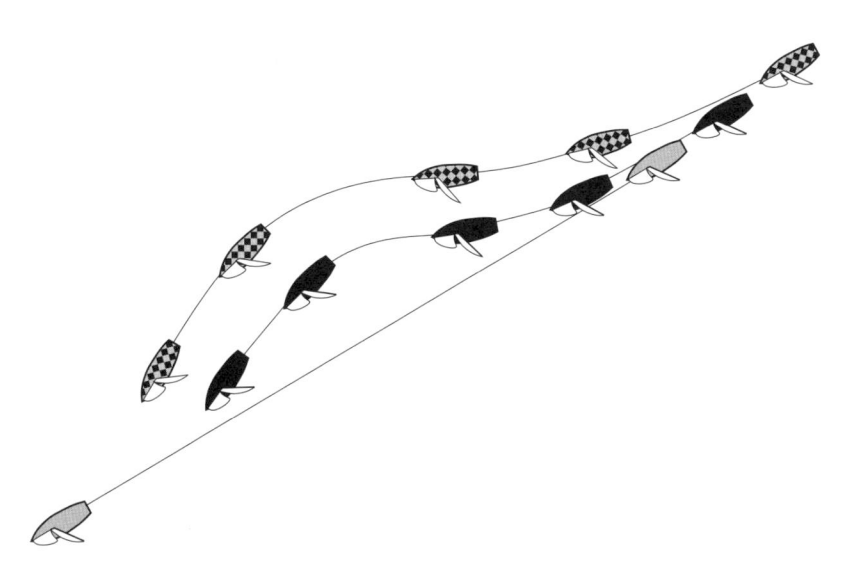

Fig. 16 - To pass another boat, you must first sail faster than them, and then make one decisive move to get by.

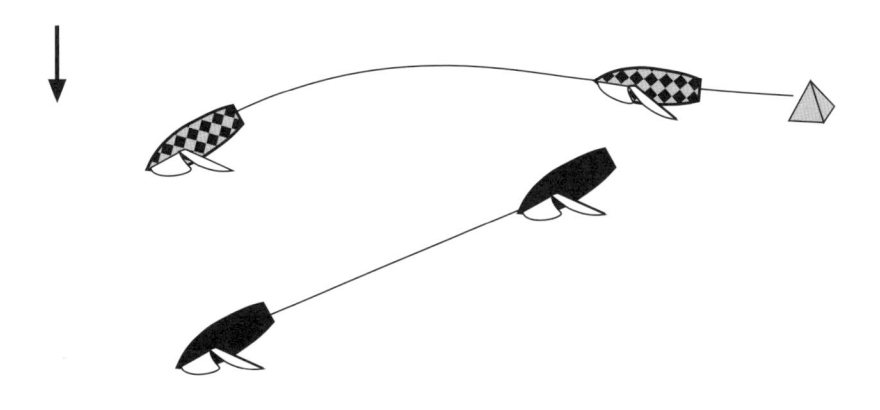

Fig. 17 - Get into the Passing Lane *on close reaches by sailing with a jib briefly before setting your spinnaker.*

Behave. Don't sail high. Catch your rival by sailing faster without sailing higher. Sail right up his transom, or aim at the leeward quarter. This non-threatening approach will save you from sailing extra distance, and it may lull the rival into complacency.

Look for an edge and make your move. Once you are close astern, look for an opportunity to pounce on your opponent's air. You'll need a puff, or a wave to give you a performance edge. Or use the element of surprise when the other crew is not paying attention. *Pounce* when they are passing around drinks, or removing excess clothing, or the guy is cleated, or the main unattended (Fig. 16).

Set, Ready, Go.

You have to pounce. *Ready, Set, Go* takes too long. You must be set to go at any time. Head up quickly. Trim the sheets. Ease the guy. Hike out. Practice your *pounce* so everyone knows the move. You will succeed if your crew pounces effectively, and the other crew fails to respond properly.

The Passing Lane—Does it Exist?

There is a *Passing Lane* on close reaches. On a shy spinnaker reach you can set up in the passing lane at the outset, by jib reaching to a position where boats with spinnakers can't get up to your line. As we discussed in *Chapter 2: Race Preparation* earlier in this book, sailing the course in miniature before the start will help you anticipate how tight the reaching legs will be (Fig. 17).

Not only does the *Passing Lane* exist; the *Get Passed Lane* exists too, and there may be times you want to get into it, as we shall see, below.

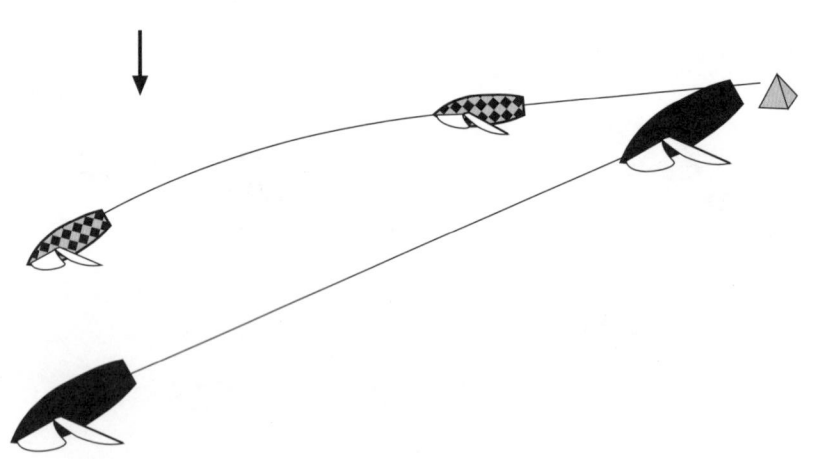

Fig. 18 - In a small boat, sail up to the Get Passed Lane *to encourage larger boats to pass to leeward.*

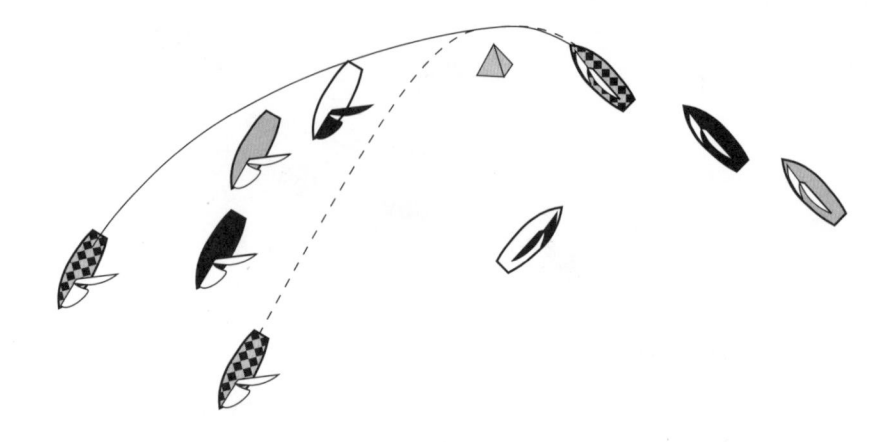

Fig. 19 - Establish a strong windward position to save yourself lots of luffing wars and aggravation.

Defending Your Position

There are several techniques you can use to protect your position and to prevent others from passing you. The correct technique depends on the circumstances. If a group of larger boats is rolling up from behind, it is a waste of time and effort to try to hold them back. When a fleet of larger boats is sailing through you, it is time to get into the *get passed lane*. The *get passed lane* is much the same as the passing lane—a couple of boat lengths to weather of the fleet line. The idea is to encourage the larger boats to sail through you to leeward, where they won't sail over your air (Fig. 18).

When the attacking boats are more like you in performance, then you must choose the appropriate defense.
- Sail fast.
  Sail faster than those behind you and extend your lead! The best defense.
- Establish a windward position (Fig. 19).
  As you start down the leg, immediately establish a position a boat length or two to weather. This can save you many boat lengths and lots of hassling later. It is much more effective than waiting to see if anyone attacks, and then responding. Setting up early sends the message: *Don't even think about going by, at least not on my windward side.*

  On close reaches establish a clear air lane by holding high initially so others can't get up to you. On a broad reach it can also work to establish weather position early, but this can leave you vulnerable, later in the leg, to boats working for an inside position and mark-room.
- Pay attention.
  Assign one crew to keep a lookout aft. If the trailing boat makes a move, respond promptly. An exaggerated response will let the other boat know you are paying attention. Make a swift, sharp turn up, then slide back down

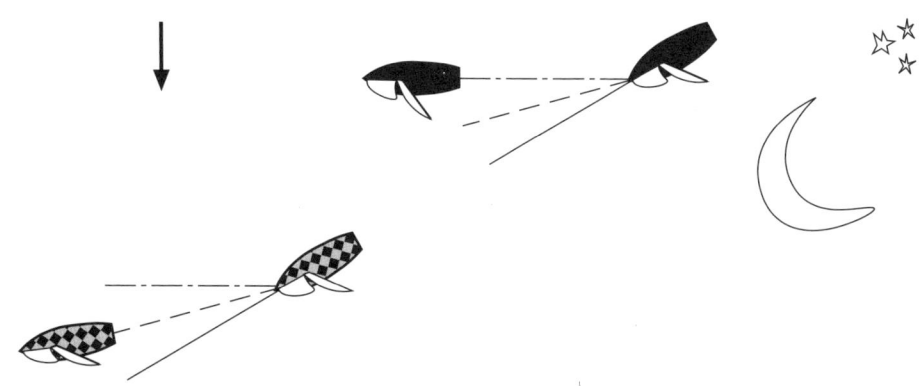

Fig. 20 - Don't over react if your air is not threatened. By heading up half as much as the attacker, you sail less extra distance—and extend your lead.

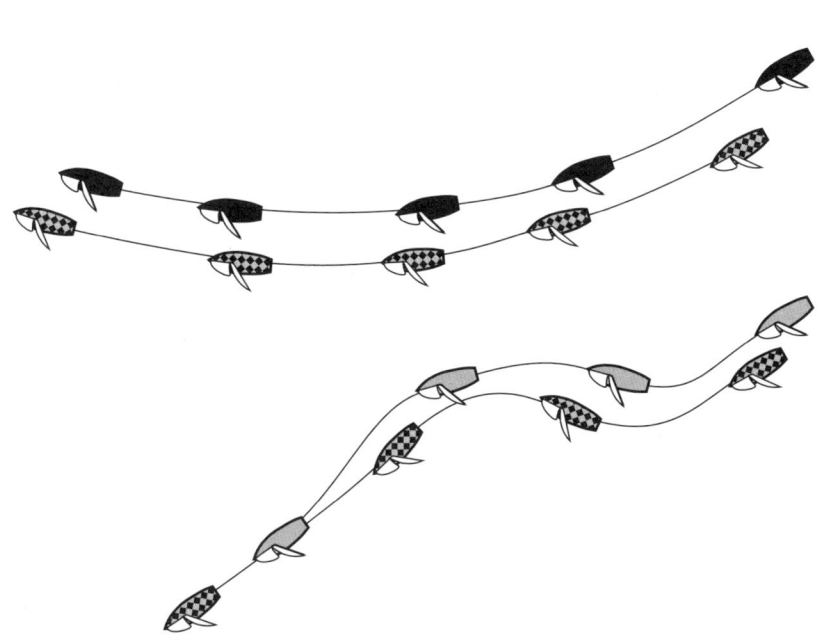

Fig. 21 - Defend with vigor, or let the attacker pass. The worst thing you can do is a halfhearted defense which takes you both "to the moon." Often a quick, preventive luff followed by a smooth return to course will give you a little breathing room.

to as close as you can to course. Holding a high line only lengthens the leg for you.

- Don't overreact (Fig. 20).

  If you have a lead of two boat lengths or more, then your response should be tempered. *The Rule of Halves* works well here—head up half as far as the rival to keep position between him and the mark. By sailing only half as far off course you will sail less distance. Don't forget: The best defense against attack is to extend your lead.

- All or nothing (Fig. 21).

  When under an immediate threat defend vigorously, or not at all. When an opponent makes a move to pass, respond hard and fast, with a vigorous luff and trim. As the attacker responds to your defense, come back down and squirt out to establish a small lead. If you are not prepared for a vigorous defense, you will be better off to let them pass and get on with it. Avoid a halfhearted luffing dual, as you will both *go to the moon*!

- Act First

  If your attacker establishes a small overlap on your weather quarter but has yet to make a full run to get over you, a preemptive luff may catch him off guard. The panicked response will leave him in disarray, and your smooth return to course will give you an edge—both in position and in psyche.

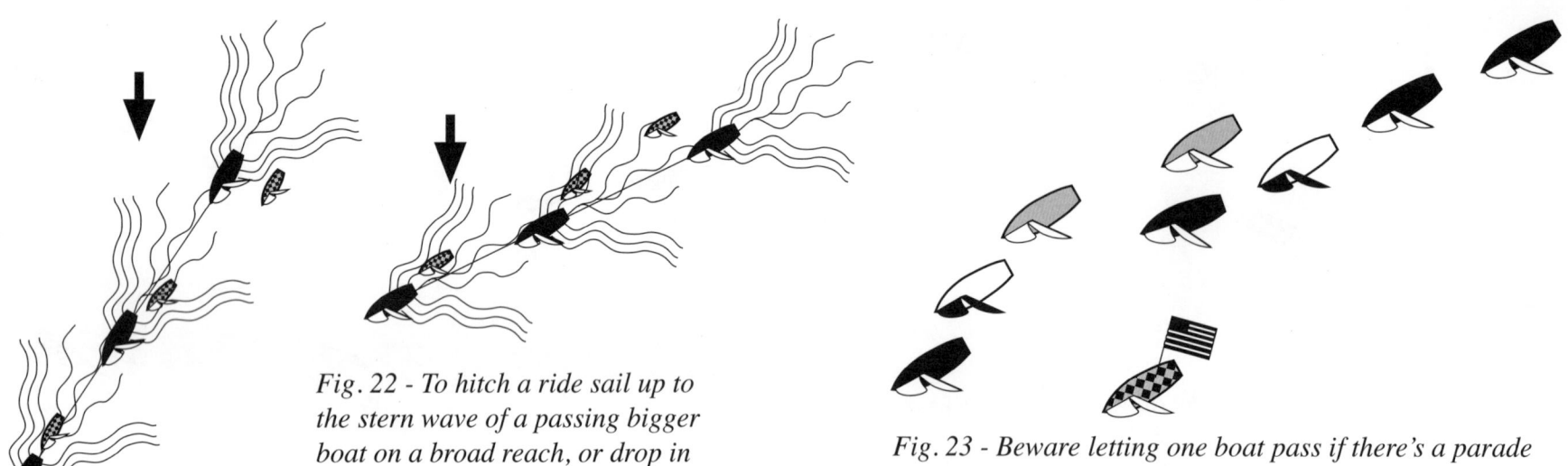

Fig. 22 - To hitch a ride sail up to the stern wave of a passing bigger boat on a broad reach, or drop in from above on a close reach.

Fig. 23 - Beware letting one boat pass if there's a parade lined up behind him.

Sometimes the battle is not worth it. To let the other boat go by either sail high and wave him through to leeward—preferred for you, but he may not take the bait, as he is likely to get stuck there—or wave him by to weather.

When he passes to weather on a broad reach, you can reach up and hitch a ride by drafting on his stern wave. On a close reach force him to pass to leeward, and try to hitch by sliding down onto his stern wave (Fig. 22). Drafting works best when heavy boats are sailing near hull speed. You will see them towing a big wake. Jump aboard! .

The biggest danger in letting one boat slip by is that the next one may be on your air before you recover. Before you know it, feels like the Fourth of July, as the whole parade passes you by. Don't forget to wave the flag! (Fig. 23).

Outside Reaches, Mark Roundings, and Inside Reaches

There are two kinds of reaches—*outside reaches* where the windward side is to the outside of the mark rounding, and *inside reaches* where the windward side is inside. Outside reaches lead to jibes, inside reaches lead to leeward marks. The tactics on the two kinds of reaches differ in some important ways (Fig. 24 a&b).

Outside Reaches

On outside reaches there are split incentives: sail up for clear air or work down for inside position at the rounding. Tactically a trailing boat can lure a leading boat up and then dive inside for room as the leader squares away for the mark. The closer you are to the mark, the more difficult it is to get the leader to take the bait (Fig. 25).

Fig. 24 a

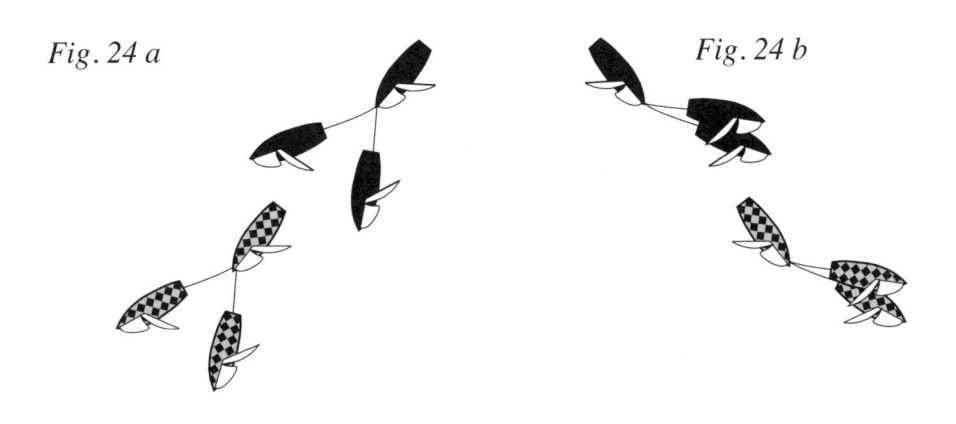

Fig. 24 b

Fig. 24 a&b - On outside reaches clear air is to the outside—you must protect both sides. On inside reaches clear air and mark-room are on same side—which you must double protect.

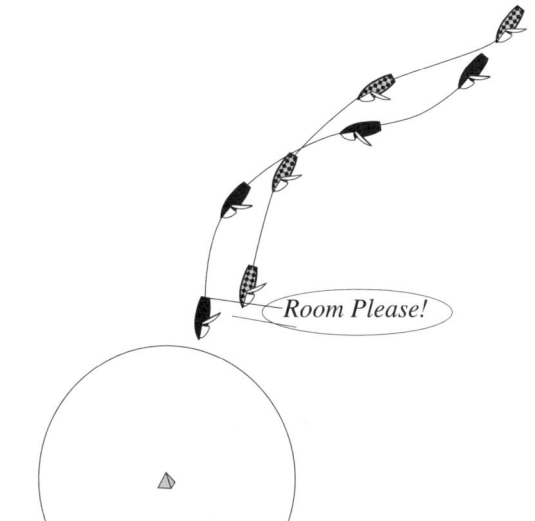

Fig. 25 - On an outside reach the trailing boat can fake an attack, and then dive inside for room.

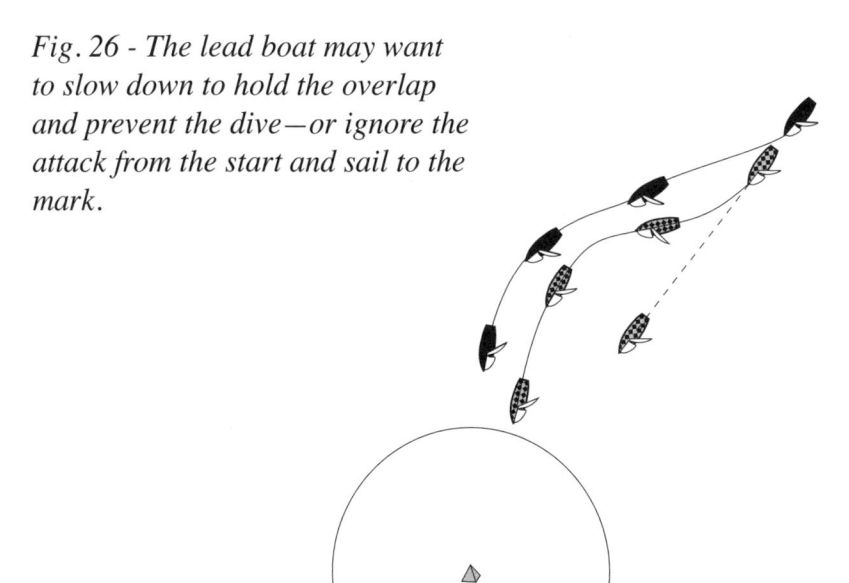

"Room Please!"

As the leader in that position, it is often *best* to hold course—don't get suckered up. There are also times, as the leader, when you may actually want to *slow down* to solidify the attackers overlap on the outside, and prevent him from diving inside as you square away! Obviously any slowing loses you distance to the rest of the fleet, but not as much as you stand to lose if the trailing boat gets mark-room and passes you at the rounding (Fig. 26).

Mark Roundings

Tactics at the jibe depend on your position finishing the inbound leg and your strategy for the outbound leg. Four general routes cover most circumstances.

Most often the preferred route is to come in wide and go out close. *In wide and out close* is preferred because it gives you control and clear air as you start the next leg. To do this you'll need to start your turn early—two or more lengths from

Fig. 26 - The lead boat may want to slow down to hold the overlap and prevent the dive—or ignore the attack from the start and sail to the mark.

Chapter 9: Reaching Strategy and Tactics

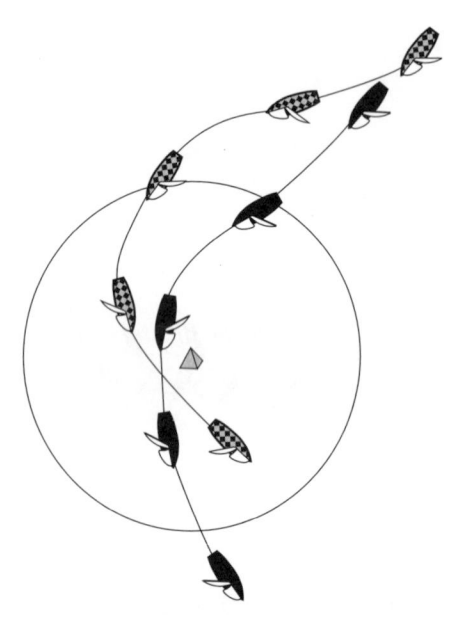

Fig. 27 - In wide/ out close is the preferred route when jibing as it establishes a strong position on the next reach.

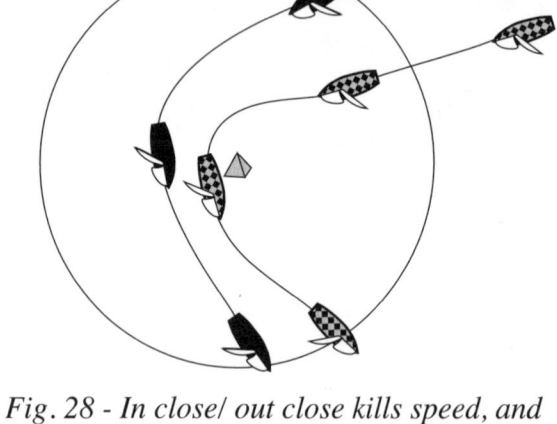

Fig. 28 - In close/ out close kills speed, and is hard on your crew, but it preserves inside position.

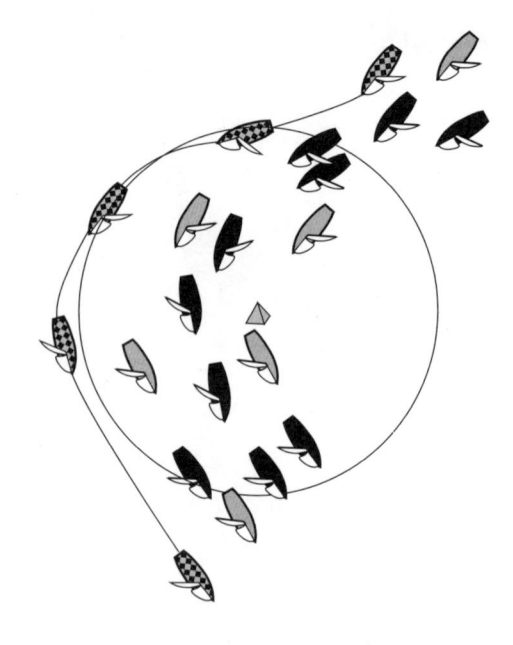

Fig. 29 - An end run can get you around a traffic jam up in light air.

the mark—in order to make a smooth turn and carry speed onto the next leg. Your goal should be to finish your turn, and be on course to the next mark, as you come alongside the jibe mark (Fig. 27).

The reverse—*in close and out wide*—happens when your approach is low. If you are clawing to the mark on a close reach then you may have no choice, and there is little risk. But if your approach is low and your rounding is *close and wide* while others are executing a *wide and close*, they will gain an inside position, limiting your maneuverability and taking your air.

In close, out close is hard on your crew, but sometimes tactically necessary. When you are the inside boat, getting room, outside boats and trailing boats will try to cut inside your transom and roll over you. Don't let 'em. Warn your crew and apologize in advance, then slam the helm to force a tight turn, spinning at the mark. Any room you can get on the approach side will help you come out close on the exit side. With a hard slam, you should be able to round close enough to keep trailing boats from cutting inside (Fig. 28).

An *end run* can be your best tactic when a large fleet converges on the mark in very light winds. These situations announce themselves with a cacophony of voices, slatting sails, and banging hulls. If you find yourself anywhere but on the inside, consider going *way* outside (Fig. 29).

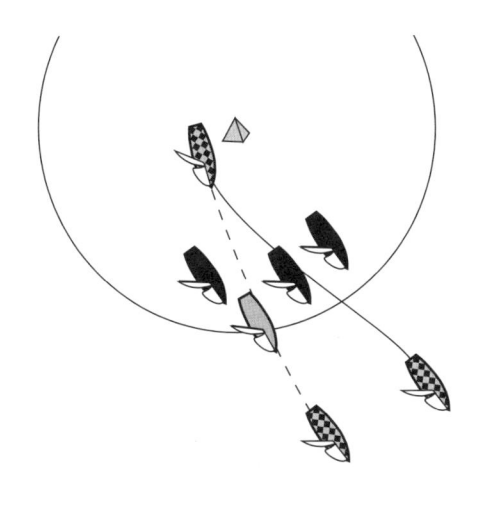

< Fig. 30 - On an inside reach establish a strong inside position to prevent attacks.
> Fig. 31a - Break out from the pack to get to the inside.
> Fig. 31b - On a broad reach, the best tactic may include a strong move to the inside and a jibe back to the mark.
>Fig. 31c - From behind, the low road and an end run can get you back in contention as others battle.

Inside Reaches

Inside reaches push the fleet far above the rhumb line, since the lure of clear air and inside position at the rounding lie on the same side. If you are the lead boat in a group, it pays to establish an inside position immediately. As you clear the jibe mark sail up a length or two before settling down on course. If you don't establish this strong position, others will be tempted to attack. You will driven up further in the end as you work to defend a weak position (Fig. 30).

If you find yourself in the middle of a crowd on an inside reach, it pays to work to the inside early. Inside position and clear air will be decisive factors, particularly as the fleet converges for the rounding (Fig. 31a).

On a broad reach the tendency to sail high can push the fleet over the mark, where it becomes necessary to jibe back. It is a common error to sail too broad at the end of an inside reach in an effort to avoid jibes. For those with the boat handling skills to jibe well there is much to be gained by sailing fast angles, and jibing into the mark (Fig. 31b).

Two other ideas deserve mention:

First, if you are part of a small group, particularly near the lead, talk with your rivals and avoid fights. "Yo, old buddy old pal, let's not us get into a snit. Let's sail fast and straight, and get away from the teaming masses, hot on our …tails." Once your lead group breaks away from the crowd, you can start infighting, but it is definitely worth it to break away first.

Second, if you are well behind, there is an opportunity for an heroic end run. Rather than get suckered up by the crowd, sail low—on or below the rhumb line—while the fleet sails high. Later in the leg, as the fleet squares away to slow reaching angles and they choke on each other's bad air, you can beam reach across the bottom of the leg and pass the crowd. Your chances for success are enhanced by light air and adverse current, and the risks are slight (Fig. 31c). I'm proud to mention that I was crewing in the Etchells North Americans one Autumn when we went from 29th to 8th in one leg with just such a tactic! (Regrettably, space does not allow me to recount how we arrived at the jibe mark 29th.)

Chapter 9: Reaching Strategy and Tactics

Final Thoughts on Reaching Tactics
Mixed Fleet Tactics

In a mixed fleet with a broad range of handicaps, the importance of tactics is diminished. You are racing the clock more than other boats. Boats nearby are obstacles, but they may not be rivals if they rate differently than you. Negotiate peace and sail your boat.

If you are in a small boat near the head of the pack as you turn down the reaches, the *get passed lane* may be the place for you. Also, work for position to hitch a ride and surf a passing boat's stern wave.

As a big boat in the lead, you must get away from the crowd. Any time you waste diddling with other boats will cost you double, as every moment you spend with slower rated boats leaves you less time to build a sufficient time margin. When working to pass a fleet of smaller boats get up and over the crowd, or well below them. Beware the low road. Although you may be able to sail through one or two smaller boats with ease the cumulative wind shadow of a gaggle of them can prevent you from getting through.

If your boat performs poorly on reaches, you should work to clog things up for the fast reaching boats. Once you round the windward mark in good position you can hold off the fast boats two ways: One is to establish a position to weather, as described earlier (See Fig. 19). The other is to set up low, and luff. This can have a cumulative effect. As you luff one boat he will push up the next boat and so on. You can clog up the entire fleet this way.

Fig. 32 - Strategically, reaches turn into runs when the reaching angle is broader than the correct sailing angle for the given wind speed.

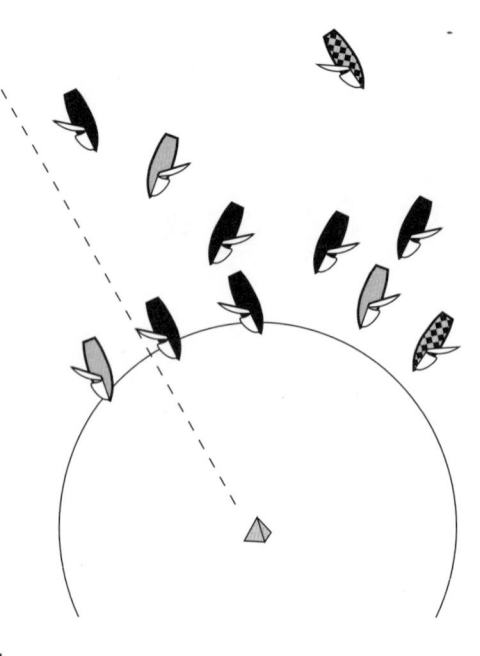

Heavy Air Tactics

While most of the forgoing tactics apply in all wind conditions, there are some special opportunities in heavy air. Light to moderate winds result in similar sailing speeds for similar boats, but speed differences can be pronounced in heavy air. As the breeze comes on, shift your focus from tactics to performance. Get clear and sail fast—the best tactic of all.

Reaching or Running?

Very broad reaches should often be treated as runs. If the angle is broader than the proper sailing angle then strategically the leg is not a reach, but a skewed run. Even if the leg doesn't initially warrant running tactics, you may need to change modes if you find yourself well above the rhumb line (Fig. 32).

For more on *Running Strategy and Tactics*, look no further than the next chapter.

Chapter 10: Running Strategy and Tactics

10.1 Introduction
10.2 Downwind Performance
10.3 Running Strategy
10.4 Running Tactics
10.5 Jib and Main Racing
10.6 Conclusion
10.7 Quiz Questions and Skill Building

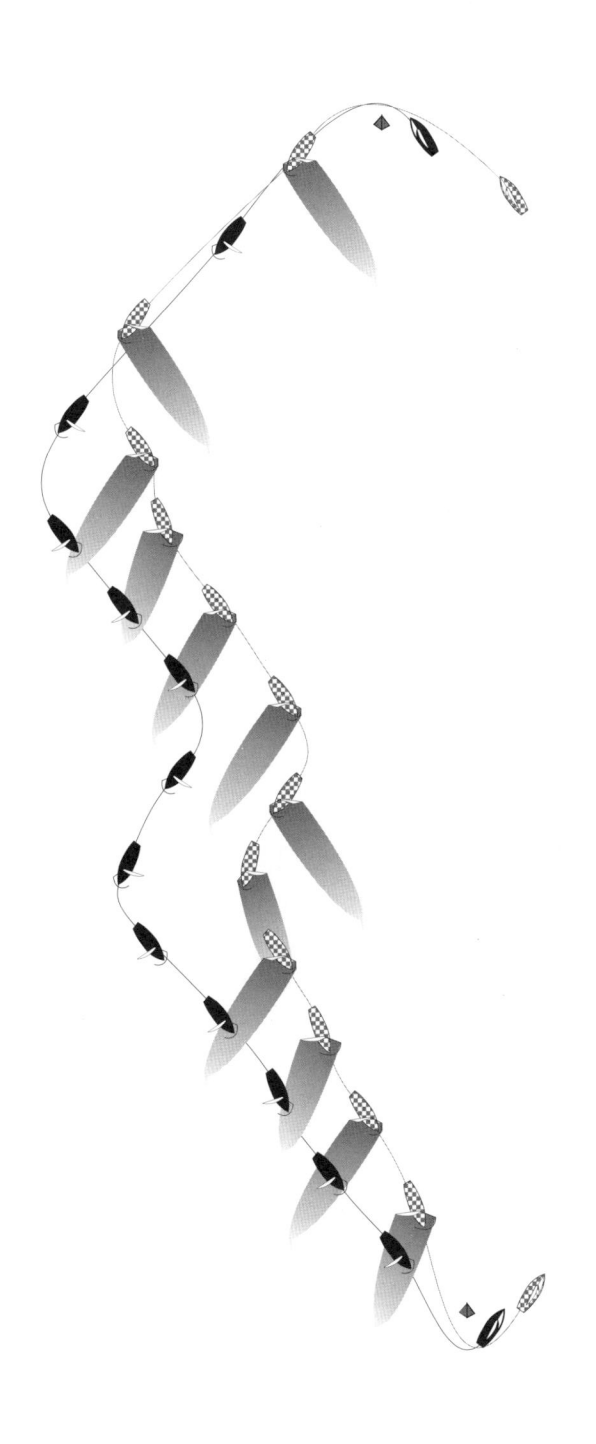

Chapter 10: Running Strategy and Tactics

Fig. 1 – Runs offer trailing boats the chance to attack. They are the only legs where the fleet tends to compress rather than stretch out.

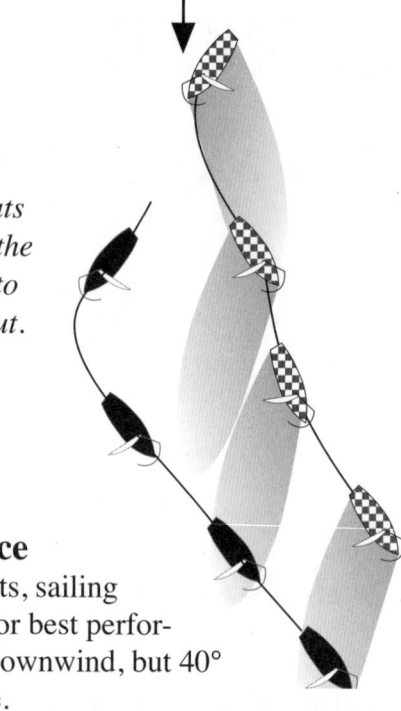

10.1 Introduction

More and more races are being sailed on windward-leeward courses, and with good reason. Tactically, running legs are much more interesting than reaching legs. Running legs offer trailing boats a real chance to attack; runs are the only legs where fleets tend to compress. By comparison, reaches often turn into parades, with the fleet stretching out (Fig. 1).

Running strategy and tactics bears little resemblance to reaching. In fact, much of running is like upwind strategy and tactics turned on its head, with several interesting variations and exceptions.

Performance and Strategy

Before we look at running strategy, we must first understand a little about running performance. We will introduce these performance concepts here in order to establish parameters for our strategy. *Performance Racing Trim* offers a much more detailed discussion of these performance issues.

Downwind performance can be divided in three segments based on wind strength: Light air, for winds from 3 to 10 knots; moderate air for winds from 10 to 14 knots; and heavy air for winds over 14 knots (Fig. 2). Boat performance changes from one segment to the next, and our strategy options change as performance changes.

Light Air Performance

In winds from 3 to 10 knots, sailing angles are very wide. That is, for best performance we do not sail directly downwind, but 40° above a dead downwind course.

Boat speed changes dramatically as the wind fluctuates between 3 and 10 knots, but the correct sailing angle changes hardly at all. In these conditions, we will jibing through about 80°—which is only slightly narrower than our tacking angles upwind (Fig. 2a).

In these light air conditions the *off in the puffs, up in the lulls* adage we advocated for reaching does not apply. Our sailing angle remains steady through puffs and lulls in light air running.

Moderate Air Performance

In moderate winds sailing angle, not boat speed, is the dynamic variable. The correct sailing angle changes dramatically—by about 5° for every knot of wind speed—from 145° in

Fig. 2 – Downwind Performance can be divided into three sectors: Light air—up to 10 knots, moderate air—10 to 14 knots, and heavy air—15 knots and above.
a – In light air, optimum performance is achieved at a high (and consistent) reaching angle about 40° above dead downwind.
b – In moderate air, the optimum angle changes dramatically with the wind speed.
c – In heavy air, we can sail straight to the mark.

10 knots of wind to 165° in 14 knots of wind. Boat speeds do increase slightly, but it is the ability to carry speed at lower and lower angles which characterizes the moderate wind segment of the performance spectrum (Fig. 2b).

Off in the puffs, up in the lulls is very much a part of moderate air running.

Heavy Air Performance

In winds of 15 knots or greater, we can sail almost directly downwind—or straight to the mark. The preferred sailing angle is influenced by waves along with strategic and tactical considerations (Fig. 2c).

10.2 Downwind Performance

With this understanding of downwind performance, we can now look at downwind strategy and tactics. Obviously, these performance parameters will dictate changes in strategy for each segment of the performance spectrum.

Two additional comments: These wind speeds and angles are fairly consistent for keelboats (sailing with spinnakers). For more details, see *North U Racing Trim*. Also, for wind speeds under 3 knots, best performance is a mystery. I suggest you keep your head down, use a smooth back swing, and follow through toward the green. Good luck!

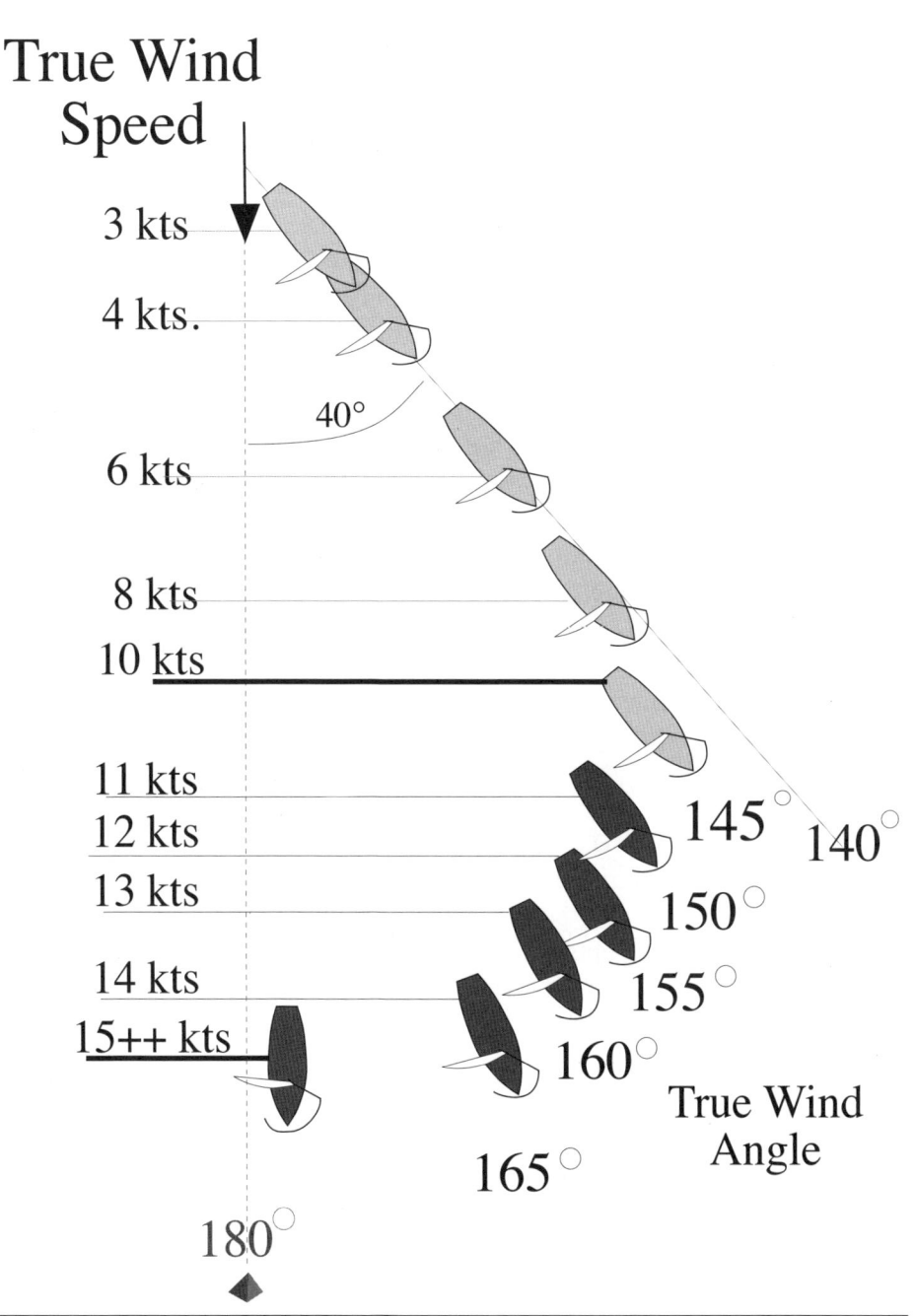

10.3 Running Strategy

As always, strategic variables are wind, wind shifts, and current. If we look at the performance cones for each sector of downwind sailing, we can see that in light air the cone is as wide as the upwind cone. For moderate and heavy air sailing, the cones are narrower. The reality is that most (too much) of our racing is done in winds of 10 knots or less. In these conditions our strategic choices are wide. The narrower performance cones of stronger winds narrow our strategic field.

As with upwind sailing, we are looking for better wind, and more favorable or less adverse current. We are also trying to take advantage of wind shifts. Downwind wind shifts are a major factor, as with upwind, but also differ from upwind in some interesting ways, as we shall see.

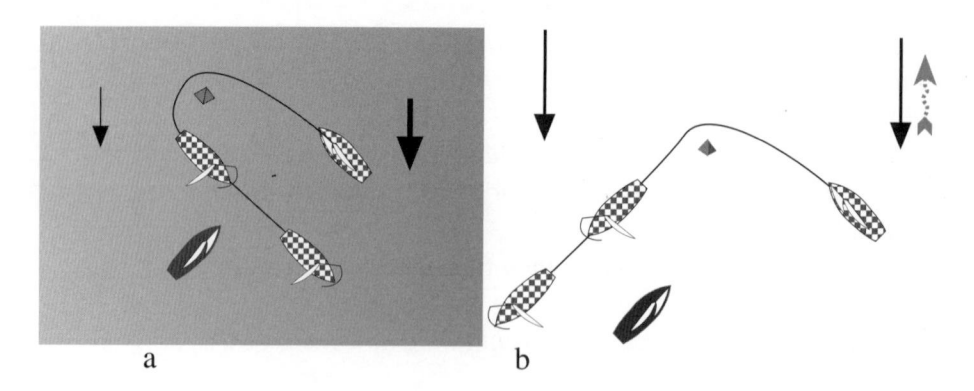

Fig. 3a,b – If the advantage upwind was due to wind, then the same side will be favored downwind. If the advantage upwind was current driven, then the opposite side will be favored downwind.

Find more wind!
Favored Side

Downwind differences in wind strength have a more pronounced impact on performance than they do upwind. It always pays to find more wind. If there was a favored side upwind due to stronger winds, then sail to the *same side* downwind (Fig. 3a). An advantage upwind due to current will be realized on the *opposite* side downwind (Fig. 3b). Note: the right and left sides of the course are named looking upwind. The right side upwind and the right side downwind are the same water.

Light Air Strategy

With a wide cone, but a narrow choice of sailing angles, light air running most closely resembles upwind strategy. Your goals should be to find more wind, advantageous current, and to play the wind shifts. Keep clear air by looking ahead and behind for open lanes (Fig. 4a).

Moderate Air

As the wind fluctuates in the moderate range, you need room to roam up and down to maintain optimum performance (Fig. 4b). Position yourself in front of the puffs, and with room to work them to advantage. Since jibes (or, I should say, *good jibes*) cost very little distance in moderate conditions, it pays to jibe in search of better wind and open space.

Heavy Air

Whereas in moderate air you must work up and down as the wind fluctuates, in heavy air there is a choice of wind angles (Fig. 4c). You can sail a little higher and a little faster or a little lower and a little slower, with little change in downwind performance (VMG). The correct choice depends on strategic issues of wind, shifts, and current; tactical concerns involving traffic, clear air, and mark rounding position; and performance considerations like surfing and control.

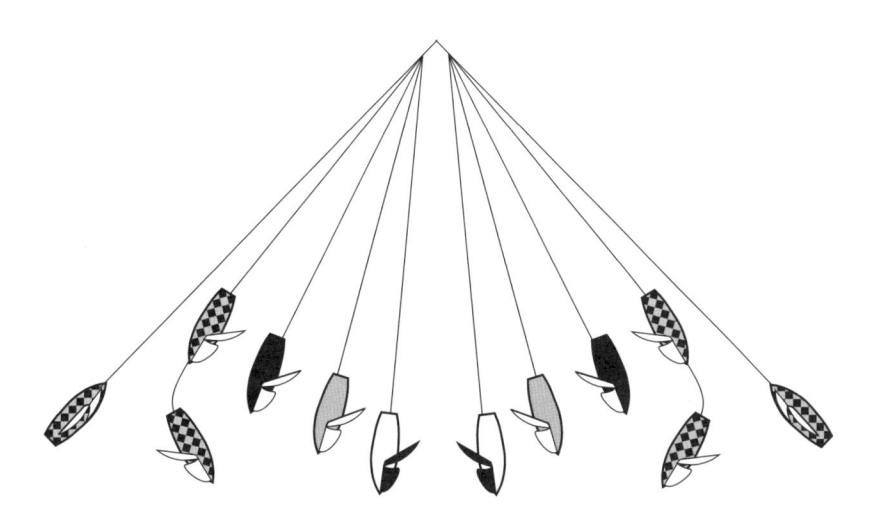

Fig. 4a,b,c – In light air we sail a wide cone – nearly as wide as the upwind cone. In moderate winds the cone narrows as the wind increases. In heavy air we sail nealry dead down wind and the playing field is narrow.

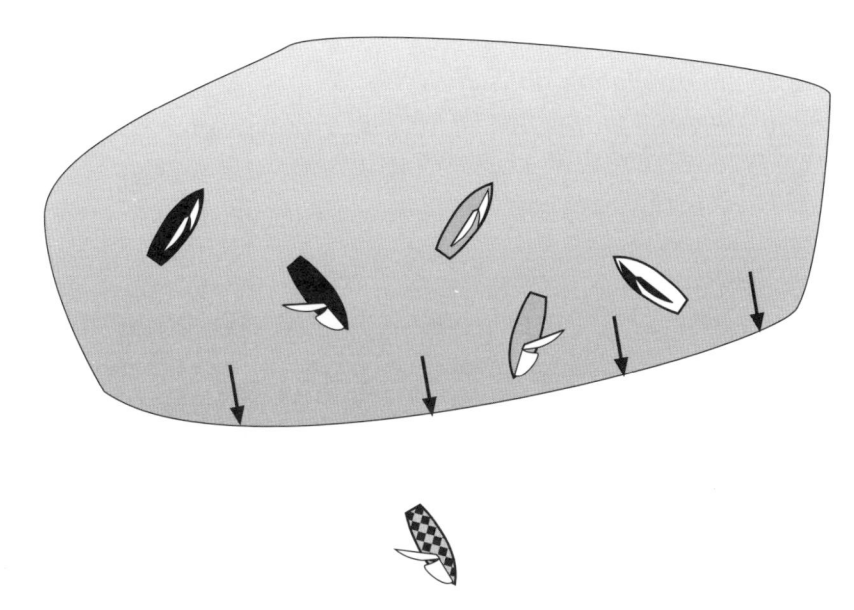

Fig. 5 – In puffy conditions look back to find more wind. Look at the water and observe other boats.

Puffs and Lulls

In puffy conditions, look back to find the puffs and position yourself downwind of them (Fig. 5). You can see them as darker patches moving across the water, and as they influence the performance of boats behind you. Pay attention to close-hauled boats as well as those on the run. Puffs are easier to read on beating boats than running boats. The proper response to a puff depends on which segment of the performance curve you are in. Remember, *off in the puffs* is wrong in light air.

Puffs and lulls are often accompanied by wind shifts. For example, puffs come with shifts from the right and lulls come with shifts from the left. It is critical to get in phase with the shifts as well as playing the puffs. We'll cover wind shifts in more detail below.

In a dying breeze, work for a position which will keep you in clear air and clear of crowds. Pay careful attention to performance, and be sure to sail fast angles as the wind gets light. In a building breeze, focus on getting to the new wind first; then match your performance to the conditions. Great boat speed is always a powerful tactic.

Fig. 6 – In oscillating shifts jibe on the lifts and sail the headed tack— the inverse of upwind strategy, where we tack on the headers to sail lifted.

Wind Shifts

Wind shifts don't stop when you round the windward mark. You need to make the most of wind shifts downwind, just as you do upwind. The trouble is that downwind shifts are trickier than upwind shifts, for a number of reasons. The upside is that if you can figure them out, it will give you a big strategic advantage.

The Main Idea

Wind shift strategy downwind is like upwind shift strategy stood on its head. Instead of sailing the lifted tack, as you do upwind, the objective is to sail on the headed tack—allowing you to sail more of a reach, rather than a run, to the leeward mark. In oscillating winds this means jibing on the lifts downwind, the reverse of tacking on the headers upwind. In persistent shifts this means sailing away from the shift in order to jibe onto the headed tack later in the leg—the inverse of sailing into the shift and tacking onto the lifted tack upwind.

So far so good, but there is more. For starters let's take a closer look at downwind strategy in oscillating and persistent shift conditions.

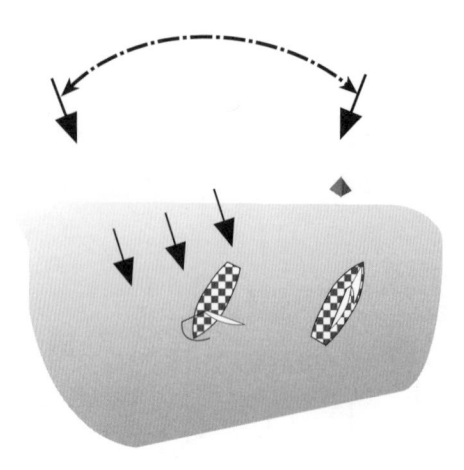

Fig. 7 – To get in phase, note the lifted tack upwind. Assume the opposite tack as you start down the run.

Oscillating Shifts

Oscillating winds are winds which are shifting back and forth, oscillating like a pendulum. In oscillating conditions your goal is to sail the headed tack downwind. Once you are on the headed tack, watch for a lift. When you are lifted, jibe to sail headed on the new tack. When you are lifted, jibe again (Fig. 6).

The first step is to get in phase as you round from the windward leg. The best way to do this is to note the headed tack as you approach the windward mark, and then get onto this headed tack at the first opportunity downwind (Fig 7).

Even when you start the leg in phase with the shifts, it is easy to get out of phase or lose track—wind shifts are difficult to detect when you are sailing downwind. If all else fails, sail the jibe which carries you closest to the mark.

Later we'll discuss techniques for detecting shifts—it can be tricky.

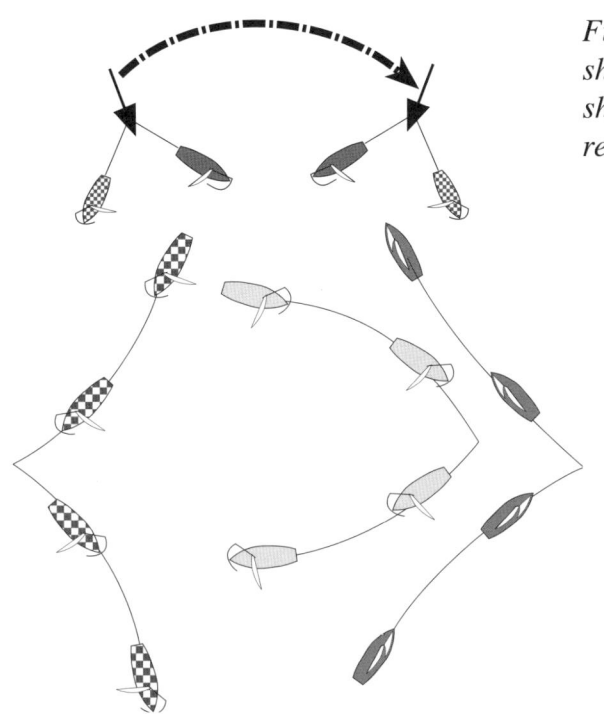

*Fig. 8 – In a persistent shift, **sail away** from the shift to get a favorable reaching angle.*

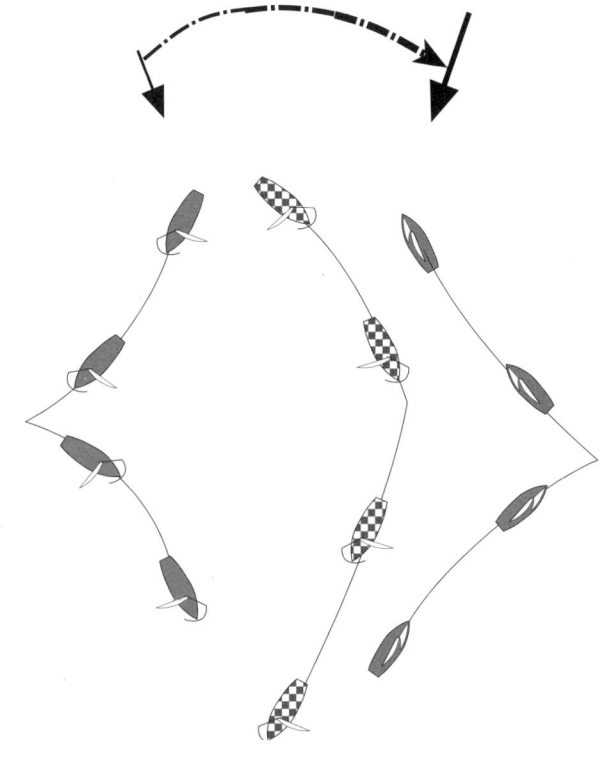

*Fig. 9 – In a building and shifting wind, ignore the shift strategy above. Sail toward the shift – **Get More Wind!***

Persistent Shifts

A persistent shift is a gradual shift in one direction, either veering consistently clockwise, or backing counterclockwise. In persistent shifts sail away from the shift downwind rather than sailing into the shift as you do upwind. By sailing away from the shift you can jibe to a closer reaching angle. Sailing toward the shift would leave you in a position more upwind of the mark, requiring a broader sailing angle to the mark (Fig. 8).

>>ALERT ALERT<< *Major Exception*: This persistent shift strategy fails in a building and shifting wind. In that case it is best to sail to the new wind—wind strength is a more important factor than wind shifts (Fig 9).

Fewer Shifts, Harder to Find

There are a couple of things which make wind shifts more difficult downwind than upwind. One is that they are more difficult to detect. There are several techniques for detecting the shifts, which we discuss more below – I promise.

The second difficulty is that there are *fewer shifts downwind than upwind*.

Whoa! Fewer wind shifts downwind than upwind! We sail upwind, and turn and sail the other way, and the windshifts turn off? How can that be? Turn the page, and find out...

Fewer Shifts Downwind!

Imagine, first of all, a Race Committee at anchor in a 10 knot wind. As they set a course, they record the wind speed and wind direction and find oscillating wind shifts every six minutes. With a wind speed of ten knots, a six-minute interval places the shifts one mile apart.

You (a very astute tactician) detect a shift three minutes before the start. How soon after the start will you hit the first shift? Three minutes, right? *Wrong!*

You would expect the next shift *at the start area* three minutes after the start. You (with any luck) will no longer be in the start area – you will be racing upwind, and meet the shift part way. Sailing at about six knots of boat speed* your upwind speed (Velocity Made Good, VMG) is about four knots. You are sailing toward the wind shifts and the closing speed is fourteen knots (10 knots of wind speed *plus* 4 knots VMG). The frequency of shifts for boats racing upwind increases to a shift every 4 minutes, 18 seconds.

As you turn downwind, you sail away from the shifts. Instead of *meeting them half way* as you were upwind, you are now *running away* from the shifts. With a VMG downwind of about four knots, the closing speed of the shifts is reduced to six knots. (10 knots of wind speed *less* 4 knots VMG.) Downwind, you experience shifts once every 10 minutes, or less than half the frequency of the shifts experienced upwind (Fig. 10a, c).

The ratio of wind shifts experienced upwind and downwind changes with the wind speed and boat performance – but not very much. In lighter air or with faster boats the differences are exaggerated to the point where the fleet experiences

*The boat speeds and VMG's used here are approximations for a 30-35 foot boat. Yours may vary.

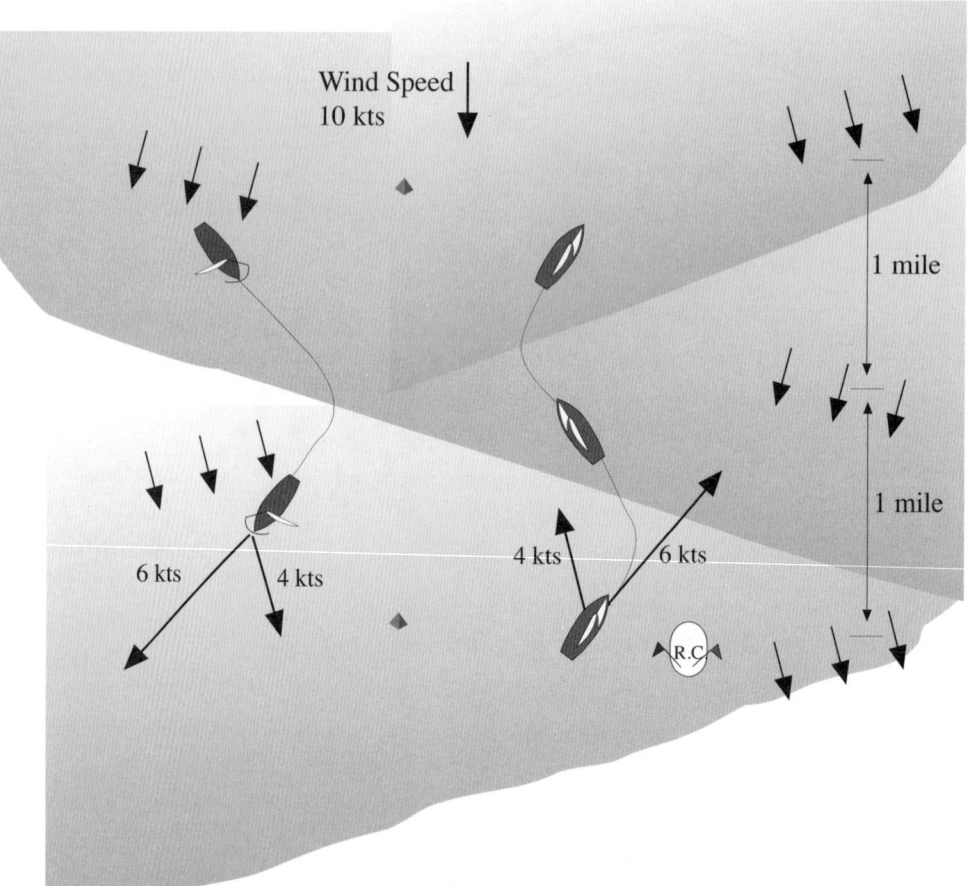

Fig. 10a – In a 10-knot wind with shifts spaced 1 mile apart, the Race Committee, at anchor, experiences a shift every 6 minutes. Boats racing upwind experience shifts every 4 min 17 sec, while boats sailing downwind only experience a shift once every 10 minutes! You will experience more than twice as many shifts upwind as downwind.

Fig. 10b – In fact, there will be times when you experience oscillating shifts upwind and one persistent shift on the downwind leg.

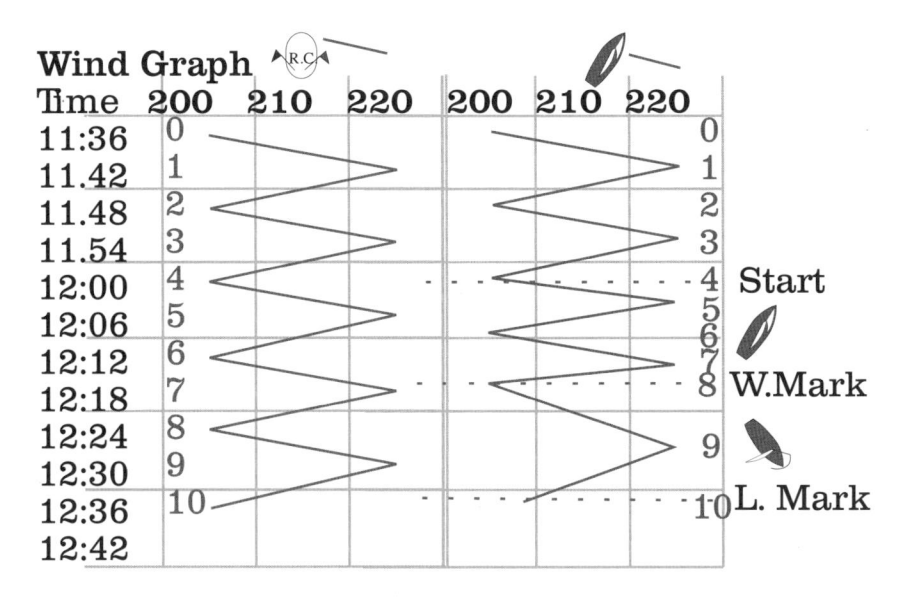

```
Wind Graph   R.C
Time  200 210 220   200 210 220
11:36  0                         0
11:42  1                         1
11:48  2                         2
11:54  3                         3
12:00  4                         4  Start
12:06  5                         5
12:12  6                         6
12:18  7                         8  W.Mark
12:24  8                         9
12:30  9
12:36 10                        10  L. Mark
12:42
```

Fig. 10c – The Wind Graphs for the Race Committee and a boat in the race show the apparent compression and elongation of the wind shift frequency as the boat races upwind and down.

only one-third as many shifts downwind as upwind. In heavier winds the ratio remains about two-to-one.

Only when the wind is *very* strong does the frequency of shifts upwind and downwind converge significantly. By then you can stop looking for shifts downwind—just hang on, hoot and holler.

There are a couple of interesting consequences to the reduced frequency of wind shifts downwind. One is the challenge of finding these infrequent shifts (which we *will* get to, momentarily, I promise). The second consequence is that oscillating shifts upwind may become persistent shifts downwind, at least for the duration of the leg.

Oscillating vs. Persistent

There will be times when you will have oscillating shifts upwind and persistent shifts downwind. By persistent shifts, we mean that there is only one shift for the duration of the leg—consequently your strategy is persistent shift strategy. This can occur any time the downwind shift frequency is more than half the sailing time of the leg, which means upwind you would experience three or four shifts (Fig. 10b).

The main point remains to sail away from the shift, and then jibe to sail headed, regardless of the frequency of shifts. Just be aware that there may not be very many shifts to hunt. One further insight: Don't be deceived by the change to persistent shifts downwind. When you turn upwind, the oscillations will return.

Find the Shifts

As we said above, one of the tricks to downwind strategy is detecting wind shifts. One way to take the mystery out of downwind shifts is properly calibrated true wind instruments. With integrated instruments, the shifts are much easier to find. It is almost like cheating. Careful calibration is a must. Otherwise it is "garbage in, garbage out."

Here's how to find the shift if you are sailing without integrated instruments. (And of course, even if you have high-tech instruments, you should use them as adjuncts to methods we'll describe, not in lieu of them.) First, after rounding the windward mark settle onto the correct tack—the headed tack you noted at the end of the beat, and the proper performance angle and speed—as described in *Downwind Performance* above, and in *North U. Racing Trim*. Once you settle, note your wind angle, boat speed, and compass course. To find the shifts, you must look for changes in this base line performance.

*Lull:
Apparent wind lighter and forward*

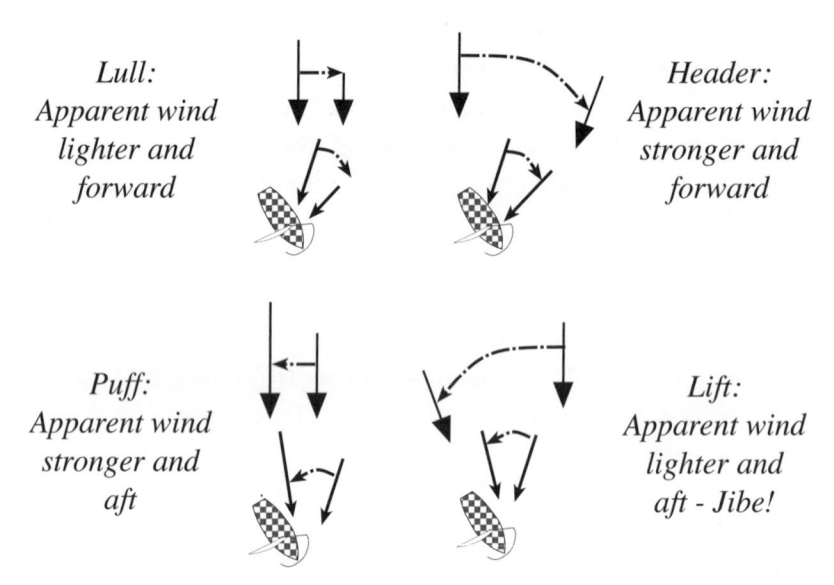

*Header:
Apparent wind stronger and forward*

*Puff:
Apparent wind stronger and aft*

*Lift:
Apparent wind lighter and aft - Jibe!*

Fig. 11 – Shifts, puffs, and lulls will change your apparent wind speed and apparent wind angle.

Fig. 12 – To find the shifts look back at other boats, and watch for the wind on the water.

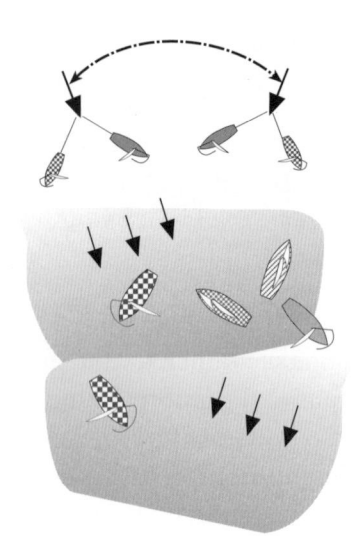

If the apparent wind speed drops, you are either in a lift or a lull (or a wind shadow or you have changed course). In a lull the apparent wind angle will initially shift forward. Your boat speed will drop. If you head up to try to accelerate you will have to re-trim to the new wind. (This is not the correct response to a lull in light air, but is correct in moderate winds.)

In a lift, the apparent wind will shift aft. You can hold your course and bring the pole back—your speed will drop, or head up to keep the original boat speed and apparent wind—at a higher compass course. The correct response is neither of those—the correct response is a jibe!

The spinnaker trimmer and helmsman must pay close attention to find the lifts. It is more difficult than detecting headers upwind, which you can read in the jib and compass, and where you can easily feel the lulls and puffs. Downwind the apparent wind angle and apparent wind speed are much more volatile. Careful study is needed to tell if a change in apparent wind is due to a change in the true wind speed, true wind direction, or in sailing angle. The spinnaker trimmer must feel changes in the tug on the sheet and in spinnaker trim, and the helmsman must feel the helm and note the course, speed, and pole angle in order to differentiate lulls from lifts (Fig. 11).

Another important tool in finding the shifts is observing other boats. When you feel a change on your boat, see if it shows on other boats. It is particularly valuable to compare your performance to the performance of boats on the opposite jibe. If performance on all the nearby boats is suffering, then you are in a lull. If boats on the opposite jibe seem to be sailing lower angles while carrying speed, that would suggest you have been lifted and ought to jibe. Also, watch performance of boats which are sailing upwind; they are still doing shift the

Fig. 13 – The impact of wind shifts downwind is huge. With a six-knot boat speed, and a 10° shift from a course 40° above dead downwind, the checkered boat will sail 90 seconds per mile faster than the white boat which ignores the shifts, and 4 minutes faster than the grey boat which gets it all wrong. Note: If boat speeds are slower, times will be greater!

easy way. If the close hauled boats in your wind neighborhood are on one tack, then try the opposite tack. In addition, be cognizant of the shift pattern you noted upwind—are the puffs all starboard tack lifts?

Finally, don't forget to look at the water. You can see puffs on the water surface. If your course changes with no discernible change in true wind speed, you are in a shift (Fig 12).

The Impact of Shifts

In winds up to 10 knots, the impact of shifts downwind is enormous, comparable to the impact of shifts upwind. In a 10° shift, the headed boat will gain 22% versus a boat which is sailing lifted. A boat working the shifts will gain 10% versus a boat which ignores the shifts. That adds up to 90 seconds per mile for boat speeds of 6 knots (Fig. 13). At slower speeds, in lighter winds, the time difference is even greater!

In moderate winds, the impact is somewhat diminished, though still huge. In heavy air, there is little room to play the shifts since the fastest course is straight to the mark.

For a boat sailing at six knots, the numbers work out like this on a per mile basis:

Boat	Course	< to Rh	VMG	1 mile time
Black	Lifted 10°	50°	3.858	15 min 33 sec
White	No Shifts	40°	4.596	13 min 3 sec
Check	Headed 10°	30°	5.196	11 min 33 sec

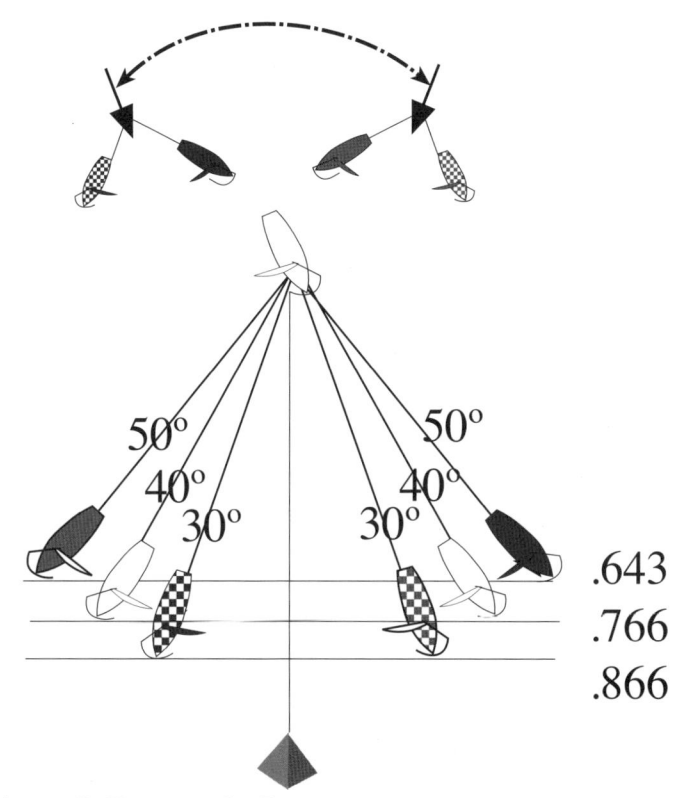

.643
.766
.866

Attack Downwind

More and more race committees are running windward leeward courses instead of conventional triangles. Part of the reason is the additional tactical challenge of running legs. To succeed, you need to use the same aggressive approach to wind shifts downwind that you use upwind. You stand to gain or lose hundreds of yards in the shifts downwind, just as upwind.

Because it is harder to do downwind, the differences across the fleet can be even greater than on a beat. Don't miss the opportunity. Get in phase by paying attention to conditions at the end of the windward leg, search for the rare and elusive shifts downwind, and jibe on the lifts!

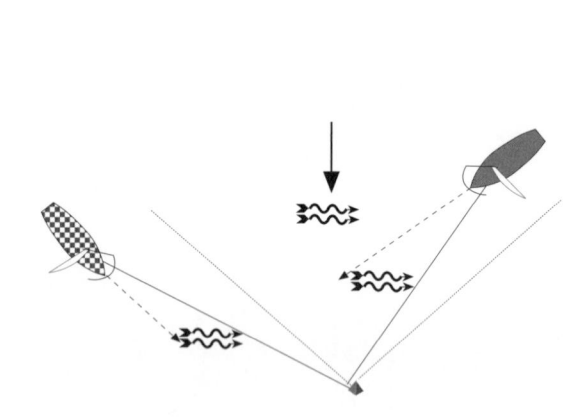

Fig. 14 – When the current is pushing across the course, it shifts the laylines. Use a COG bearing to call the layline.

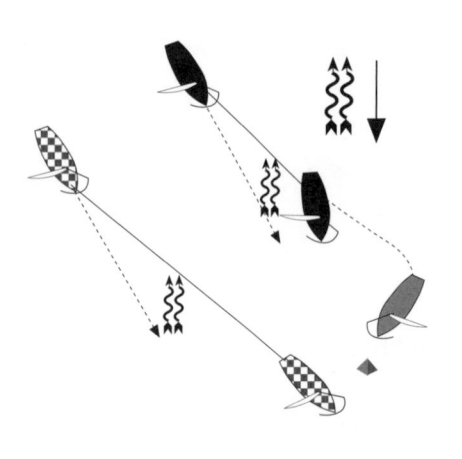

Fig. 15 – When the current is against you, it is easy to jibe too early and miss the layline. If necessary, jibe again rather than force a low angle against the current.

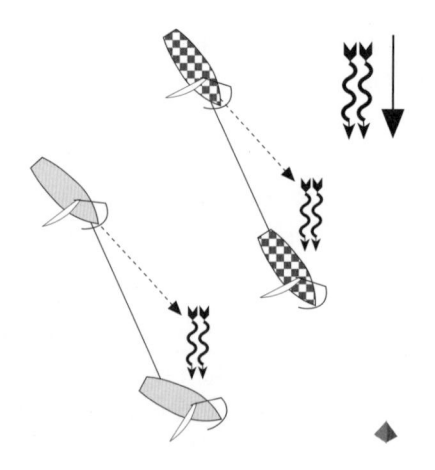

Fig. 16 – When the current is behind you, you can jibe early and let the current sweep you down to the mark.

Current

Favored Side

Strong current can become the singular strategic concern. If there was a favored side to the course on the beat, and the advantage was current driven, then sail the *opposite side* on the run. (See fig. 3b., earlier)

Uniform Current

If the current is uniform over the length of the leg, then it will skew the course and shorten or lengthen the sailing time on the leg. When the current is running across the course determine the Course Over the Ground—COG (or Course Made Good—CMG) by sailing past a buoy at the proper wind angle and taking a back bearing. Use this information to determine laylines to the leeward mark. Depending on whether you approach the mark from the up current or down current side, it is easy to over- or under- stand the mark (Fig. 14).

When the current is against you, the biggest impact is on the approach to the leeward mark. Boats will jibe onto what appears to be a proper angle, only to have the current push them up and force them to sail a lower, and slower angle in order to avoid more jibes. As they slow down, the impact of the current is greater, and the problem is compounded. Avoid this error by determining your COG and then use that bearing to call your layline (Fig. 15). Furthermore, if you find you have not compensated sufficiently jibe again. (Your crew can handle it—you've practiced.)

Current from astern shortens the leg. The danger here is overstanding the leeward mark. You need to establish your COG to call the layline. When in doubt, jibe early and let the current carry you down. You can get away with cheating the

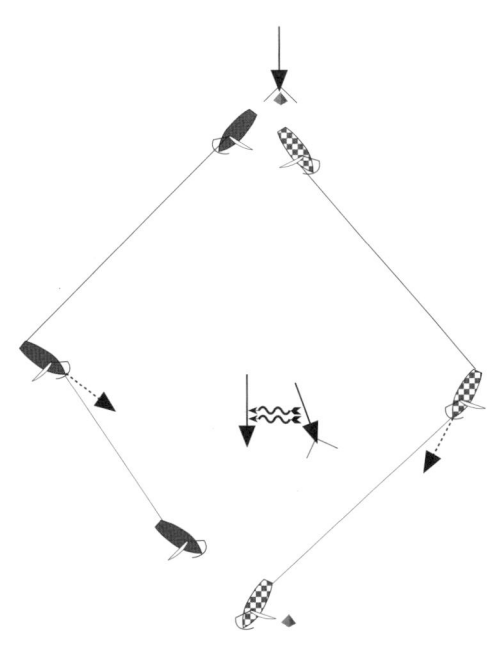

Fig. 17 – If you know the current will be stronger later in the leg, set up on the up current side of the course while the current is weak so you will have the current on your stern when it is strongest..

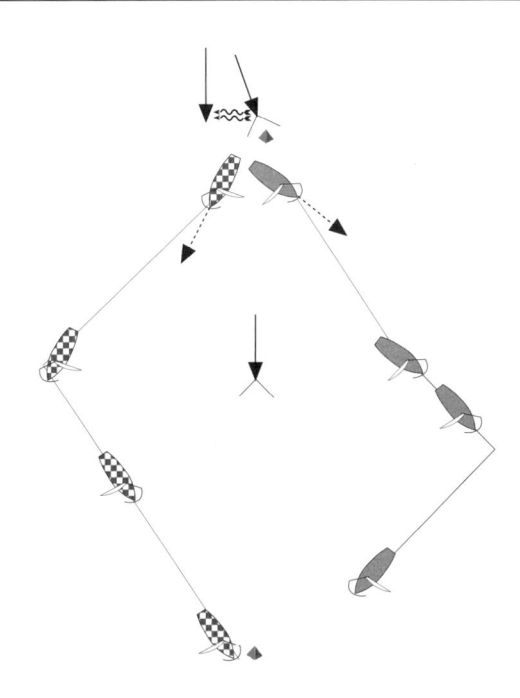

Fig. 18 – When the current is stronger early in the leg don't fight it. Sail the jibe which is headed by the current to get out of it most quickly.

layline here, unlike when you are against the current. Also, warn your crew. The mark will sneak up on you before you expect it. Get the jib ready early (Fig. 16).

Non-Uniform Current

When the current is crossing the course and it is stronger in the beginning or end of the leg, your current strategy is to minimize the distance sailed through the water. As you might have guessed, you should seek a position where you can let the current help you when it is strongest.

If the current will be stronger later in the leg, then position yourself up current while the current is weak and let the current sweep you down to the mark. In doing this you will get the added benefit of a sailing wind header during the current portion of the leg. If you sail to the down current side initially, then you will end up fighting the current later on. Your troubles would be compounded by a less favorable wind angle as well (Fig. 17).

If the current is stronger early, don't fight it. Let it sweep you down and correct for it later. Sail the jibe which is headed by the current until you run out of current, and sail the other jibe later (Fig. 18).

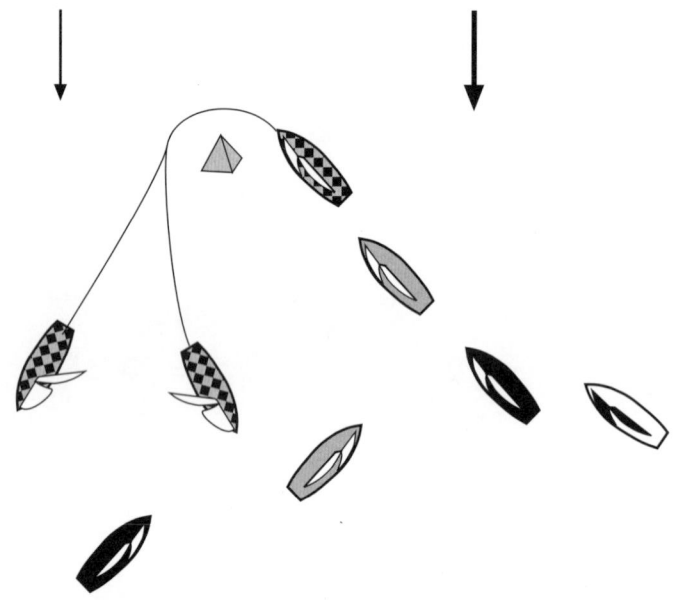

< Fig. 19 – As you finish the beat, plan your rounding. Which way do you want to go? An immediate move to the favored side will give you a jump on the competition but beware of jibing into the traffic and bad air of boats coming upwind.

> Fig. 20a,b – To attack those ahead, chase them to the sides of the course, then as they jibe, jibe inside to put your wind shadow on top of them.

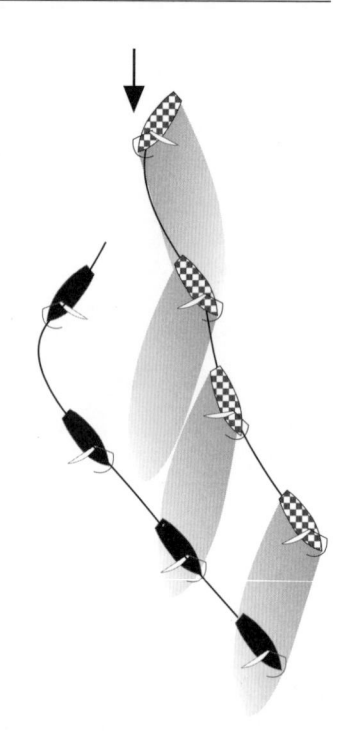

10.4 Running Tactics

With our strategic game plan set based on expected wind, wind shifts, and current; we will use tactics to put our plan into place.

Beginning of the Leg

As you round, get onto the favored jibe (either the headed jibe in shifting winds or the jibe which will take you to the favored side of the course) as quickly as possible. A decisive tactical move can allow you to break away at the rounding while others are still sorting out their options (Fig. 19).

If the right is favored, a jibe set is the quickest way to hit that side. Just beware that on a port broad reach you must stay clear of all boats sailing upwind. [Author's note: As you master the skills presented in this book, you no doubt will find that you often round in front of your fleet. Consequently, you will frequently be sailing back through them as you start down the run. Such are the burdens of leadership.]

In a big fleet, use a bear-away set to a fast reaching angle to break out of the wind shadow at the top of the leg. Once clear of the crowd, jibe or carry on, as strategy dictates.

Attack those Ahead

Running legs give trailing boats the chance to attack leaders. Early in the leg, you get in the attack position. Later in the leg, you attack. Chase the boat(s) you want to attack as they sail to the sides of the course, then attack by jibing inside as they come back. If you try to get on their air as they sail to the outside, you leave them an escape route. It is better to be patient, and attack while sailing toward the middle (Fig. 20a).

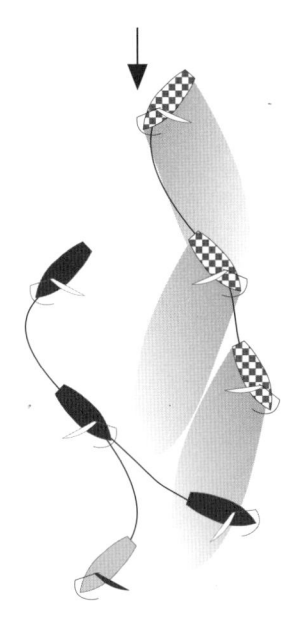

< Fig. 21 – To defend your air either reach up to break through the wind shadow or jibe away.

> Fig. 22 – To keep clear air, look back and position yourself in a lane of clear air. As boats jibe, their wind shadows' shift. Anticipating the position of a clear lane is tricky.

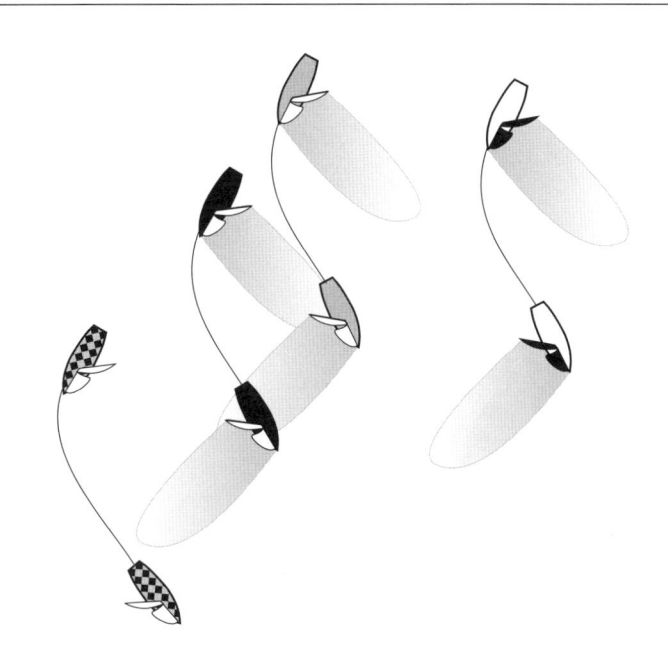

To make your attack work, you should jibe early and sail down on your rival, cutting off the escape route. Sail down until the rival is aligned with your windex. If you are within three or four mast heights, you will have an impact. Watch to see his spinnaker curl as he enters your shadow … and look back to be sure no one is doing the same to you (Fig. 20b).

The closer you get, the greater your effect. If the leader jibes back out, you do the same. Get into attack position and be ready to strike again when he jibes in. Your frequent attacks will challenge each boats jibing skills. Practice those jibes.

Keeping Clear Air

As a lead boat, the challenge is it to keep clear air while implementing your strategy. Work the shifts or favored side, and look for lanes which will allow you to sail the middle in clear air. If you are threatened by a pack of trailing boats chasing you to the outside of the leg you may need to jibe early and reach up to break across their wind shadow.

Remember, jibes (which is to say, *good jibes*) cost very little. Be a moving target. Don't let attackers set up on you. As you work toward the favored side, a quick jibe and jibe back can throw off an attacker; or give you a position for a later jibe which will allow you to break through to the inside. If you find your air threatened, reach up to break through or jibe away immediately. Don't delay (Fig. 21).

Sailing down the middle of the leg can be difficult in the middle or forward sections of a large fleet. Look for lanes of clear air and try to find a position inside a pack of potential attackers. Anticipate their jibes to keep out of their shadows (Fig.22).

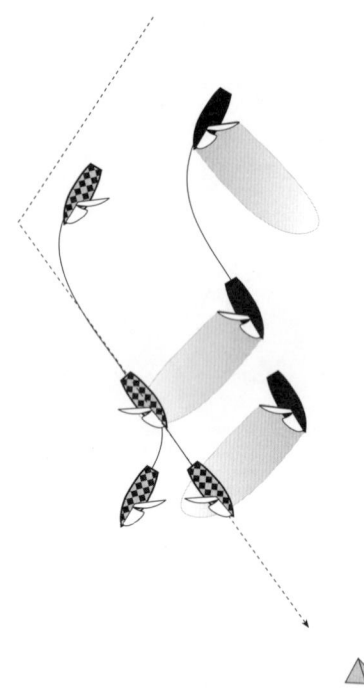

Fig. 23 – Sailing into the corners presents the same hazards downwind as upwind. Once you are in the corner, you lose your strategic flexibility and you are subject to attack with no way to escape.

Fig. 24 – If the leg is skewed so one tack is longer than the other, try to sail the long tack first. The short tack will lead you quickly to a corner, and the hazards found there.

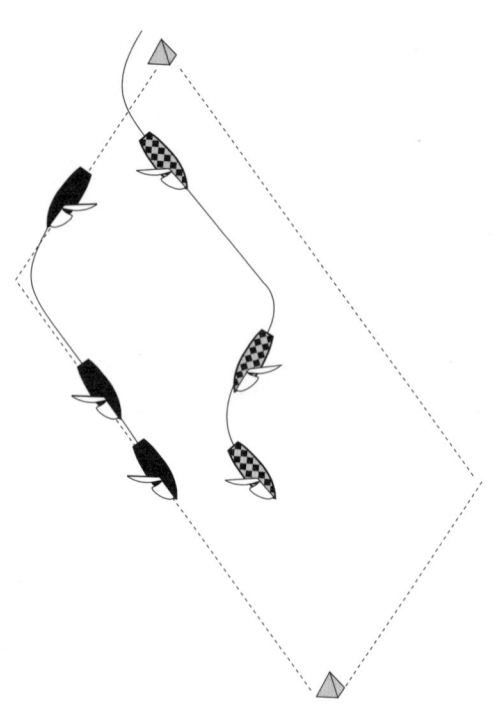

Of course, as difficult as it may be to sail the middle, it is recommended. Sail to the corners only when there is a clear and definite strategic advantage. As with upwind sailing, it is usually best to…

… Avoid the Corners

As upwind, the corner leaves us strategically spent, unable to take advantage of changing winds, vulnerable to attack, and devoid of tactical options (Fig. 23).

The corners are easy to reach if the run is skewed—so that you will spend substantially more time on one tack than the other. It is generally best to sail the long tack first—just as we do upwind. The danger in sailing the short tack first is that we quickly may find ourselves in the corner (Fig. 24).

Of course, if the run is so heavily skewed that no jibe will be required, then it is no longer a run but a reach, and reaching tactics apply.

End of Leg Positioning

As the fleet converges at a leeward mark rounding, your weapons are: speed, positioning, and right of way. To achieve speed, work through a proper reaching angle into the mark. Avoid the trap of forcing the boat too low to avoid jibes late in leg. With proper crew work, extra jibes at the end of the leg will not mess up your spinnaker take down and rounding. (See *Performance Racing Trim* for Boat Handling details!)

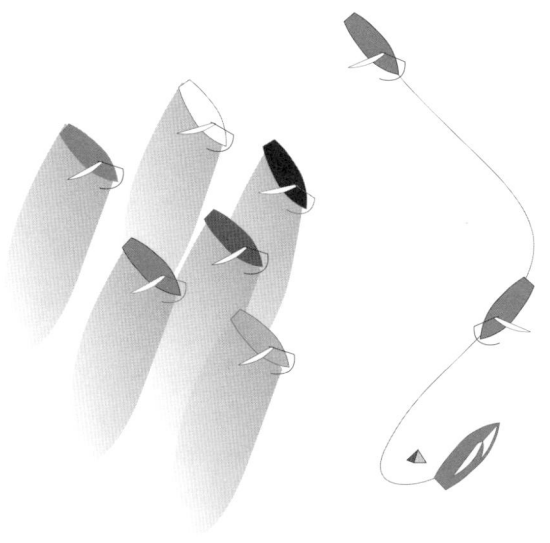

Fig. 25 – An approach on starboard provides clear air, right of way, and inside position. It also requires a jibe drop of the spinnaker. Tactical prowess is achieved through superior boat handling!

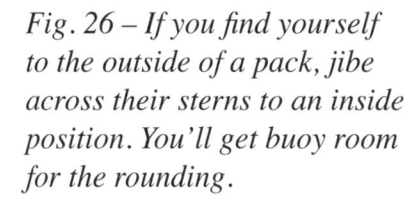

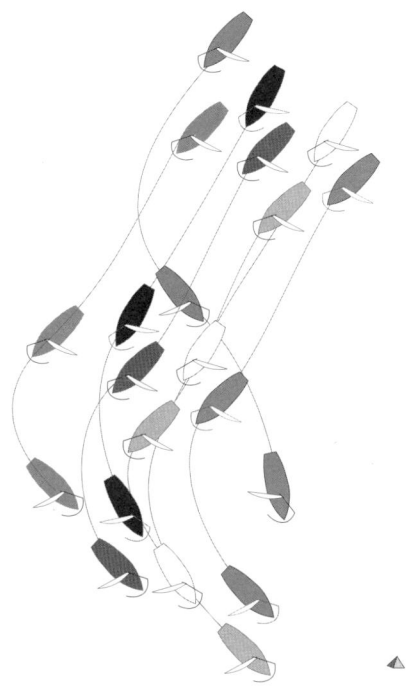

Fig. 26 – If you find yourself to the outside of a pack, jibe across their sterns to an inside position. You'll get buoy room for the rounding.

Inside position and right of way often go hand in hand. A starboard tack approach into the mark gives you both. The rounding, from a starboard broad reach to port tack close hauled, is not as difficult as you might imagine, though it might be worth practicing once or twice before you try it in competition. Incidentally, it is surprising how often inside position at the end of the leg can be traced back to a jibe set or early positioning to that side early in the leg (Fig. 25).

If you find yourself on the outside of a pack in the later stages of a run, make a bold move to the inside. There is little at risk and much to be gained. Even if you can't pick off the entire pack at the rounding, you may get room from a bunch of them; and if not then you round behind, just as you would have from the outside (Fig. 26).

You Can Do It, If You Can

Have I mentioned the role of good boat handling in tactical success? Tactical ideas are only as good as the boat handling and boat speed they accompany. There is a special thrill to the teamwork of attacking a rival, and watching their boat-handling unravel under your team's attacks.

Fig. 27 – When racing under jib and main; wing the jib, heel to weather, and sail slightly by the lee for best speed.
Since the performance cone is narrow, you can use your wind shadow to attack boats ahead.

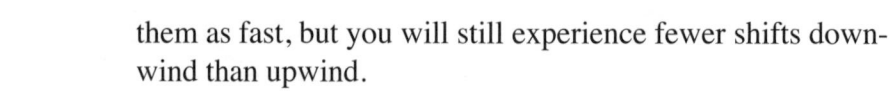

10.5 Jib and Main Racing

If you are racing non-spinnaker, with just jib and main then tactics change in several ways.

Narrow Cone

The performance guidelines described at the beginning of this chapter do not apply. For best downwind performance under jib and main; sail wing and wing, directly at the mark, and slightly by the lee, with windward heel. (See *North U. Racing Trim* for more trim details.)

Strategy

Sometimes the course to the mark is on the cusp between carrying wing and wing and sailing a jib reach. If you will have to sail part of the leg running wing and wing, and part broad reaching with the jib to leeward, then you can use standard strategic criteria to decide when to reach and when to run. Wind strategy calls for running off in puffs, and reaching up in lulls. Current positioning is more critical than with spinnakers as boats are relatively slower. In shifts, try a direct course, altering trim as winds oscillate. You will experience more shifts than under spinnaker, as you will not be running away from them as fast, but you will still experience fewer shifts downwind than upwind.

A run which is sailed entirely on starboard resembles an outside reach, while a port tack run resembles an inside reach, as described in the previous chapter.

Tactics

Since the performance cone is narrow, defending boats have a difficult time escaping an attack. As an attacker, put your wind shadow on the bow of the lead boat and reel them in.

On a skewed leg you can attack leaders by sailing over their air on a broach reach before settling on their air, wing and wing. If you are in the lead, do most of your reaching first, across the windward edge of the cone. If you run first, you may find yourself reaching in bad air later on. Try to save some of your reaching for the final segment of the leg, as the extra speed and maneuverability gives you an advantage as boats converge at the mark (Fig. 27).

10.6 Conclusion

Downwind legs present all the strategic and tactical challenge of upwind sailing with the added challenge of spinnaker handling and trim. While most racers are attuned to upwind strategy and tactics, many mistakenly treat runs like reaches—creating real opportunity for those who appreciate the difference.

Sail fast, hit the shifts if you can find them, and keep clear air. Our next topics are downwind mark roundings, finishes and rules.

10.7 Quiz Questions and Skill Building

1. How can you anticipate the wind angle on an upcoming reach?

2. How does the expected wind angle of the next leg affect your approach angle to a jibe mark?

3. You approach the windward mark on a port lift in an oscillating breeze. How does this affect your initial sailing angle on the reach (on starboard tack)?

4. When might you not *try to pass a boat ahead of you?*

5. Would you ever want to slow down on a reach?

6. What sort of wind conditions make it possible to catch a tow from another boat? What types of boats provide the best tows?

A hand bearing compass is a great tool for running tactics, just as it is upwind. Use your "puck" to sight across an LEP to determine position, judge port/starboard crossings, and to call laylines. Also, use the puck to measure performance against other boats. As bearings change, you are gaining or losing. In this way you can determine if you are sailing the correct angle or too high/fast or too low/slow.

One area you can work on is communication, in describing another boats performance—particularly a trailing boat. Discuss the terms you will use. Performance should be described in relation to your boat in a consistent format; i.e. distance back, distance high or low, sailing angle and speed. E.g. "Dennis is 1 length back, on our line, sailing slightly higher and faster."

Your tactician will need to stay a step ahead, anticipating initial conditions on the reach—strategically and tactically—during the final segment of the beat. At times he may not be able to know what will happen—will you round ahead or behind some of your rivals? In that event, he may still be able to tell you on the approach that upon rounding you will either: Sail high with the jib on a course of xx° or set immediately on a course of yy°—I'll call it as soon as I can by saying either "jib reach at xx°" or "spinnaker set to yy°."

Quiz Answers

1. How can you anticipate the wind angle on an upcoming reach?

There are a number of ways to anticipated the wind angle. The first is to sail the course in miniature before the start (as described in *Chapter 2 - Race Preparation*). You can use that info as a baseline, and factor in any changes to conditions since that time.

You can also compare the compass course for the leg to the wind direction. As you get to know your boat, you should catalog the highest effective true and apparent wind angles for carrying a spinnaker in different wind speeds.

2. How does the expected wind angle of the next leg affect your approach angle to a jibe mark?

If the next leg will be a close reach, then be sure to come in high and jibe early so you can exit the jibe mark with a high, inside line.

If the next leg will be broad, then your approach angle is not so critical. As long as you don't have other boats hot on your heels, you can sail wide coming out of the mark onto a broad reach.

3. You approach the windward mark on a port lift in an oscillating breeze. How does this affect your initial sailing angle on the reach (on starboard tack)? How about on a run?

Sailing a reach in oscillating winds, we treat the shifts similar to a puff / lull cycle, sailing off in the headers, and up in lifts. With starboard headed, we'd want to sail low initially on the reach, as long as we could do so and still maintain clear air.

On a run, we'd do a bear away set to starboard tack and sail headed until we detect a lift.

4. When might you not *try to pass a boat ahead of you?*

Approaching a mark there are times when it is best to work for an inside overlap rather than try to pass on the outside.

5. Would you ever want to slow down on a reach?

There are a number of times you might want to slow down as you approach a mark. As an inside boat, sometimes you want to slow down to keep an outside boat overlapped outside. If the outside boat falls astern, they might try to dive inside.

Also, as a trailing boat, you can get an inside overlap too early, sail up into bad air, and then lose the overlap as you slow down.

As a lead boat, you might want to slow to let an inside boat get an overlap inside, and then give them bad air, so you can accelerate and break the overlap.

6. What sort of wind conditions make it possible to catch a tow from another boat? What types of boats provide the best tows?

In full-power hull speed conditions you can hitch a ride on the stern wave of boats up to about 20% faster than you. Heavier boats throw bigger wakes, and are easiest to hitch on.

Chapter 11: Downwind Rules, Mark Roundings, and Finishing

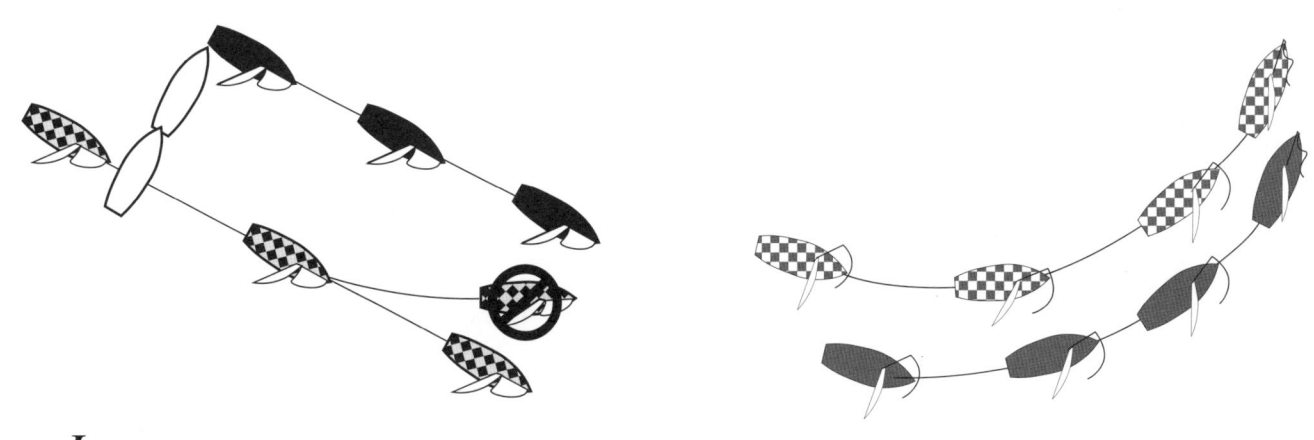

11.1   Introduction
11.2   Downwind Rules
11.3   Mark Rounding Rules and Tactics
11.4   Finishing Rules and Tactics
11.5   Quiz Questions and Skill Building

Chapter 11: Downwind Rules, Mark Roundings, and Finishing

11.1 Introduction

In this chapter we will cover downwind rules, mark rounding tactics and rules, and finishing tactics and rules. Right of way can change quickly. A clear understanding of the rules is needed if you are to receive your due and fulfill your obligations. Furthermore, many offwind and rounding tactics involve the rules, so an understanding of the rules is essential to tactics.

The rules for upwind sailing and upwind mark roundings are covered in Chapter 8 – Upwind Tactics.

11.2 Downwind Rules

The same-tack rules predominate on reaches. Rules 11 and 12 cover windward/ leeward and overtaking situations. Rule 15 covers acquiring right of way, Rule 16 addresses altering course, and Rule 17 covers proper course issues. As we move from reaches to runs, we must add consideration of opposite tacks (Rule 10).

Windward/ Leeward

The leeward boat always has the right of way. Stop Repeat: The leeward boat always has the right of way; the windward boat shall keep clear.

The interaction of windward and leeward boats depends on how the overlap was established. When a boat is passing to windward, a leeward boat may change course as she pleases, constrained only by Rule 16.1, which requires that she give the other boat room to keep clear. The windward boat must use the room provided and promptly keep clear (Fig. 1a).

Fig. 1a – When a boat is passing to windward, a leeward boat may change course provided she gives the windward boat room to keep clear.

If the overtaking boat establishes an overlap to leeward within two boat lengths, then he shall not sail above her proper course (Rule 17) (Fig. 1b).

The definition of *keep clear* requires that the windward boat establish his overlap in such a way that the leeward boat could change course without immediately making contact with the windward boat. In other words, when the windward boat establishes his overlap, he must allow himself room to keep clear.

Other Downwind Rules

Two other downwind situations deserve mention. First, a boat clear astern must keep clear (Rule 12). Second, a starboard-tack boat has right of way over a port-tack boat

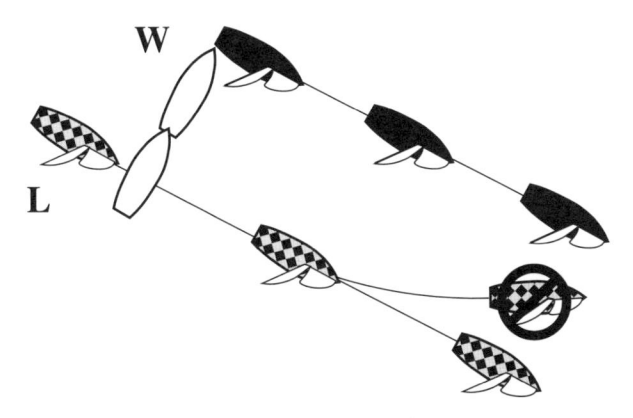

Fig. 1b – A leeward boat which establishes an overlap from astern shall not sail above her proper course.

Fig. 2 – The Checkered boat has right of way over the trailing boat as a boat clear ahead, and over the lead boat by starboard/port.

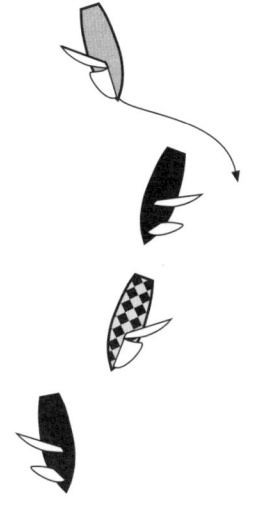

(Rule 10). Just as upwind, you are better off to take a starboard boat's stern than to risk a foul—or be forced into a sudden jibe. Note also that the port starboard rule applies even when coming from behind on a run. The clear astern rule applies only to boats on the same tack (Fig. 2).

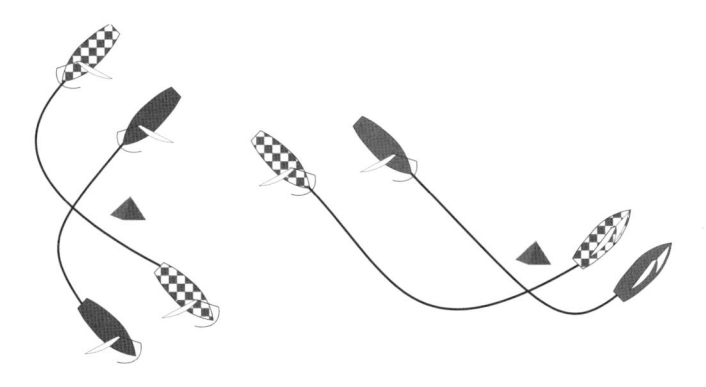

Fig. 3 – When rounding alone, use a smooth turn to carry speed. Come in wide and go out close for best position, as the checkered boat is doing.

11.3 Mark Rounding Rules and Tactics

Mark roundings on reaches and runs have a set of rules and tactics which are distinct from windward mark roundings.

Rounding Alone

In wide, out close.

When rounding an offwind mark alone, complete the turn and be on course for the next leg as you pass the mark. The wide turning radius necessary to hold speed through the rounding requires that you start wide of the mark in order to finish close. Practice wide-and-close roundings wherever you are, under sail or power, to improve your feel for your boat's handling characteristics. You'll find you need a two boat length radius to carry speed well through a turn (Fig. 3).

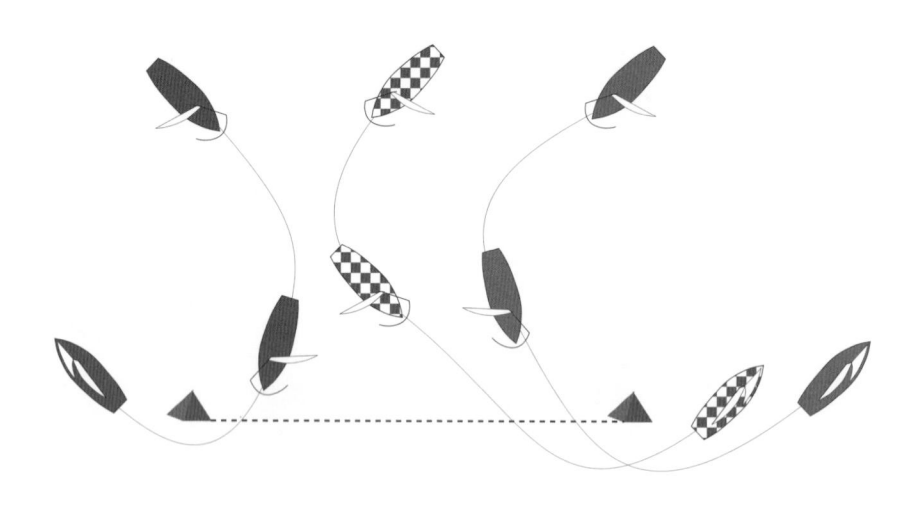

Fig. 4 – When rounding through gates, pick the favored side – then change your mind at the last instant to challenge your crew! The rules are the same as those at leeward marks.

Fig. 5 – As the outside boat reaches the three length zone, any boat overlapped inside is entitled to room at the mark. The grey boat does not get room, and the white and black boats are entitled to room regardless of what may happen later. (See Fig. 6.)

The wide-and-close rounding carries speed through the turn and places you to windward with clear air and freedom to maneuver. Proper roundings save boat lengths. A proper rounding at a leeward mark lets your carry reaching speed up to a close-hauled course. A proper rounding at a jibe mark protects your air if the next leg is broad, and gives a little extra height when struggling on a close reach.

Although this section is short, its importance cannot be overstated. Usually you round alone. Proper roundings can save half a minute or more on a six-legged course.

Rounding through Gates

When the leeward mark is set as a gate, you must choose which side to round. Much like a starting line, the choice depends on three factors: which mark is to the favored side, which end is furthest upwind, and which mark is least crowded. As these factors are often in conflict, the decision can be difficult. If the gate is set out of square to the wind by 10°, then the advantage at the upwind end equals half the distance between the marks. Equally difficult are the boat handling gyrations needed to accommodate a last minute change of tactics (Fig. 4).

Once an end has been selected, then the rules and tactics are like those at any single mark. Just beware the rules as you crisscross with a competitor who has selected the other end!

Rounding with Company

When rounding with company, Rule 18: Passing Marks and Obstructions governs. This rule is the source of many protests and appeals, most of which involve the elusive three boat length zone.

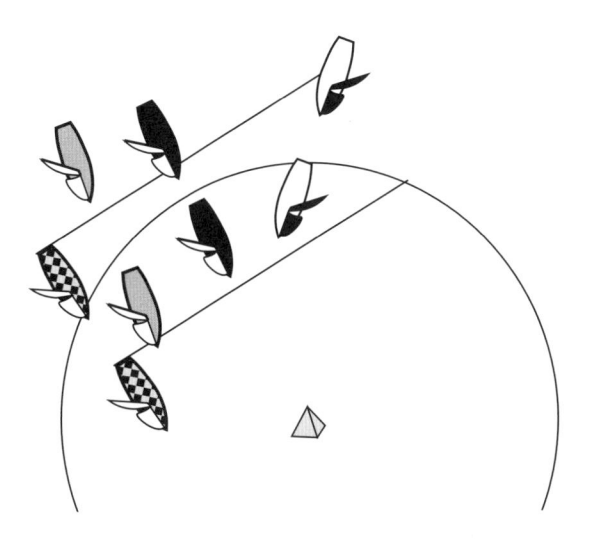

Fig. 6 – Moments later the grey boat has achieved an overlap, and the black and white boats have lost theirs. The mark-room rights are unchanged: No room for grey, room for black and white.

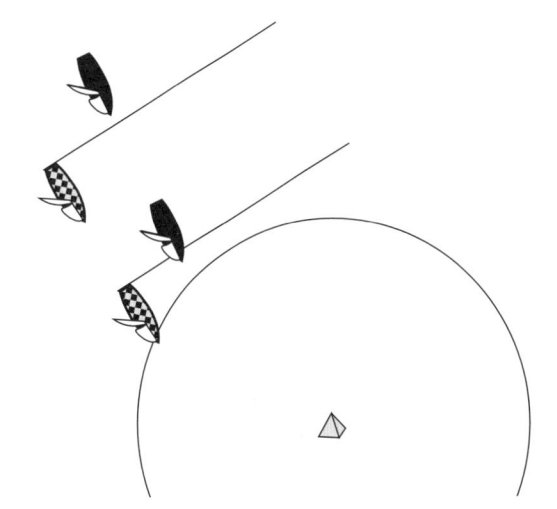

Fig. 7a – Since the inside boat does not have an overlap earlier, he must show that he achieved an overlap on time.

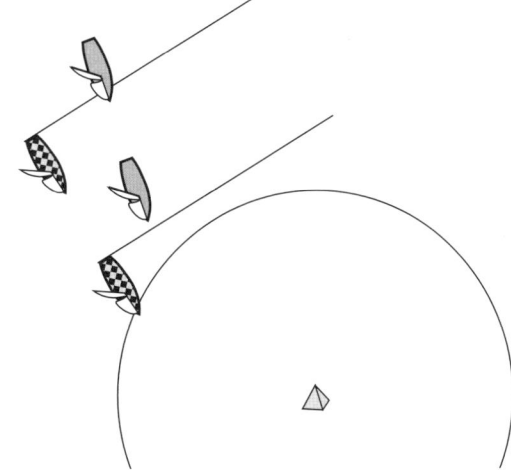

Fig. 7b – Here the inside boat has an overlap, and the outside boat claims to have broken it. So the burden falls to the outside boat to show that it was broken.

The Three Hull Length Zone

When approaching a mark with company, the question is whether the boats were overlapped before reaching the zone – which is three hull lengths from the mark. Any boat overlapped to the inside is entitled to room (Fig. 5).

Late Breaks & Overlaps

If an inside boat establishes an overlap after the outside boat reaches the three length zone, she is not entitled to room. The overlap must exist before the lead boat hits the zone. Similarly, if an inside boat has an overlap at the zone, she is entitled to room even if the overlap is broken a moment later (Rule 18.2b). To repeat: Room requirements are established when the lead boat reaches the zone. Anything which happens after that time is of no consequence (Fig. 6).

Approaching the Zone

The situation prior to reaching the zone is determinative if there is a dispute (Rule 18.2d). A skipper claiming to have established or broken an overlap just before reaching the zone must established his claim beyond reasonable doubt if protested (Fig. 7a&b).

Therefore, though no hail is required, it is good practice as you approach the zone to establish the situation—overlap or no. Don't wait until you're in the zone to open communications.

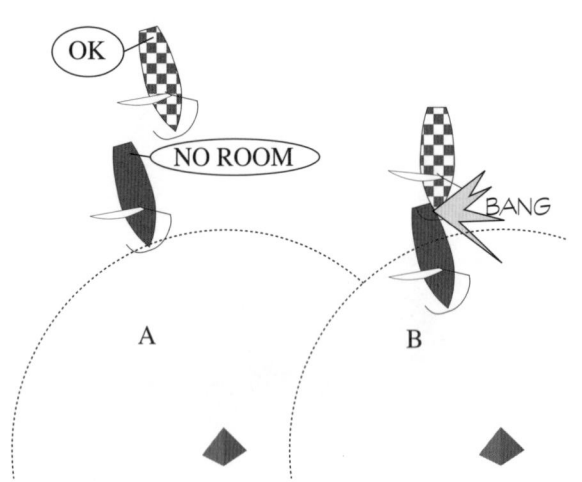

Fig. 8 – The inside boat asks the outside boat if there is an overlap. The outside boat hails, "3 lengths, no overlap, no room." Accepting this, the inside boat turns to go outside, and hits. Well, what do you know – there must have been an overlap.

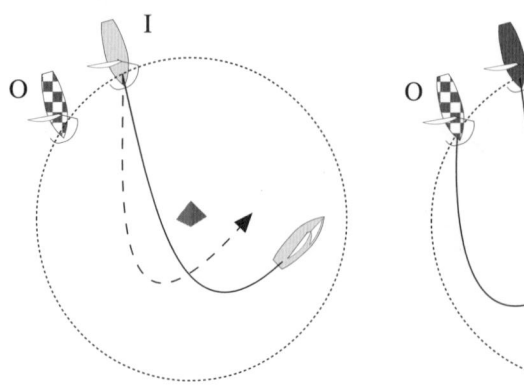

Fig. 9a – An inside windward boat is only entitled to room to sail to the mark, not a tactical wide-and-close rounding.

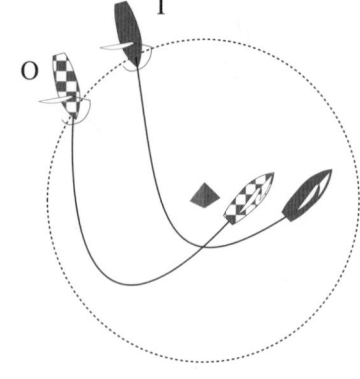

Fig. 9b – The outside boat should make a tactical turn to end up behind, not outside, the inside boat.

A Gentleman's Sport

Given the occasional differences of opinion about the exact position of the three boat length zone, prior discussion can be critical. As an inside boat you should ask the outside boat to call the overlap and the three boat length zone. Put the burden on the outside boat. Is it too much to expect an honest appraisal from our rival? "Do let us know if we've got an overlap at the zone, won't you?"

It certainly is easier for the lead boat to call the situation. From the helm, he can more easily judge an overlap at his stern and your bow than you can from your helm. And he is also in a better position to call when his bow reaches the three boat length zone. You, after all, may still be nearly five lengths from the mark when his bow reaches the zone.

So go ahead, put the burden of sportsmanship on him.
You can trust those you race against to be fair and honest.
Of course, if sportsmanship fails, you can always fall back on the rule of law. When the outside boat hails…
Three boat lengths, no overlap, no room!
…you turn smartly to the outside to stay clear. If you hit, then you have *proof through performance* that there was an overlap. If it comes to a protest you will need to establish that both boats were traveling at the same speed on parallel courses, and that you made an immediate turn when hailed (Fig. 8).

And if you don't hit—well, then I guess you didn't have an overlap after all. But chances are your rival has been so preoccupied with the mark-room call that his rounding will be a mess, and you will pass him in short order regardless.

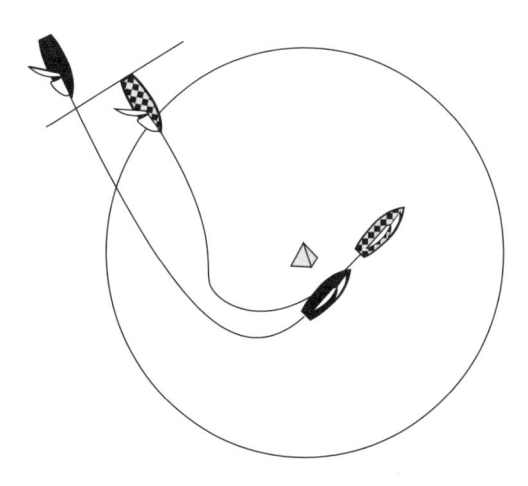

Fig. 10 – If the outside boat is clear astern, the inside boat had right of way and can make a tactical rounding.

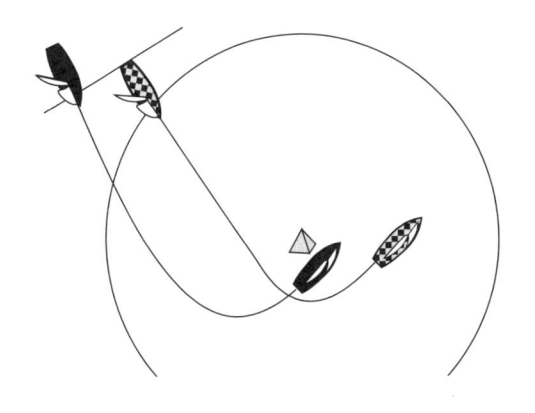

Fig. 11 – If the outside boat has an overlap, the inside boat is entitled to room to sail to the mark, not a tactical wide-and-close rounding. The outside boat will end up in better position.

Fig. 12 – An outside boat must give an inside boat room if she can. Here the white boat arrives too late for space to be made.

How Much Room?

An inside boat is entitled to room to make a safe (concentric) rounding. An inside or clear ahead Right of Way boat can make a tactical (wide-and-close) rounding (Fig. 9a). As a first approximation, one boat length of room is not too much; and in some conditions more room is justified. On the other hand, an inside boat has taken too much room if another boat manages to sneak inside. Protest if this happens, but as an outside boat never let the inside boat touch you. Stay clear and protest, and you will be safe. Once there is contact, you may be in trouble.

The existence of an overlap is important even if the inside boat is leading the outside boat. If the inside boat is clear ahead, she may make a tactical wide-and-close rounding. If the outside boat has an overlap the inside boat is restricted to a safe rounding (Fig. 10).

As an outside boat, be sure to let the inside boat know if you have an overlap. By restricting the inside boat to a safe rounding, you will be able to get a better position around the mark; on the inside boat's hip (Fig. 11). If the inside boat makes a tactical rounding, you will likely end up directly astern of the inside boat, in bad air, as in Fig. 10.

"Able to Give"

The outside boat must give room if she is able to give room. A boat establishing a late inside overlap (just prior to 2 boat lengths) may not be entitled to room. If the outside boat cannot give the room, due to a crowd of boats outside her, for example, the inside boat is not entitled to it (Fig. 12).

If the inside boat has a long-established overlap, then she is entitled to room, and the outside boat must plan in anticipation of giving room. But if the inside boat gets an overlap at the last moment, it may not be possible to get room (Rule 18.2e).

Chapter 11: Downwind Rules, Mark Roundings, and Finishing

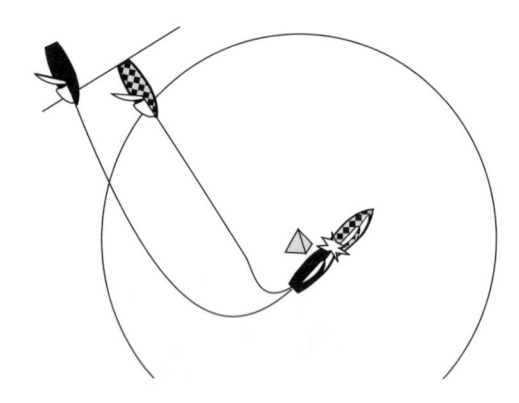

Fig. 13 – Beware: No Brakes! As the inside boat makes a sharp turn at the mark, he will slow dramatically. Don't hit him from behind.

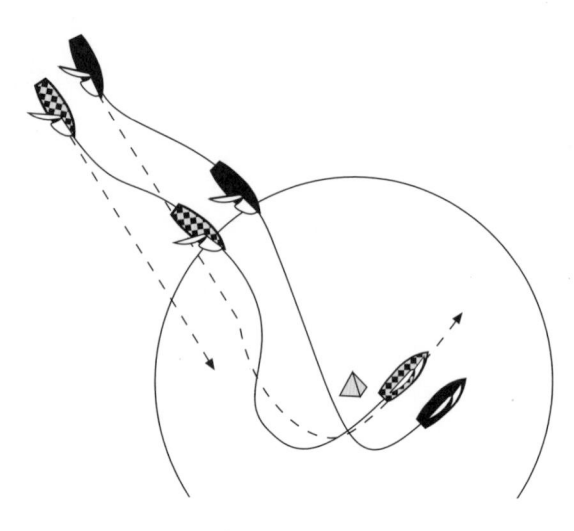

Fig. 14 – Before reaching the three length zone, luff the inside boat to force a poor rounding; allowing you to get a position on his quarter as you round.

Rounding Tactics

Following are some tactical tricks you can use at roundings. If your tactics are good coming down the leg, you should only rarely find yourself giving room.

Use a Tactical Rounding. The inside boat is not allowed to make a tactical rounding, but you still should. If you are giving room, swing wide and follow on the inside boat's transom, rather than pinwheel to the outside. If you pinwheel you may end up blanketed with no way to escape. (See Figs. 10 & 11.)

No Brakes! As you swing wide to follow, be careful not to hit the lead boat from behind as you accelerate. His sharp turn at the mark may leave him dead in the water. As the lead boat, it is a good idea to slow down and force the outside boat to the outside (Fig. 13).

Force a Bad Rounding. When you are giving room, you can try to force the inside boat into a bad (in close and out wide) rounding by sailing high as you approach the mark. If you force the inside boat onto a high line approaching the mark, she will have trouble making a good rounding. You can then take room as necessary to round into a controlling position coming out of the turn (Fig. 14).

Watch for Vultures. When you are giving room warn those behind you not to cut in. Plenty of advance dialogue (and threats) may be necessary to ward off those not entitled to room. Tell them early, before they've decided to try to force their way in (Fig. 15).

The Big Wheel. If you are on the outside of three or four boats with others close behind, you can follow inside or sail around the outside. If you cut in, you may be required to give room to late arrivers. Your strategy for the next leg can help you plan whether to pinwheel outside or try to cut inside (Fig. 16).

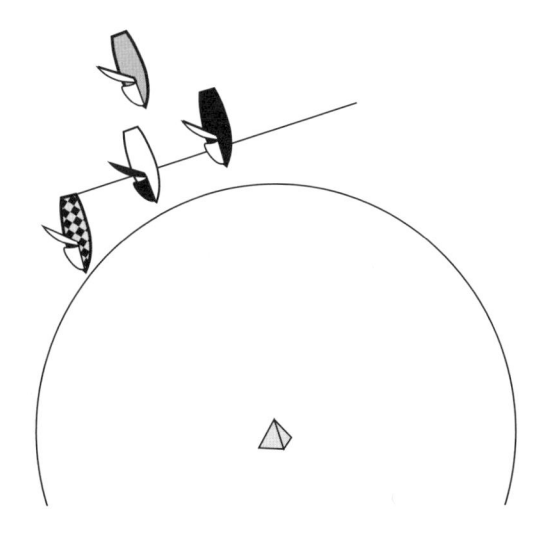

Fig. 15 – Watch for Vultures: When you are giving room, be sure to hail those not entitled to room to keep them from trying to force their way in.

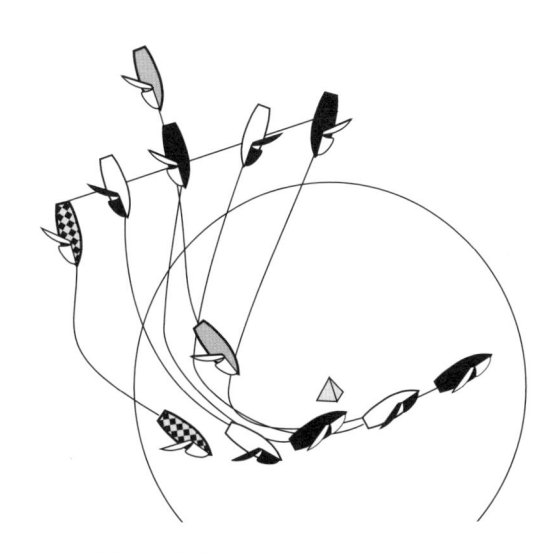

Fig. 16 – While giving room, these outside boats are late entering the 3 boat length zone. By the time they enter the grey boat has an overlap and is entitled to room.

Fig. 17 – Negotiate Early: Don't wait for the three boat length zone to start your negotiations.

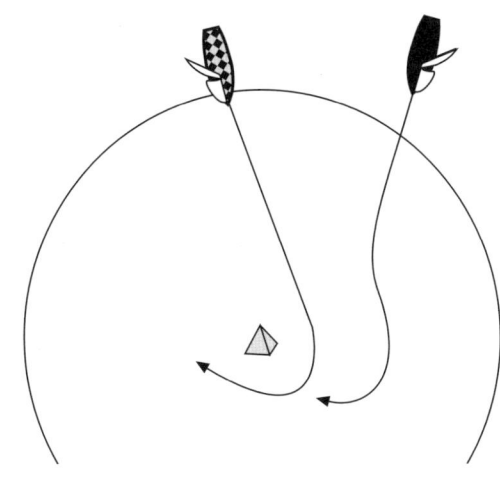

Fig. 18 – Downwind inside the three boat length zone mark-room takes precedence over starboard/port.

Negotiate Early. Do not wait until the three boat length zone to start negotiations, especially at a crowded rounding. Tell all boats nearby what you expect, and be sure to warn potential vultures against forcing their way through. Appoint a spokesman to handle inter-boat dialogue. While one crew member negotiates your rights, the rest of the crew should keep sailing (Fig. 17).

Room or Starboard? At starboard roundings and starboard gates, inside port tack boats are entitled to mark-room once they reach the zone (Fig. 18).

Many places (and races) are won and lost at the corners. To win you must position yourself carefully, negotiate diplomatically, and handle your boat smoothly.

Chapter 11: Downwind Rules, Mark Roundings, and Finishing

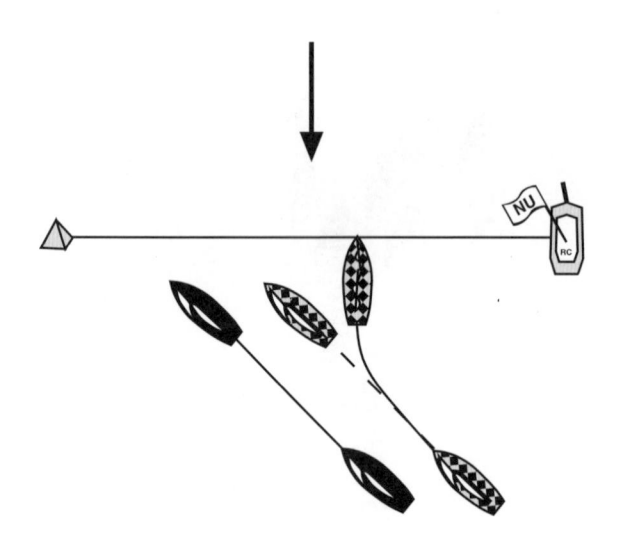

Fig. 19 – Shoot the finish and save a few seconds.

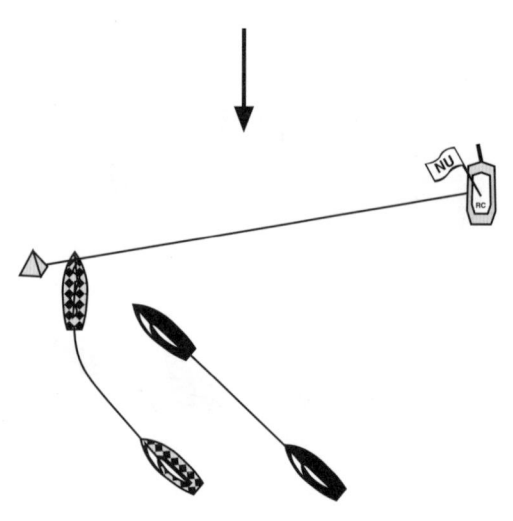

Fig. 20 – Pin end favored. Tactics are like windward mark tactics with marks to port.

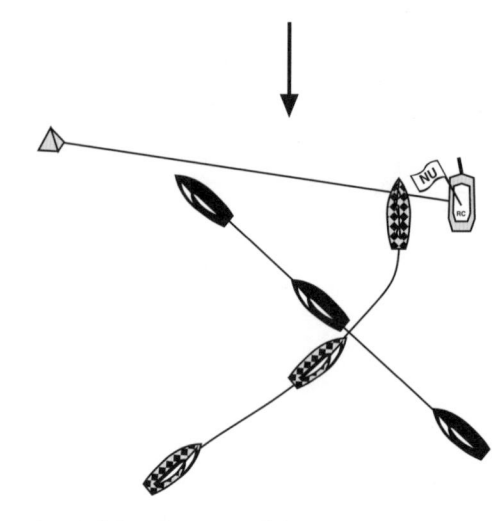

Fig. 21 – Boat end favored. Tactics are like windward mark tactics with marks to starboard.

11.4 Finishing Rules & Tactics

Finishing Tactics depend on what kind of race you are in. In one design or level-rated racing, your goal is to finish ahead of as many boats as possible; finishing tactics are then similar to positioning tactics approaching a mark. In handicap racing, the goal is to finish as soon as possible; in this case avoid boat-on-boat duels and sprint to the finish. There are times in handicap races when a level-rated competitor is close at hand and both situations apply simultaneously.

Finishing Tactics Upwind

You should shoot the finish by turning up into irons and coasting the last boat length or two. By shooting you are able to shorten the distance sailed while coasting at nearly full speed (Fig. 19).

A finish line has a favored end, much like a starting line. When finishing upwind, the favored end is the end furthest downwind – opposite of the favored end for a start. Your finishing tactics then focus on the laylines to the favored end.

As you approach the finish, you want to stay below all laylines until you have determined which end is favored; then only the favored end laylines are significant.

There are several ways to determine the favored end. If it is the old starting line, you can determine the favored end based on the line bearing and the present wind. If it is a new line, then you must make your determination based on observation. If you cannot figure out the favored end by observing boats ahead—such are the burdens of leadership—then your own tacking angles can tell you which end is favored. If port

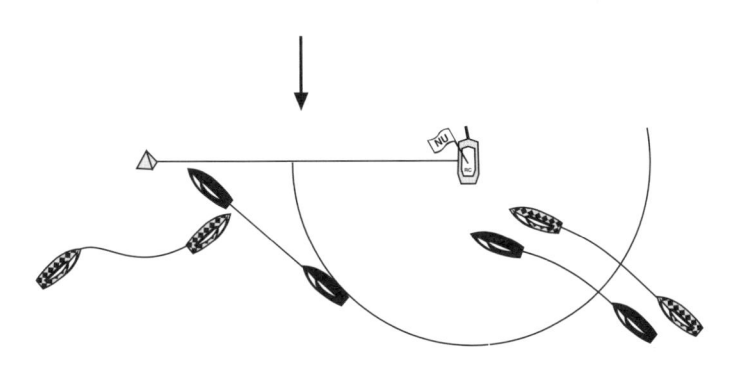

Fig. 22 – Rules at an upwind finish are the same as those at a windward mark: Starboard/Port for boats on opposite tacks; mark-room for boats on the same tack.

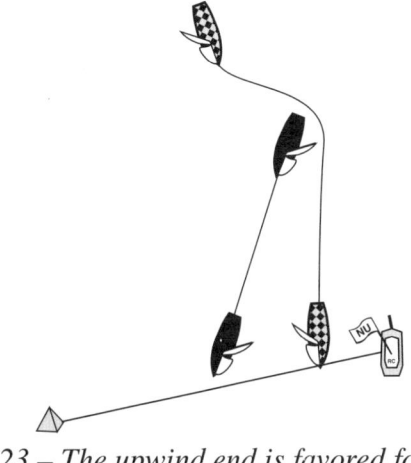

Fig. 23 – The upwind end is favored for a downwind finish. Sail proper angles and shoot the finish by coasting on a run.

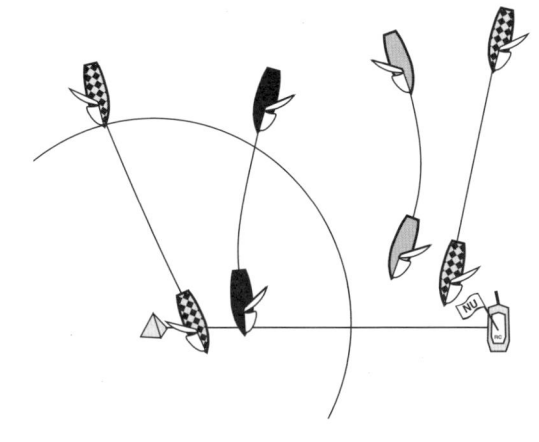

Fig. 24 – Near the ends, mark-room rules prevail. At the middle of the line, the downwind sailing rules govern.

tack is more nearly parallel to the line and starboard more nearly perpendicular, then the port end of the line is favored; as you pass under the port end you would be sailing extra distance parallel to the line, and vice versa. (See Figs. 20 and 21.)

Upwind Finishing Rules

The rules at an upwind finish are like those at an upwind mark rounding. Starboard/port prevails, and a windward boat may call for room if overlapped at the three length zone. You are not required to cross a finish line. Once any part of the boat or equipment crosses the line you may clear yourself in any direction, provided you do not interfere with those still racing (Fig. 22).

Finishing Tactics Downwind

Finishing tactics downwind focus on the favored end, just as they do upwind. We want to sail proper reaching angles and finish at the favored (upwind) end (Fig. 23).

Tactics to reach the favored end are the same as those approaching any leeward mark. Clear air is essential to good speed. A finish line does offer some flexibility though. If the line is near square, you have some latitude on where to go in search of clear air.

You can shoot the finish downwind and coast twice as far as you would upwind. Bear off to a run and coast to the line with your reaching speed (Fig. 23).

Downwind Finishing Rules

The rules at the finish line are the same as those on the course; near the marks the mark-room rules apply (Fig. 24).

11.5 Quiz Questions and Skill Building

1. How do the windward / leeward rules at starts differ from the rules on reaches and runs?

2. A boat with no overlap calls for room. What should you do?

3. A windward boat mast abeam hails "Mast Abeam." How should you respond (aside from suggesting he buy a new rule book)?

4. When might you need to slow down as you approach a mark?

5. If you are the outside trailing boat, does it matter if you have an overlap with an inside boat?

6. In a mixed fleet, whose boat lengths are used for the three-length-zone?

Wide-and-close turns are the best route around marks. Practice them all the time—under sail and under power—even in your car. You will quickly learn your boat's appropriate turning radius. Remember, a wide smooth turn carries speed.

It is also good to practice jamming a tight turn around a mark— coming in close and trying to stay close by jamming your turn. Practice accelerating out of the turn.

There are also times when you will need to slow down—such as when you are inside but NOT entitled to room. You'll need to stall and let the outside (lead) boat pass. Oversteering is the best way to do this. (For some this requires no practice.) Another way is by over-trimming.

Time speed distance test. With your spinnaker flying, sail past a mark and start a stopwatch. Go through your mark rounding routine:. Upwind controls on, jib up, spinnaker down, and turn upwind. How long did it take, in time and distance?

Quiz Answers

1. How do the windward / leeward rules at starts differ from the rules on reaches and runs?

As they are written, there is no difference. In practice, there is a difference in that there is no proper course before the start. In all cases, the leeward boat has the right of way (Rule 11), and may alter course provided she gives the windward boat room to keep clear (Rule 16.1).

2. A boat with no overlap calls for room. What should you do?

First, try to talk him out of it. If he forces his way in, give room and protest – do not deny room, and do not get into a collision.

3. A windward boat hails "Mast Abeam." How should you respond (aside from suggesting he buy a new rule book)?

Turn towards him, and when he hails and fails to respond, protest. The mast abeam rule was dropped in the last century.

4. When might you need to slow down as you approach a mark?

To keep from going inside when you are not entitled to room, or to keep an outside boat overlapped to the outside, so they can't cut inside and claim room.

5. If you are the outside trailing boat, does it matter if you have an overlap with an inside boat?

Yes. If you are an outside, leeward boat, then the inside boat is entitled to room for a safe rounding. If you lose the overlap, the inside boat becomes clear ahead, and is entitled make a tactical (in wide, out close) rounding, which will make it much tougher for you to round and have clear air.

6. In a mixed fleet, whose boat lengths are used for the three-length-zone?

Your boat lengths. You give room to boats overlapped inside you when you reach your three-length-zone. Each boat uses its own lengths.

Chapter 11: Downwind Rules, Mark Roundings, and Finishing

Chapter 12: No More Tactics

12.1 The Trouble with Tactics...

The trouble with tactics is that you have to deal constantly with factors you can't predict or control. Strategy, which is based on wind and weather, obviously has a high degree of uncertainty, particularly for the narrow coastal areas in which most of us sail. Yet the weather is relatively tame compared to the erratic behavior of your competitors, around whom you must base your tactics. These people are clearly irrational—after all, they choose to spend their leisure time, and considerable funds, going nowhere at 6 miles an hour!

At the same time, tactics have an enormous impact on race results. As we have seen, hundreds of yards can be gained (or lost) in a matter of minutes. The weather, and your ability to predict it, has a big impact on racing success.

By comparison, boat handling and boat speed are quite pedestrian. Performance differences are measured in tenths of a knot. A better tack may save you half a boat length. While a wind shift may bring a huge gain (or loss) in a matter of moments, gains from boat speed accrue slowly, over time.

The upside of boat speed and boat handling is that they are completely within your control. You don't need to rely on any outside factors, or predict the unpredictable. Your boat handling and boat speed can be good every day.

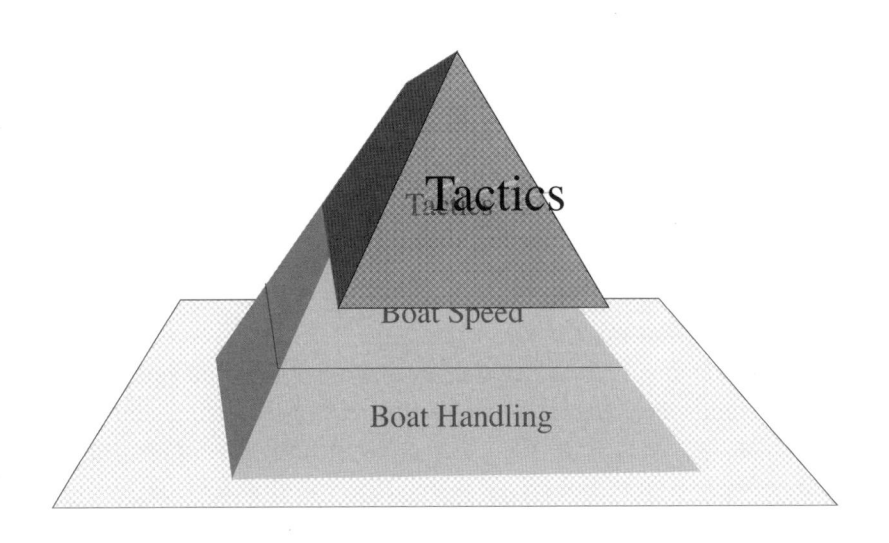

In the performance pyramid, boat handling is the base. You won't be able to race successfully until you can sail well: get sails up and down, tack and jibe, accelerate, and maneuver without hesitation. Your boat handling must be second nature, so you can pick your head up, look around, and do tactics.

Boat speed is the next building block. If you are fast, you'll soon find you are clever tactically. If you are slow, then tactics won't save you.

Often racers lamenting tactical woes actually have boat handling and boat speed problems. If they are slow off the starting line, and are forced to tack away to the unfavored side, that is not a tactical problem.

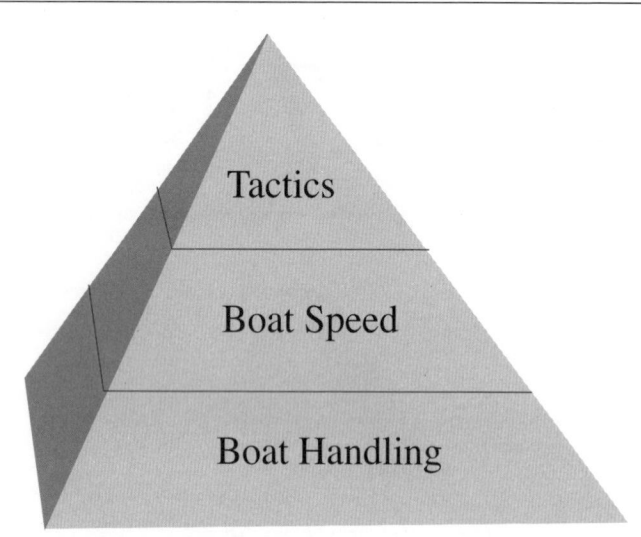

THE PERFORMANCE PYRAMID:
Not only do Boat Handling and Boat Speed form the base of the pyramid, they are also performance factors entirely within our control. Tactics, on the other hand, involves weather and other boats—factors which are decidedly unpredictable.

When your boat handling is second nature, and your boat speed is second to none, you will find that, all of a sudden, you are a tactical wizard.

You should use tactics and strategy to advantage when you have an edge—when you can predict what is going on and control events. When you can't predict what is going to happen, your best tactic is to minimize the impact of weather, and focus your attention on boat handling and boat speed.

Often the best strategic objective is to minimize the impact of the unknown and let your boat speed prevail. Tactically this means putting your boat in a position where you can sail full speed, in clear air, free from crowds; yet without sailing to the strategically fraught edges of the course.

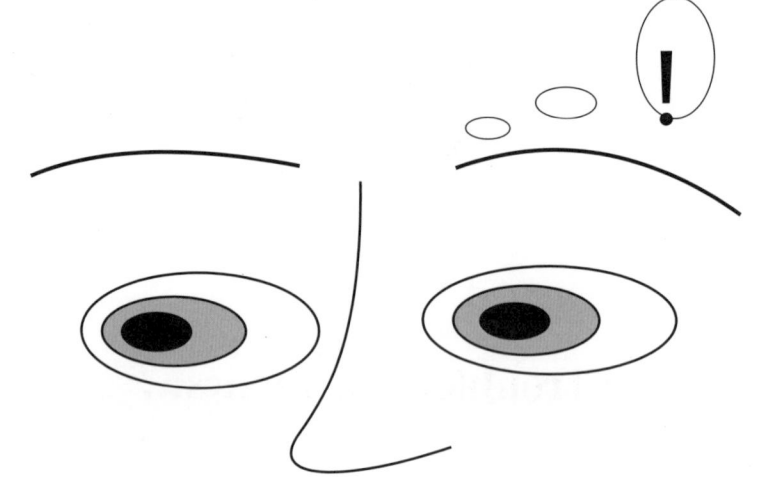

Conclusion: Good luck in all your racing…
…and don't believe everything you read!!

12.2 The End

Part of the attraction of sailboat racing is its complexity. From athletic to intellectual, from interpersonal to introspective, from reflex to endurance—we are challenged in every way. When you have mastered all the skills, you can quit. Until then, keep trying.

As you work to master the skills, never let the theory get in the way of what actually works. Let the theory serve as a starting point, not an end. Keep testing, keep working to find what works. Then make up a theory to explain it…

Remember that this is, in the end, a sailboat race. On a good day you may win a sailboat race. On a bad day, generally the worst thing that will happen is you lose a sailboat race.

Finally, thank you for reading *North U. Tactics*; I hope you have enjoyed it. In parting let me wish you luck in your racing.

Appendix 1: Learning The Rules

App. 1.1 The Rules
App. 1.2 The Four *Right of Way* Rules
App. 1.3 The Four Limitations
App. 1.4 *Mark-Room* and Other Rules
App. 1.5 Appeals & Protests
App. 1.6 Next Steps

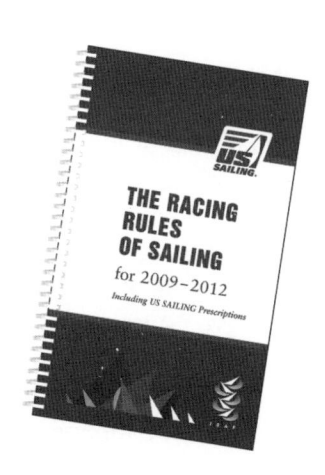

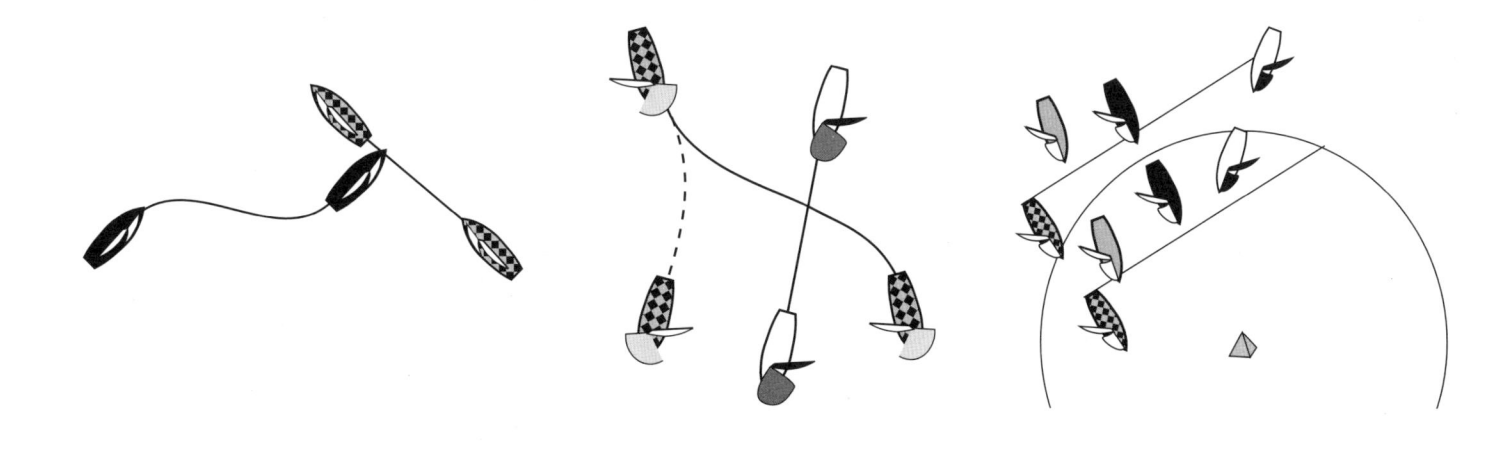

Appendix 1: Learning The Rules

App. 1.1 The Rules

This chapter will introduce and answer a few questions about the rules. Specific rules and situations are covered in the chapters related to the situation (i.e., upwind rules are covered in *Chapter 8: Upwind Tactics*).

The fundamental goal of the rules is to prevent collisions. Our racing rules are derivative of The Rules of the Road which govern shipping. But the purpose of the rules goes beyond "preventing collisions at sea."

As Dave Perry explains it, "the rules are the game. Without rules we would have no game. If we don't sail by the same rules, we are not playing the same game."

It is true, the right-of-way rules are basically the same as the rules used to prevent collisions between ships at sea. But they do much more. From the rules, we get much of our close-quartered tactics, for it is the rules which define what we can and cannot do. Furthermore, the rules are more than just right-of-way rules. *The Racing Rules of Sailing* cover how races are to be run and how violations are handled. The rules also govern sailing situations which do not involve right of way between boats.

While any racing sailor should be familiar with the full rule book, we will start by covering the Right of Way rules, their General Limitations, and the Mark Room rules.

The US Sailing rule book runs 153 pages, yet all the Right of Way Rules fit on a single page, the General Limitations take one additional page, and the Mark Room rules take two pages.

Fig. 1 - Rule 10: On Opposite Tacks. A port tack boat shall keep clear.

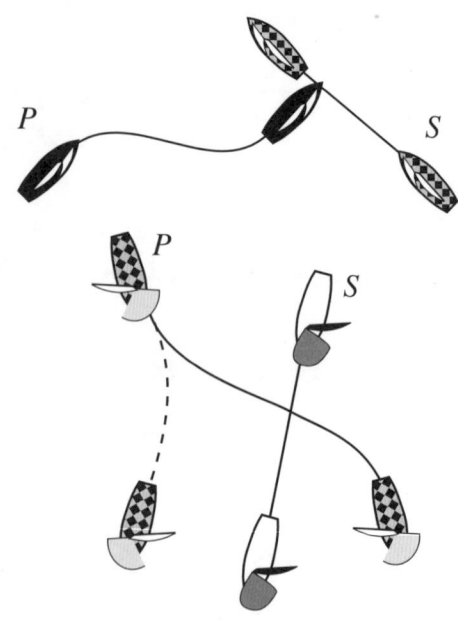

App. 1.2 The Four Right of Way Rules

Their are only four right-of-way rules. If you are new to the rules, you should start by learning these. They cover most situations. Once these are clear look at the four General Limitations which temper the right of way and govern the transitions and conflicts between the right of way rules.

Rule 10: On Opposite Tacks
A port-tack boat shall keep clear.

The starboard–port rule is one we use every race. It applies whenever boats are on opposite tacks, even if one is sailing close-hauled and the other is running.

A close crossing situation upwind is a common source of protests, and the port-tack boat rarely survives such a protest. What the port-tack boat sees as a clear crossing the starboard-tack boat may see as an unacceptable risk. (Fig. 1)

Fig. 2a

Same Tack Rules:
Fig. 2 – Rule 11: Same Tack, Overlapped. Windward boat must keep clear.

Fig. 2b

Fig. 3 – Rule 12: Same Tack, Not Overlapped: The boat Clear Astern must stay clear.

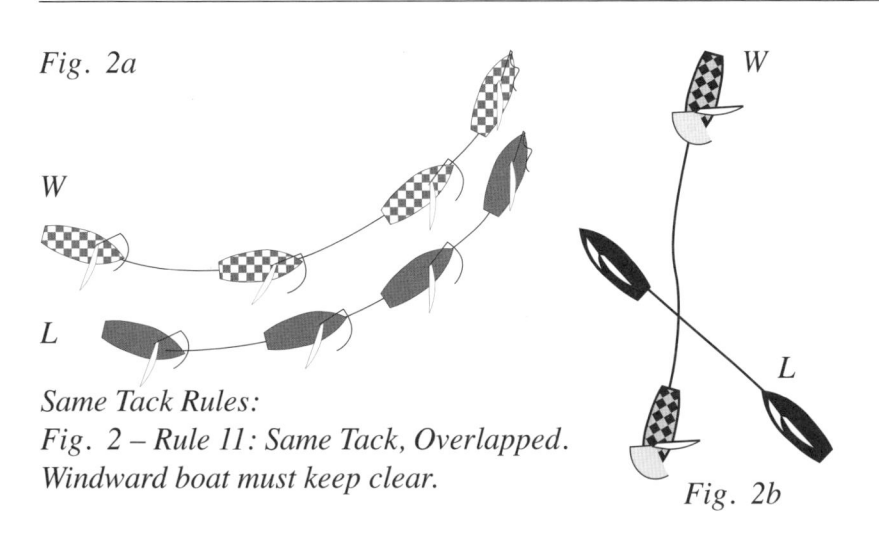

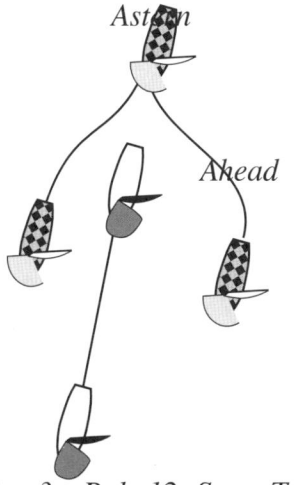

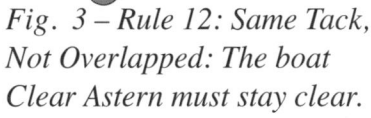

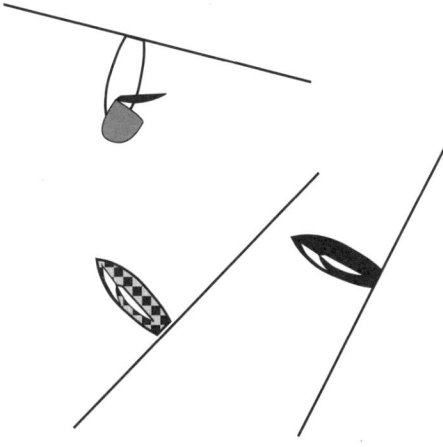

Fig. 4 – Black is clear astern of Checkered. Since neither is clear astern White and Black are overlapped, and White is likewise overlapped with Checkered.

Rule 11: On the Same Tack, Overlapped
A windward boat shall keep clear.

The windward–leeward rule is one of the simplest in the book. The leeward boat has right of way and the windward boat must keep clear (Fig. 2a). This rule applies to all boats on the same tack and overlapped even if they are on different points of sail (Fig. 2b).

Wow. We are half way through the Right of Way rules.

Rule 12: On the Same Tack, Not Overlapped
A boat clear astern shall keep clear.

An overtaking boat must keep clear of a boat clear ahead. This rule, like the windward–leeward rule, applies to boats on the same tack regardless of point of sail (Fig. 3).

To differentiate Rules 11 & 12 we need to define an overlap: A boat is clear astern if she is aft of a line abeam of the stern of the boat clear ahead. Otherwise, they are overlapped (Fig. 4).

Once again, while the rule itself is straightforward, the transitions to windward–leeward and starboard–port are addressed in General Limitations.

Rule 13: While Tacking
A tacking boat shall keep clear of other boats.

Rule 13 actually starts, "After passing head to wind..". During the initial part of tacking – from close-hauled to head to wind – the rule does not apply. It is only during the second half of the tack – from head to wind until she is on the new close-hauled course that the rule kicks in. If you head up from close-hauled and then abort the tack and bear off to your old course, then you have not tacked, and Rule 13 never applies.

The most common infraction of Rule 13 occurs when a

Fig. 5 - Rule 13: While Tacking is seen most commonly when a port tack boat tacks in front of a starboard boat.

Fig. 6a - When Check completes her tack she must give Black room to keep clear. Black need not anticipate Check acquiring right of way.

Fig. 6b - When Check tacks she creates her own burden. Black need not give Check room to keep clear. (But Black must avoid a collision if possible.)

port tack boat tacks in front of a starboard tacker. For the tack to be legal S must be able to hold course until P completes her tack before starting an evasive maneuver (Fig. 5).

Consider this before you tack in front of a starboard boat: Suppose S starts her evasive maneuver earlier than she had to. How are you going to prove she could have waited?

Right of Way Rules

So that's it: All four Right of Way rules. The only right of way rules in the entire 153 page rule book. Next we'll take a look at the General Limitations. Only four of them too.

App. 1.3 General Limitations

The four right of way rules are limited by four General Limitations in Rules 14 –17. These limitations constrain the Right of Way boat and also govern the transition between Right of Way rules. Here they are:

Rule 14: Avoiding Contact

Even if you have the right of way, you must avoid contact with other boats. Once it is clear that the keep clear boat is not keeping clear you must act to avoid contact.

Rule 15: Acquiring Right of Way

"When a boat acquires right of way, she shall initially give the other boat room to keep clear, unless she acquires right of way through the other boat's actions."

A couple of examples: One is a boat coming from astern and acquiring an overlap to leeward. As the overtaking boat establishes her overlap she must allow the newly burdened boat room and time to keep clear (Fig. 6a).

Two others involve tacking: With two boats on port, when one tacks to starboard she must allow the newly burdened boat room and time to keep clear, as above. With two boats on star-

Fig. 7 - A right-of-way yacht may alter course, as long as she gives the keep clear boat room to do so.

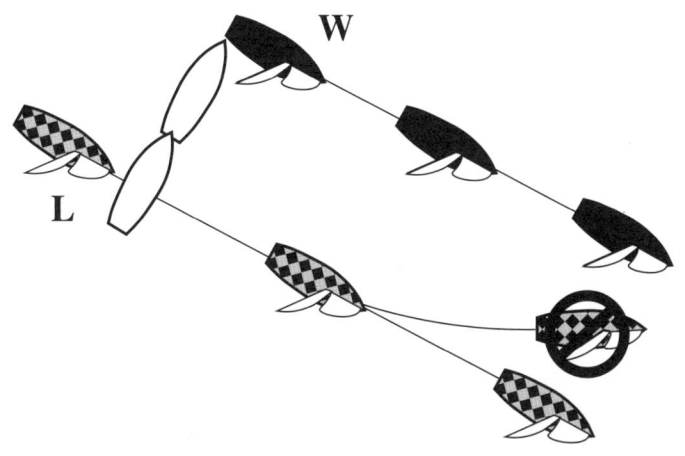

Fig. 8 – A leeward boat which establishes an overlap from astern shall not sail above her proper course.

board, when one tacks to port she is not afforded any room or time, as she created her own burden (Fig. 6b).

Rule 16: Changing Course

"16.1 When a right-of-way boat changes course, she shall give the other boat room to keep clear." As with Rule 15, Rule 16.1 (and 16.2, which further constrains a starboard boat when a port-tack boat is ducking) provides the keep clear boat with time to adjust to changing circumstances. The most common situation where this rule comes into play is when leeward boat luffs a windward boat. With a substantial overlap the leeward boat can luff aggressively and the windward boat must respond. With a small overlap of Leeward's bow to Windward's stern, Leeward must allow room for Windward's stern to swing down as Windward responds to Leeward's attack (Fig. 7).

Rule 17: On the Same Tack; Proper Course

This one can be a bit confusing: If a leeward boat got her overlap from clear astern she is not allowed to sail above proper course. Note that this does not change the right of way – the windward boat must still keep clear – it just constrains the leeward boat to a course no higher than the course she would sail if the windward boat were not there (Fig. 8).

What's the rationale? I'm not sure; but here's one thought: If an overtaking boat tries passing to windward the leeward boat can head up to defend her air; whereas if the overtaking boat passes to leeward she is not allowed to luff. In the first case the boat is allowed to defend her air – a defensive posture. Whereas an overtaking boat is not allowed to attack. The rules are set up as a shield: you can defend; but not as a sword: you are not meant to attack with protection from the rules.

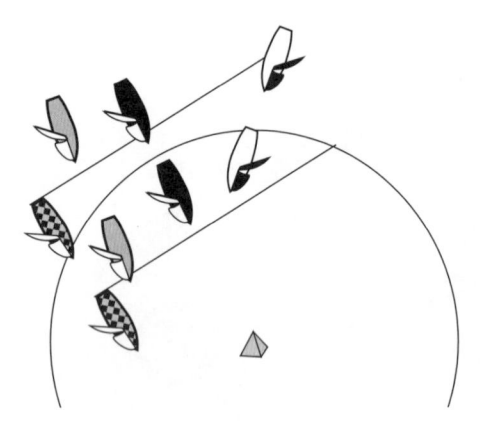

Fig. 9 – Check owes room to Black and White, but not to Grey. Mark-Room is set by overlaps at the 3 length zone. Later changes do not matter.

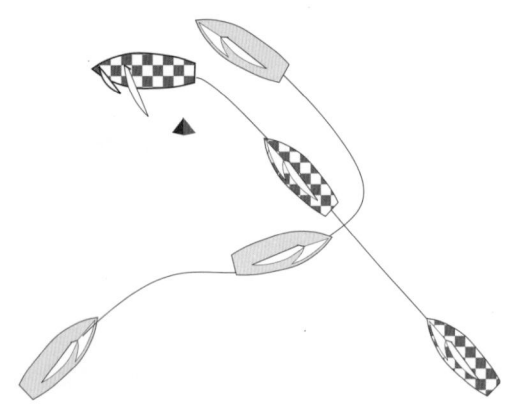

Fig. 10 – At a windward mark Mark-Room rules to not apply to boats on opposite tacks. Starboard/ Port prevails.

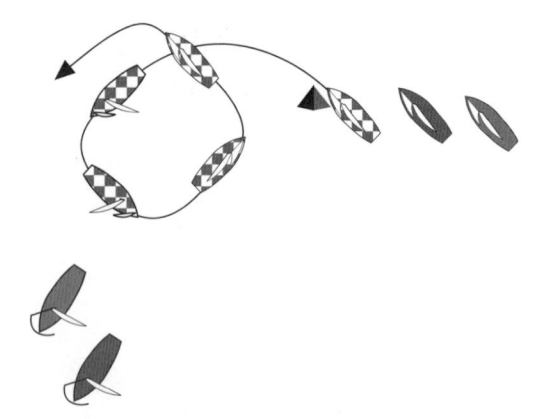

Fig. 11 – If you hit a mark you must do a One-Turn Penalty.

App. 1.4 Mark-Room and Other Rules

Rule 18 covers Mark Room. Portions can be quite complex and the language confusing to the point where you can lose track of the major points. Here are the essentials:

When boats are overlapped, the inside boats gets room.

When boats are overlapped when the first of them reaches the three boat length zone, the inside boats gets room even if the overlap is later broken (Fig. 9).

When boats are NOT overlapped when the first of them reaches the three boat length zone, the clear ahead boats gets room even if an overlap is later established (Fig. 9).

Rule 18 does NOT apply between boats on opposite tacks at a windward mark. The regular Port/ Starboard rule applies (Fig. 10).

Mark-Room is covered in more detail in *Chapter 8: Upwind Tactics* and *Chapter 11: Downwind Rules, Mark Roundings and Finishing*.

A Few Other Rules

While the Right-of-Way Rules which govern situations when boats meet, get most of the attention, there are other rules you need to know.

There are Fundamental Rules in Part 1 of the Rule Book which address safety, fairness, and responsibility, and the rules of Part 3, which detail how races are run. There are rules on scoring, and on the conduct of protest hearings, and special rules for match racing and team racing.

Rule 44 explains the Penalties for Breaking Rules. Usually if you interfere with another boat then you must do a Two Turns Penalty. If you hit a mark, a one turn penalty is required. (Fig. 11).

One of my favorite parts of the Rule Book is Appendix H which explains the procedures for weighing wet clothing.

We won't rewrite the rule book here. Get one and read up. The best time is early April, before sailing season, when you should be doing your taxes.

App. 1.5 Appeals and Protests

Q. What are the Appeals?

A. When you join US Sailing, you will get a rule book. You will also want to get a copy of the US Sailing Appeals and International Sailing Federation (ISAF) Cases.. The Appeals and Cases provide clarification and interpretation of the rules.

As you become comfortable with the basic workings of the rules you can develop a more thorough understanding by studying the appeals and cases.

Download or order the appeals at:
http://raceadmin.ussailing.org/Appeals.htm
Download the International Cases at:
Go To: www.sailing.org/   and search "case book"

Q. What do I need to know about Protests?

A. Sooner or later you are going to have to defend your actions on the race course before a jury. Obviously you will want an understanding of the rules. More importantly, you will need to present your information about the incident in a clear, precise manner. Give facts, not generalizations. Be specific. Listen carefully to what others say and question anything you disagree with. Search for inconsistencies in the story offered by others.

Sit in on protest hearings. The process is described in the Rule Book Appendix M. It helps to sit in on hearings and watch the rules in action. Most juries and parties to a protest will allow you to observe (in silence). Protest hearings range from boring to fascinating. Observing a hearing can give you some insight into the application of the rules. It will also be invaluable preparation for the day you are a party to a protest.

Sidebar: Do the Rules Make Sense?

Do the Right of Way Rules make sense?

Working backwards, would it be better if Rule 13 gave a tacking boat the Right of Way, and the other boats had to keep clear? I think not. How about reversing Rule 12, so a boat in front had to keep clear of an overtaking boat coming from clear astern? Nah.

The rationale for the Rule 11: Same Tack, Overlapped revolves around clear air: The windward boat is in clear air, while the leeward boat's wind may be blanketed, compromising her maneuverability. The more maneuverable windward boat must keep clear.

And what about Rule 10: Opposite Tacks? Well, somebody has to have the Right of Way! But there's more to it than that: Old ships would dock with their port side against the dock, opposite their steerboard (starboard) side which had the rudder (when rudders were not on centerline), keeping the rudder in deep water. Thus, on port tack the ship would heel to starboard, immersing the rudder; while on starboard tack the rudder would be lifted and maneuverability compromised. Thus, the more maneuverable port-tack boat must keep clear. Great story, and it might even be true.

App. 1.6 Next Steps
More on Learning the Rules

If you race sailboats in the United States, you should be a member of the United States Sailing Association. As a member you'll be supporting the group that oversees the sport, administers the rules, and provides guidelines and training for race manager, judges, measurers and umpires. Join.

US Sailing also offers a handy Quick Guide to help you learn the rules. It really is handy.

While I'm at it, let me put in a plug for Dave Perry's book, *Understanding the Racing Rules of Sailing* and David Dellenbaugh's DVD *Learn the Racing Rules*. If you want to study the rules, get the book and DVD. These are the two best sources for rules info. Both make great gifts....

Don't let your limited knowledge of the rules be an obstacle to racing. Learn the four Right of Way Rules, get a sense of the Limitations and Mark-Room Rules, and go racing. As your racing and sailing get better make a growing knowledge of the rules part of your learning; but don't let the rules stop you from racing.

Dave Perry's book, "Understanding the Racing Rules of Sailing" and David Dellenbaugh's DVD, "Learn the Racing Rules" are great next steps in your rules education... (And they make great gifts.)

If you race in the Unites States, you should join the United States Sailing Association
     Visit WWW.USSailing.org or call 800 877-2451

You'll receive a rule book, member discounts on entry fees and merchandise, and other benefits too numerous to mention. Most importantly you'll be supporting the group that runs our sport.

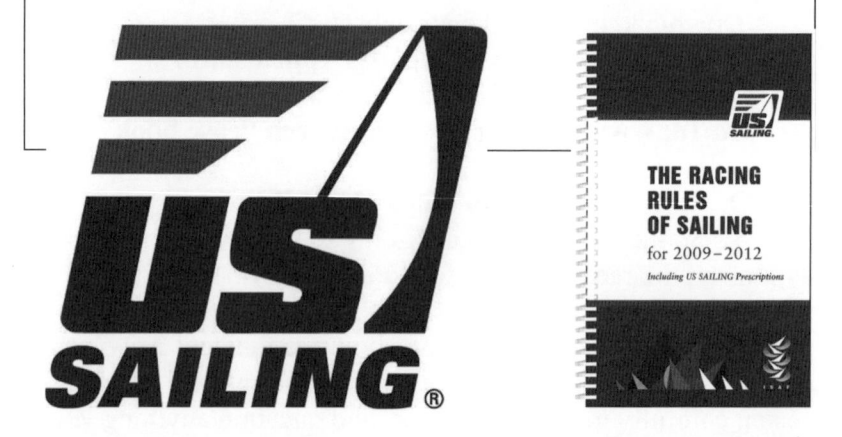

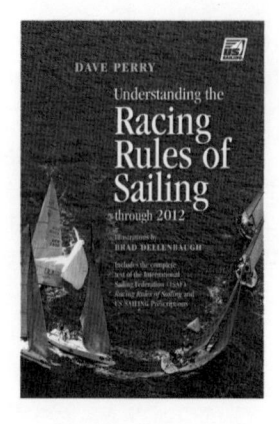

APPENDIX 2: SPECIAL TOPICS

App 2.1 Mixed Fleet Racing
App 2.2 Big Fleet Racing
App 2.3 Distance Racing

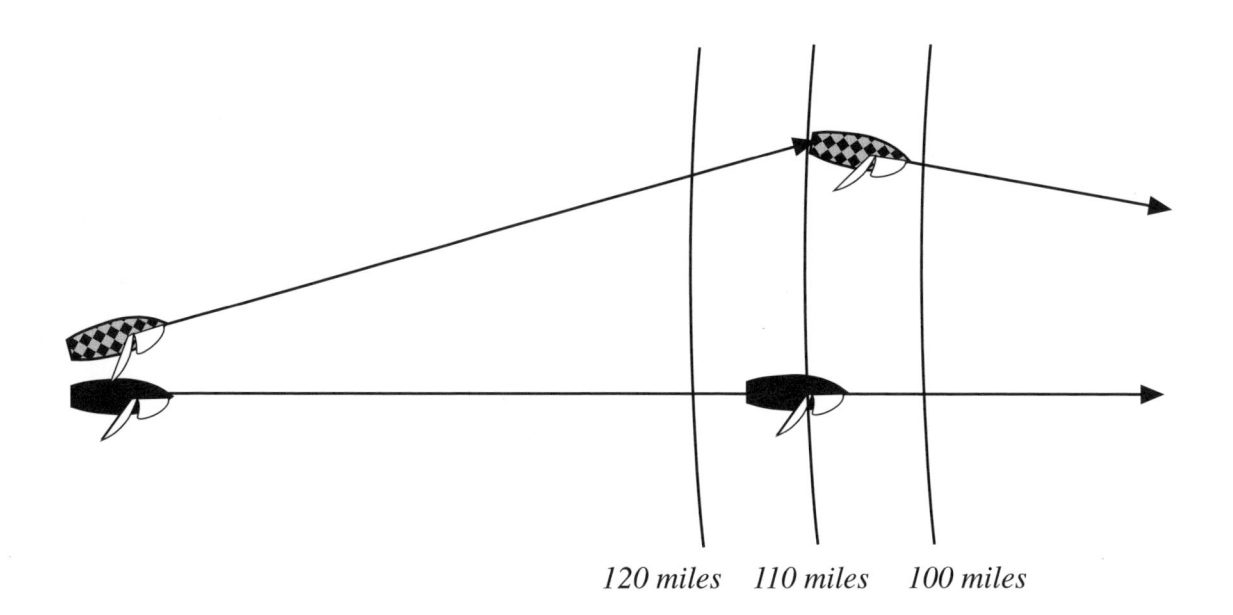

120 miles   110 miles   100 miles

Appendix 2: Special Topics

App 2.1 Mixed Fleet Racing

The Strategic Imbalance

The type of fleet you race in will effect your tactics. One-design or level-rated competition is more tactical. Your closest rivals are the boats nearby. In racing with a wide spread of handicaps, your closest rival may not be within reach. In fact, with some scoring systems the final handicaps aren't figured out until after the race when conditions are entered.

Handicap racing is strategic. You race the clock, not boats. Stay clear of other boats and get around the course fast. The only exception is approaching the finish near a level-rated competitor. In that situation, you must balance the tactical concerns for finishing in front of the rival with the overall strategy of beating the clock in a mixed handicap fleet.

Small Fry & Big Fish

When racing a relatively small boat in a mixed fleet, there is a tendency to get pushed to the side in search of clear air, as the larger boats take up the center. The smaller boats must pay particular attention to finding lanes of clear air in which to pursue strategy. A degree of patience is also called for. Sitting in the bad air of a bigger, faster boat may be tolerable for a short time, if it allows you to go the right way.

The challenge for big boats is to stay clear of the smaller boats. Big boats do well if they can get away clean at the start. If they get caught up in the crowd, they suffer.

When a smaller boat can hang on upwind and the next leg is a reach, they often should get into the Get Passed Lane. See Chapter 9: Reaching Strategy and Tactics for details.

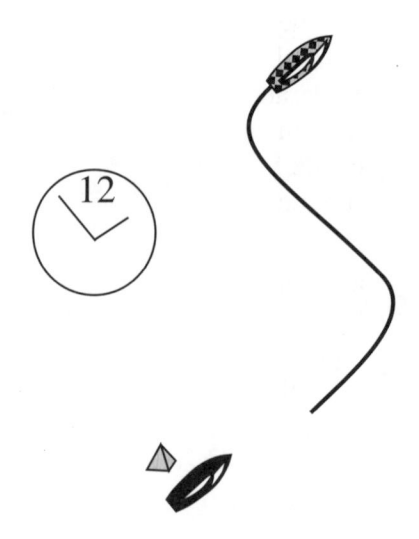

Fig. 1 - Racing in a handicap fleet puts an emphasis on strategy. You are racing against the clock, and your nearest rival may be nowhere in sight. One-design racing is more tactical. The boats nearby are your biggest concern. In a mixed fleet, take times at marks to see how you are doing on corrected time against your closest rivals.

How Are We Doing So Far?

In the final legs of a race, take the times of boats as they round the marks and figure out corrected positions. If you are saving your time on the fleet, then conservative tactics are called for; if you are behind on corrected time, then a more daring strategy may be in order (Fig. 1).

App 2.2 Big Fleet Racing

The transition from the regular weekend fleet to a championship fleet can be painful. Big fleet tactics differ in several ways from tactics in moderate sized fleets. The first difference is that the penalties for even slight mistakes are magnified. Big fleet racing emphasizes the fundamentals: great speed, sound strategy, and fluid boat handling.

Starts

Starts become increasingly critical. You must get off the line with clear air and good speed. At the same, time starts become increasingly difficult. It is easy to get lost in the crowd, and easy to underestimate the effects of turbulence and bad air on your approach.

You've got to push hard to keep clear air. A luffing start is often the only way to stay in the front row. Once you fall into bad air, you may never recover (Fig. 2).

Sailing off the line is a sprint to keep clear air. Just sail fast. The tactician can watch to see how the breeze is settling in, but it won't matter if you aren't in the front row.

Up The Beat

If you find yourself going the wrong way early, you'll have to wait until things open up during the first half of the beat to remedy the problem.

As the fleet converges at the windward mark, the middle of the course becomes a mess of boats, chop, and turbulence. If you are not in the top ten, avoid the middle as you approach the mark. Overstand to get well clear of the crowds. (The trick, of course, is to arrive in the top ten rather than the middle twenty. Life is tough in the rat race.)

Downwind

You must defend your air. If one boat rolls over you, ten may go by before you recover. Work for inside position at the marks, and start your buoy room discussions early to keep things orderly in your crowd. Speed and boat handling reign.

Go Home a Winner

Going to a big time regatta for the first time can be an eye opening experience. If you go in humble, you may be able to save yourself from humiliation. Try to achieve consistency and you will do well—at some events, finishing in the top ten every race wins the regatta. Take some time to look at the boats of the top sailors, and talk with them about technique. Learn your lessons at the championship, and use your new skills to beat up on the competition back home.

Fig. 2 - There is a strong emphasis on fundamentals when racing in a big fleet. At the back of a big fleet, sailing up the middle will leave you gasping for air.

App 2.3 Distance Racing Strategy

Success in distance racing is more than a simple extension of round-the-buoys technique. Strategy involves a bigger picture of weather changes over a period of days. Crew organization includes setting a watch system to take advantage of your crew's skills. Motivation changes as you are often racing against the clock, out of sight of your nearest rivals. Concerns about safety, provisioning, and health demand added attention. The basic principles of success around the buoys remain intact—sail fast, go the right direction—but achieving these objectives becomes a more involved process.

There are six basic elements to distance racing strategy. They start with the fundamental approach of sailing to the finish. To that we will add strategies for sailing fast, planning for weather, and boat-for-boat positioning. We will also look at special strategies for catching up from behind and night sailing.

Sail Toward the Finish

Draw a line from the start to the finish. Follow that line. This may not sound like a real breakthrough, but more races are won with this strategy than any other. Use this strategy as your starting point, and modify from there. When in doubt, return to this approach (but not to the original line): Draw a new rhumb line from your present position, and follow it.

Sail Fast

Sail fast means more than sailing our best, straight up the rhumb line. Usually we can sail substantially faster by sailing a few degrees off the rhumb line. The goal is to get as close to the finish line as fast as we can. Sailing straight down the rhumb line may not do it.

By sailing up (or down) 10° off the rhumb line, we may get closer to the finish line faster. Sailing 10° off the rhumb line increases our sailing distance by less than 2%. If our speed is more than 2% faster 10° off course, then we may be better off sailing off the rhumb line. Here are some numbers on the

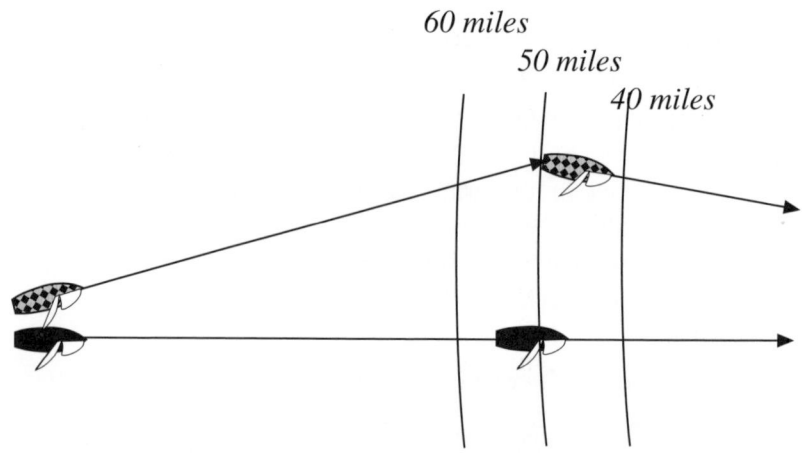

Fig. 3 - The fundamental distance racing strategy is to sail toward the mark. One reason to modify fundamental strategy is in order to sail fast. By sailing an angle slightly off the rhumb line, we may be able to sail dramatically faster and be closer to the finish line when the next weather change arrives.

extra distance you sail in a 100 mile race by sailing 5, 10, 15, and 20° off course for half the distance to the finish, and then aiming at the finish:

° Off Course	Distance Sailed
0	100 miles
5	100.4
10	101.5
15	103.5
20	106.4

On a 35 foot boat, in 10 knots of wind, bearing off 10° from close hauled will increase speed from about 6 knots to 6.6 knots. By sailing 1.5% further you go 10% faster! Heading up 10° from a broad reach creates the same result. A 20° change of course adds less than 7% extra distance! Sail Fast (Fig. 3).

The old adage "what goes up must come down" (or vice versa) does not necessarily apply. In a distance race the weather will change. Who knows what will be up and what will be down tomorrow morning? All things being equal, you want to be closer to the finish line.

To sail fast means you want to avoid sailing upwind and downwind during a distance race. If the finish is upwind, sail fast beat mode—foot off, never pinch—on the favored tack, or toward the next new wind. If the course is downwind, then tack downwind at optimum angles.

Our goal is to be the closest boat to the finish line when the weather conditions change. By sailing a little faster on a course slightly off the rhumb line, we can achieve that goal. The only time we lose is if the weather never changes.

Which leads us to our next strategy modifier: The weather.

Weather Strategy

Navigators define a distance race as a race through a series of weather changes. One of the tricks to weather strategy is to make good use of the forecast. From my experience, one lesson on weather strategy stands out above all else: Sail the wind, not the forecast.

Coastal forecasting is notoriously difficult. Changes in the weather, and the pace with which they will occur, are hard to predict. Many distance races have been lost by boats in perfect position for a change that arrives while the victors are drinking champagne.

Distance racing requires an understanding of weather and weather system movements over the duration of the race. In order to plan long term strategy, you must have the big picture of what the weather will do. Get all the weather information you can, from every available source, and keep a record of the forecasts. It is best to start tracking the weather a few days (or weeks) before the race to get a sense of how the systems are moving.

Tracking the forecasts for several days prior to the race will help you see trends in the forecast. If, for example, an early forecast predicts a front 24 hours into the race, and a more recent forecast suggests the front will arrive 36 hours into the race, then you can guess that the weather system movement is slowing (and perhaps the front will never arrive).

During the race update your forecast with weather radio, your own observations (is the barometer changing as forecast?), and via the Internet. If you can set your boat up to have web access during a distance race, then you can get weather data and forecasts from NOAA and other public sites.

One skill you need is the ability to interpret forecasts and apply them to your specific area. During the race, tracking reported conditions in the area will help you distill the forecast. By tracking reported conditions you can chart the advance of changing weather, judge its pace, and predict its impact on your specific area.

Your basic strategy should remain a race to the finish, in the existing conditions, until you can confidently predict what will happen to the weather, and when. Only then should you modify your strategy to suit the predicted weather.

When you are confident of the forecast what should you do? As conditions change you want to be 1) the boat closest to the finish 2) the boat closest to the new wind.

Here's an example: Day two the 1987 Annapolis to Newport race. We're in the midst of a glorious spinnaker surf, roaring along on starboard jibe in 20-25 knots of wind, somewhere off the Jersey shore. The weather radio is forecasting continued southerlies and sweltering conditions.

Thomas Dolby is raging from the Rick's boom box: We'll be the Pirate Twins Again. The tape ends and auto ejects. WCBS News Radio 88 AM takes over from New York. We are still out of range of the New York NOAA station, but WCBS forecasts relief from the heat wave, and north winds by sunset.

"Beautiful sleeping weather" the weatherman raves, "A break from the heat."

Hearing this forecast, we split jibes to the north and meet the front shortly after sunset, in position to close reach along the coast, while the boats offshore are beating upwind. Never mind sleep. It is a beautiful night for racing (Fig. 4).

Moral: Use every available source to get the most up-to-date weather information available. Only when you know what the weather will do should you alter your strategy.

Boat-for-Boat Strategy

Stay with the fleet. Until you have reason to do otherwise, and you are sure you are right, stay with the fleet. This is particularly true early in the race. You are better off to sail with the fleet (and sail fast) in the early going. You want to enter the final segment of the race in a position to win. An early gamble can quickly turn a long race into a long delivery.

As the race progresses and you refine your weather forecast, try to lead the fleet to the new wind. The first boat to the new wind gets the biggest advantage from it. If you are sailing upwind this usually means footing toward the shift, rather than sailing hard on the wind. If you are sailing downwind, then it pays to reach up a little extra to get to the shift. On a reach, find the fastest reaching angle to carry you to the new breeze.

Sometimes the best strategy is to lock on to your chief rivals in the race and simply sail against them. Having a competitor close at hand keeps everyone more attentive.

Strategy from Behind

If you are behind, there are a couple of options to consider. One is to simply follow the competition and drag them down from behind with superior speed. Over a long haul a little speed advantage adds up—don't be impatient.

The other option is to sail fast regardless of the angle. Your goal should be to reach to a position abeam of the competition—translate your distance behind into height. In a short

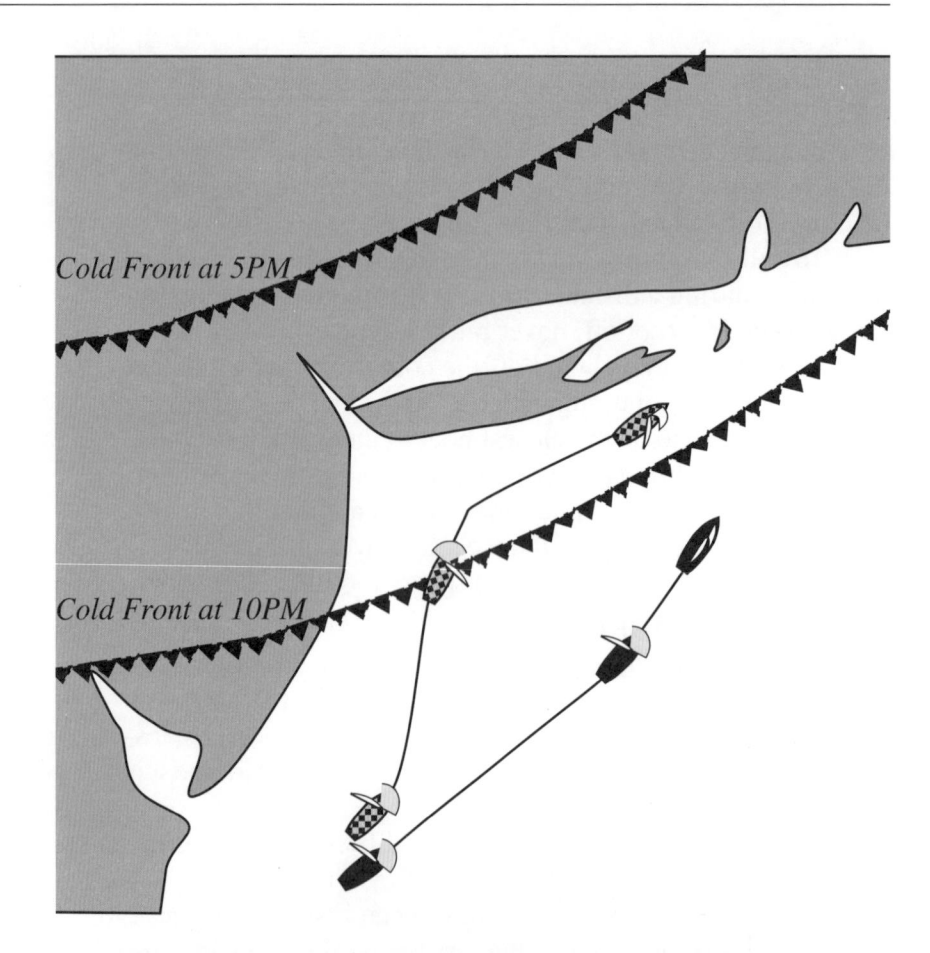

Fig. 4 - Weather Strategy: The basic idea is, **Sail to the new wind.** *The danger is sailing the forecast, when it may not come true. Sail the wind you've got until you are confident in the forecast; then go to the new wind.*

In the Annapolis to Newport Race several years ago a cold front came off the New England coast the second night out. Boats which had worked to a position inshore were able close reach in the new wind, while boats offshore had to sail hard on the wind.

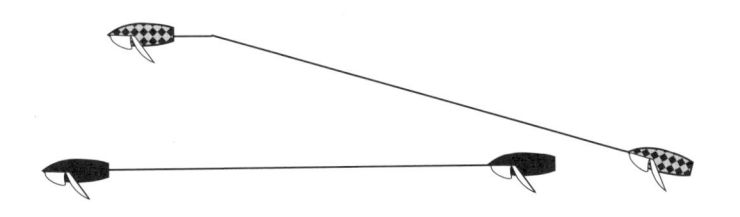

Fig. 5 - Strategy from behind. If you have superior speed, then be patient and drag them down from behind. If speed alone won't do it, then try to convert your distance behind into lateral distance. Sail a course high or low of rhumb line for extra speed. The lateral separation could work to your advantage in a favorable shift or change in the weather; whereas an unfavorable shift may simply put you back where you were.

race, this is not likely to work because "what goes up must come down" etc. But in a distance race conditions will change; the height could as easily become an advantage as a burden (Fig. 5).

Night Strategy

Distance races are often won at night. Become nocturnal. Sail hard during the day; sail harder at night to overcome the difficulties of darkness. A watch system which allows longer sleep during the day and shorter watches at night is preferred. Three four-hour watches by day, and four three-hour watches by night works well.

Be conservative. Be ready for the next change. Without the visual clues available in daylight, sudden changes are more likely. Keep the boat organized. Before dark, do your housekeeping and make sure things are in order. Clear clutter, check your coils and sail packing, pre-navigate so you know what to expect. If you need to run your engine to charge the ship's batteries, it is best to do that during daylight hours too.

Finishing Strategy

Once the last weather change has occurred, distance racing strategy becomes short course strategy. When a level-rated rival emerges in the predawn light on the final morning of a long race, it is exciting to be aboard as adrenaline kicks in and carries you to the finish.

Two notes of caution: First, don't start your sprint to the finish so early that the entire crew collapses before the end; enforce the watch system until the last watch. Also, remember that you are racing the clock as well as the boats you can see. Avoid getting caught up in a feud with one other boat.

Conclusion: Putting it All Together

A winning strategy is only one ingredient to successful distance racing. Distance racing involves a whole series of new challenges, from crew organization and provisioning to night sailing and safety considerations.

There is great satisfaction simply in sailing well and finishing a long race. There is a greater thrill to take up the challenge and return victorious.

Private coaching, on your boat…
  …because there is no boat like your own

RACE AND WIN
We can show you how, working with you and your crew, on your boat.

STOP GUESSING
Rig tuning, spinnaker handling, mainsail shape, helming. We will answer all your questions.

FOR YOUR CREW
After all you have put into your boat and equipment, get North U. Coaching for your crew.

ON YOUR BOAT
Can you think of a better place?

WITHIN YOUR BUDGET
Our regional staffing puts expert instruction within your reach. Let us design a program to match your needs and interests.

LEARN MORE
Our training covers every facet of racing trim, tactics, and boat handling. *Call or visit to learn more.*

North U.
800 347 2457 • 203 245 0727
www.NorthU.com
Turning sailors into racers and racers into winners since 1980

TACTICS SEMINAR ON CD-ROM
The Boats Move!
The companion to this book, our revised *Tactics CD* puts Racing Tactics in motion. The CD covers starting, upwind, and downwind topics, including strategy, tactics, and rules. In addition to animation of the book illustrations, the CD includes photos, photo sequences, hours of video, and an interactive windshift simulator.

The CD features a voice over by the author, Bill Gladstone.

NORTH U. TRIM
The most complete book on modern racing performance
To win races you've got to sail well, and sail fast. Tactics alone won't do it. Written by Bill Gladstone, *North U. Trim* covers boat handing and boat speed in the same easy accessible style as *North U. Tactics*.

The new edition covers helming, mainsail, genoa, and spinnaker trim, plus sets, jibes, and douses for both conventional and asymmetric spinnakers. A special chapter on *Trim Solutions* provides insights into the most baffling performance problems, while drill and skill building suggestions will help your transform your crew into a team.

TRIM SEMINAR ON CD-ROM
See Trim in Action!
The TRIM CD puts performance in motion, and shows how changes in trim change the sailing characteristics of your boat. The interactive *sail shaper* allows you to see how changes in angle of attack, depth, and twist change sail shape. In addition, coverage of boathandling topics shows the most up to date techniques for spinnaker sets, jibes and douses, for both conventional and asymmetrical spinnakers.

In addition to animated graphics, hours of video and 100's of photographs, the TRIM CD features a voice over by the author, Bill Gladstone.